The Black Death and
Pastoral Leadership

University of Pennsylvania Press
MIDDLE AGES SERIES
Edited by
Edward Peters
Henry Charles Lea Professor
of Medieval History
University of Pennsylvania

A listing of the available books
in the series appears at the
back of this volume

The Black Death and Pastoral Leadership

The Diocese of Hereford in the Fourteenth Century

William J. Dohar

University of Pennsylvania Press

Philadelphia

Library of Congress Cataloging-in-Publication Data to come
Dohar, William J.
   The Black Death and pastoral leadership : the Diocese of Hereford in the fourteenth
century / William J. Dohar.
      p.   cm. — (Middle Ages series)
   Includes bibliographial references (p.) and index.
   ISBN 0-8122-3262-3
   1. Herefordshire (England) — History. 2. Church work with the sick — England —
Herefordshire — History. 3. Medicine, Medieval — England — Herefordshire — History.
4. Black death — England — Herefordshire — History. 5. Pastoral theology — England —
Herefordshire. 6. Herefordshire (England) — Church history. 7. Plague — England —
Herefordshire — History. 8. Fourteenth century.
I. Title. II. Series.
DA670.H4D64 1994
942.4'4 — dc20   ·94-33224
                                                                           CIP

Cover: Memorial brass of John Trillek, Bishop of Hereford, 1344-1360, Hereford Cathedral.
Permission granted by the Dean and Chapter of Hereford.

For Elizabeth Dohar

Contents

viii   Contents

List of Figures and Tables

Preface

This book is meant to contribute in some small way to a very large subject. It began with and has been sustained by an abiding interest in medieval religion and how fourteenth-century people struggled to find some sense and meaning in the face of unprecedented calamity and death. Historians have traditionally referred to the Black Death and the subsequent period of epidemic plague in medieval Europe as a critical time marking the transition from one age of prosperity and achievement to another of struggle and adversity. If the Black Death and its many repercussions were of such significance to medieval people, what difference might all of this have made to the medieval church? In reading about the topic, I soon realized that its range was far broader and its dimensions more complex than I could hope to pursue in a single comprehensive study. And since my historical interests are in the area of medieval pastoral care and the ways in which the church carried out its mission, I decided to restrict my study to a single diocese and its pastoral leadership during and immediately following the Black Death. A study on religion in the time of the plague remains to be written. The larger questions are still there but I hope this book has at least diminished them somewhat. I also hope that this excursion into local history will prompt other such analyses of regional churches in order to find piecemeal what seems so elusive and imposing on the grander scale.

Like any book, this one too has its own history. It began simply enough as a conversation with Fr. Leonard E. Boyle, O.P. in his office in Toronto over ten years ago, took on the graver proportions of a doctoral dissertation and, after years spent in Toronto, Hereford, Oxford, and Notre Dame, has reached its current and final state. But along the way many important lessons have been learned about history and book-writing, about the Black Death and medieval pastoral care, and much more besides. Christopher Cheney once chided historians, in his gentle manner, to remember that medieval records may be likened to children of a former time who do not speak unless spoken to and in any case will not speak to strangers. I hope that I have spoken and listened carefully to the records and documents that inform this study. Hereford is rich in ecclesiastical archives from the fourteenth century and its bishops' registers are mines of information for the pastoral care and administration of that diocese. But there are inevitably *lacunae* in the documentation, critical points where the narrative is broken and the historian is challenged to span the distances between the firmer ground of unembellished records with a combination of interpretation, deduction, and guess work. All these elements will be found in good supply in this book: the records which tell a story about the fourteenth-century church with impressive detail and interpretations where I reach to make sense of it all. I am hopeful for and welcome the advice and criticism of my readers in this regard.

Last, this book owes much of its content and its completion to many mentors, colleagues, and friends. Leonard Boyle taught me how to listen to medieval records and to speak to them patiently; he and the late Michael M. Sheehan, C.S.B. of the Pontifical Institute of Mediaeval Studies followed this work with great patience and diligence and saved me from numerous errors. Donald Finlay, C.S.B., former Librarian of the Pontifical Institute and St. Michael's College libraries, provided indispensable aid in acquiring materials, documents, and books. I am equally grateful to his library staff in those days, in particular, Mary English. Penelope Morgan, Honorary Librarian of the Cathedral Library of Hereford, guided me patiently through the archives in her care, as did Sue Hubbard, Head of Record Services of the County Council of Hereford and Worcester, with the bishops' registers. In the first seasons of my research in England, Norman Tanner, S.J. of Campion Hall and Barbara Harvey of Somerville College were sources of instruction and encouragement when I needed both. I am also grateful to Joseph Goering of the University of Toronto and to Michèle M. Mulchahey and Timothy Haskett of the University of Victoria, whose friendship and intellectual support over the years have been rare gifts. John Van Engen and Thomas Kselman of Notre Dame and John Shinners of St. Mary's College spent a lot of time reading this book in its earlier stages and offered insightful comments for which I am very grateful. Wilson Miscamble, C.S.C. urged on progress patiently and with great support. John Sherman and Delton Cajetano helped with images and graphs, and David Klawiter shared his wide knowledge of computers and programs with generosity and forbearance. Research for the book was made possible in part by support from the Institute of Scholarship in the Liberal Arts, College of Arts and Letters, University of Notre Dame. Finally, there were many friends along the way who kindly sat me at their tables and spoke about this book and its subject in ways more helpful than they can know: Jo Ann Zannotti,

Tom Peterson, Lynn Anne Mulrooney, Lee Klosinski, Dan McCurrie, and Donna McCurrie. My own family has been very patient and consolingly interested in this work since its inception and my mother, to whom the book is dedicated, has been unfailing in her encouragement. The Basilian communities in Toronto at St. Michael's College and the Pontifical Institute as well as the Jesuits of Campion Hall, Oxford gave me a home as well as friendship and learning during my years of study and research. To my own religious family of Holy Cross, without whom this book would very likely have never been written, I owe immeasureable gratitude for material and personal support.

Abbreviations

Alberigo	*Conciliorum Oecumenicorum Decreta*, ed. J. Alberigo et al. Bologna, 1973.
BRUO	A. B. Emden, *Biographical Register of the University of Oxford to A.D. 1500*, 3 vols., Oxford, 1957–59.
CCR	*Calendar of Close Rolls, preserved in the Public Record Office*, London, 1893–1954.
CPL	*The Calendar of Entries in the Papal Registers relating to Great Britain and Ireland, Papal Letters, 1198–*, 14 vols., William Henry Bliss and J. A. Twemlow, eds., London, 1893 on.
CPP	*Calendar of Entries in the Papal Registers relating to Great Britain and Ireland, Petitions to the Pope A.D. 1342–1419*, vol. 1, ed. W. H. Bliss, London, 1896.
CPR	*Calendar of Patent Rolls preserved in the Public Record Office*, London, 1891–1916.
Councils and Synods	*Councils and Synods with Other Documents Relating to the English Church*, vol. II, parts 1 & 2 (1205–1313), ed. F. M. Powicke and C. R. Cheney, Oxford, 1964.
DDC	*Dictionnaire de Droit Canonique*
EETS, o.s.	*Early English Text Society*, original series
EHR	*English Historical Review*
HCA	Hereford Cathedral Archives
HDR	Hereford Diocesan Registry
JEH	*Journal of Ecclesiastical History*
Provinciale	W. Lyndwood, *Provinciale sue constitutiones Angliae*, Oxford, 1679.
Reg. Cantilupe	*Registrum Thome de Cantilupo, episcopi Herefordensis, 1275–1282*, ed. R. G. Griffiths and W. W. Capes. Canterbury and York Society ii, 1907.
Reg. L. Charlton	*Registrum Ludowici de Charltone, episcopi Herefordensis, 1361–1370*, ed. J. H. Parry. Canterbury and York Society xiv, 1913.

Reg. T. Charlton	*Registrum Thome de Charltone, episcopi Heforden-sis, 1327–1344*, ed. W. W. Capes. Canterbury and York Society ix, 1913.
Reg. Courtenay	*Registrum Willelmi de Courtenay, episcopi Hereford-ensis, 1370–1375*, ed. W. W. Capes. Canterbury and York Society xv, 1914.
Reg. Gilbert	*Registrum Johannis Gilbert, episcopi Herefordensis, 1375–1389*, ed. J. H. Parry. Canterbury and York Society xviii, 1915.
Reg. Mascall	*Registrum Roberti Mascall, episcopi Herefordensis, 1404–1416*, ed. J. H. Parry. Canterbury and York Society xxi, 1917.
Reg. Orleton	*Registrum Ade de Orleton, episcopi Herefordensis, 1317–1327*, ed. A. T. Bannister. Canterbury and York Society v, 1908.
Reg. Swinfield	*Registrum Ricardi de Swinfield, episcopi Heforden-sis, 1283–1317*, ed. W. W. Capes. Canterbury and York Society vi, 1909
Reg. Trefnant	*Registrum Johannis Trefnant, episcopi Herefordensis, 1389–1404*, ed. W. W. Capes. Canterbury and York Society xx, 1916.
Reg. Trillek	*Registrum Johannis de Trillek, episcopi Herefordensis, 1344–1361*, ed. J. H. Parry. Canterbury and York Society viii, 1912.
Statutes	Henry Bradshaw and Christopher Wordsworth, eds. *Hereford Consuetudines; Statutes of Lincoln Cathedral*, 2 parts in 3 vols., Cambridge, 1892–7.
TRHS	*Transactions of the Royal Historical Society*
TSAS	*Transactions Shropshire Archaeological and Natural History Society*
TWNFC	*Transactions Woolhope Naturalists' Field Club*
VCH	*Victoria County History*
"Visitation"	"Visitation Returns in the Diocese of Hereford in 1397," ed. A. T. Bannister, *EHR* 44 (1929): 279–89, 444–53; (1930): 92–101, 444–63.
Wilkins, *Concilia*	David Wilkins, ed. *Concilia Magnae Britanniae et Hiberniae*, 4 vols. London, 1737.

Introduction

The great plague that ravaged Europe in the middle years of the fourteenth century and was later darkly described in the popular imagination as the Black Death affected every aspect of medieval society. The changes that followed were certainly uneven. Communities, even households, differed in the manner and range of effects. Some places were wiped out by the plague, others were left relatively untouched. But even those who seemed to merit some mysterious protection from death suffered the indirect effects of the epidemic. The disruption of trade, insecurities of movement and commerce, the political and social strains augmented by the plague and the attendant epidemics of fear and confusion had their affects on people during the time of plague and for years to come.

It was not that death was an uncommon sight in fourteenth-century Europe, even on a grand scale. England and other countries had suffered through severe famines earlier in the century and war between England and France was draining both kingdoms' coffers as well as much of their life's blood. But the trials of lean years could be forgotten with a few good harvests. As for the anxieties of war, these could be lost for a while in the cause of nationhood and the promises of spoil, victory, and peace. The plague which swept across western Europe from the Mediterranean to the Hebrides in five years could not be measured in such comprehending terms. To be sure, medieval people had known plague and even marshalled certain precautions against it. But the pestilence that struck in the mid-fourteenth century was of a far different kind, more virulent than any had known. By conservative estimates, at least a third of the European population died in the course of this epidemic and subsequent bouts of plague.

As a subject of history, the Black Death has not suffered from a lack of attention. The general bibliography is vast and has grown considerably in the last thirty years. The historical significance of the Black Death has been at the center of numerous scholarly debates: whether, for instance, the epidemic was a turning point in late medieval society and inaugurated new perceptions and institutions, or whether it accelerated trends that had already begun to take place before the 1340s. Local historians, demographers, and economic historians have tended to dominate the discussion on plague as a force of change in medieval society.[1] The recurrent nature of bubonic plague and the coincidence of other factors such as climate, diet, geography, and population density have broadened the terms of discussion. Historians of medicine, long interested in the subject, have focused their attention on the nature of the disease itself, the aetiology of plague and the range of possible effects within medieval urban and rural communities. Studies have been devoted to rat populations, the transmissibility of the disease, and the mutations that may have occurred in the plague bacillus from the middle ages to the present.[2]

While demographic and local studies have refined our understanding of how the plague affected the social and economic structures of the societies in which it occurred, relatively little work has been done on the church in the time of the Black Death. The more recent work, at least for England, has delved more into the temporal than the spiritual sides of the question of the plague's impact on the church.[3] Religious studies in this larger historical topic are perhaps fewer on account of the durability of a handful of books and articles written early in this century. The works of Augustus Jessop, Francis Gasquet, and G. G. Coulton have all had a remarkably long life in the literature on the plague and the English church.[4] All three searched original documents such as episcopal registers, monastic cartularies, and the records of the Crown to gauge the effects of the plague in England. But, at least in the case of Gasquet and Coulton, their powerful skills as historians were occasionally blunted by confessional differences and their divergent approaches to the subject of religious history. Of the same generation but of a different style, A. H. Thompson provided a surer and less polemical method to his studies of the plague in York and Lincoln dioceses.[5] There he examined more carefully the evidence for clerical mortality in the episcopal registers of William la Zouche (1342–1352) and John Gynewell (1347–1362). Though rightly praised for his critical and unbiased work in ecclesiastical records, Thompson did not go much beyond the plague years themselves and restricted much of his discussion on the effects of the epidemic to clerical mortality rates based on institutions to vacant benefices. His lead was taken up in a more inclusive way by J. Lunn in a 1937 Cambridge doctoral dissertation entitled "The Black Death in the Bishops' Registers."[6] Like Thompson, Lunn approached the larger question of the plague's effects on the English church by searching the institution records of extant bishops' registers. His findings and more importantly his interpretations of what the plague mortality might have meant to church institutions have been lost with his dissertation, though at least Lunn's statistics were salvaged in works by Coulton and J. F. D. Shrewsbury.[7]

Apart from these several studies, very little recent work has been done to advance the discussion of the plague's effects on the English church.[8] The general works by Philip Ziegler and Robert Gottfried, and Graham Twigg's scientific reappraisal have drawn most of their information on clerical mortality in English dioceses from the earlier works cited above.[9] There is good reason for this: Gasquet, Coulton, and Thompson pored over volumes of archival materials and manuscript registers to obtain their data and reach conclusions on the plague's impact on church and society. But an overdependence on such works may also create some historiographical problems. For one thing, the question of the plague's impact can be too narrowly conceived. Death was the most impressive of the plague's effects, but it was not the only one. Changes in households, local communities, and society as a whole radiated from the direct and mortal effects of the epidemic to produce a complex of disruption and change. These subsequent or long-term effects, too, need to be assessed. Also, the traditional means of estimating clerical mortality have been limited to examinations of institution lists, records of church vacancies reported and filled. A regular mechanism in local church administration, institutions climbed dramatically in number during the plague years signaling great changes in the parish churches and in their pastoral leadership. But other records, less direct in their report of death, can suggest other means of estimating this sort of change in a local church.

Whether contemporary students of this subject depend on earlier findings or not, it is curious that relatively little work has been done in recent times on the question of the plague's effects on the church and religion. The question is important not only because religious records — the administrative archives of numerous dioceses — survive to tell the story of the plague's movements and effects in local areas, but because medieval Christians viewed the pestilence in ways that were essentially religious. Moral theologians and canonists of the medieval church had consistently stressed the interrelationship of physical infirmity with the condition of the soul. It was commonly held that spiritual healing was more salutary to the Christian than the cure of bodily disease and the Fourth Lateran Council in 1215 underscored this perception when it decreed that physicians of the body should before all else admonish the patient to seek first the healer of souls. With spiritual health restored, the application of physical medicaments would be of greater benefit, for "when the cause is removed the effect will pass away."[10] The proper treatment for diseases of the body as well as the spirit were the sacraments of the church, in particular the balm of absolution received in the sacrament of Penance. The curative features of medieval religion and, specifically, the ministries entailed in pastoral care had been too long a part of religious perceptions to be jettisoned when they were most critically needed, at the approach of death. This was precisely what pastors and most medieval Christians had in mind when news of the impending plague was first broadcast through English parishes.

There was little doubt in the mind of a fourteenth-century prelate such as Archbishop Zouche of York that souls would fare no better than bodies were they not healed of the corruption of sin. In mid-summer, 1348, he indicated as much to the clergy and people of his diocese in a letter that was reiterated by other bishops at about the same time.

> As human life on earth is warfare, there is little wonder that those who wage war on the miseries of this world are sometimes disturbed by uncertain events, at times favorable, at others adverse. For Almighty God at times allows those he loves to be chastised since, by an outpouring of spiritual grace, strength is made perfect in infirmity. Therefore, who does not know what great death, pestilence and infection of the air hangs about various parts of the world and especially England these days. This indeed is caused by the sins of people who, caught up in the delights of their prosperity, neglect to remember the gifts of the Supreme Giver.[11]

No one would be spared, the archbishop warned, unless the people turned back in earnest prayer to God whose mercy is greater than his justice. The surest defense against this plague was a cleansed heart, an earnest supplication to God.

Zouche was joined by other bishops in the southern province who issued similar mandates with the hope that the entire country would be mobilized against the epidemic with prayers and acts of charity. John Gynewell of Lincoln had issued his mandate "ad orandum pro pestilentia" on July 25, three days before Zouche raised the alarm in the north. Not long after, on August 17, Bishop Ralph of Bath and Wells ordered the clergy and people of his diocese to fast and pray in anticipation of the pestilence.[12] William Edington of Winchester ordered the cathedral chapter to recite special prayers, especially "the long litany instituted against pestilences of this kind by the holy Fathers." The custom called for the monks of the cathedral to organize penitential processions, leading the people barefoot and with heads bowed through the marketplace of the cathedral city, fasting, and reciting as often as possible the *Pater Noster* and *Ave*. The procession ended at the cathedral with mass, which all were to attend patiently and completely. As the other bishops had done, Edington attached an indulgence of forty days as added encouragement to the pious execution of his mandate.[13] To the west in Exeter, Bishop Grandisson issued his own orders for prayers on October 30 and John Trillek of Hereford ordered customary liturgies sometime earlier that month for the churches of his diocese.[14]

None of these bishops imagined that their mandates which were, in effect, the first pastoral responses to the impending plague, would turn the hearts of English Christians solely on their own merits. First, the word must be published abroad and bishops relied on the customary structures of diocesan, capitular, parochial, and religious authorities to mobilize their clergy and their laity in the face of this crisis: the mandates for prayers and participation in the sacraments were conveyed first to the archdeacons and then to the local deans and religious heads, who would see that parish priests addressed their congregations on the matter. Once the concerns of the shepherds had reached the flocks, the purpose of the mandates hinged on the earnest efforts of local clerics who would preach the necessary message of conversion and due penance, lead the people in processions, and stand ready to receive penitents for confession.

As we can see from Zouche's letter, prelates did not hesitate to claim a place of spiritual leadership in the holy warfare that was required at this time. Nevertheless, the church's abilities to shepherd, guide, console, and minister in time of plague were all potentially compromised and severely so by the impact the disease had on the church itself. People were urged to prayer and to the church's sacraments, but they could not always apply these spiritual medicaments on their own. Their priests were responsible for gathering them in prayer, theirs was the duty to bless and absolve, to feed with Christ's Body and Blood, to preach some message of consolation in the midst of fear and death. But priests were falling as well to the disease. Many who remained in their churches, facing the possibilities of contagion daily, died in the execution of their duties. Others quit their parishes and fled for whatever safety they thought they could obtain. In either case, congregations were left without priests or the sacramental care of the church, those same sacraments that were assurances of Christ's presence and healing.

Through pastoral letters such as Archbishop Zouche's and widely held views of the relationship between sin and death we have some sense of what was expected or hoped for in an epidemic. But we have less an understanding — at least in more precise ways than have been offered in the traditional and general studies on the subject — of what happened to the church during and after the Black Death. How, in fact, did the church manage to accomplish its pastoral aims, especially when it was both refuge and victim during this calamity? And, once the plague had spent its force, how did the church manage in after years to continue its pastoral mission? Were there changes in the institutional and pastoral life of the diocese and, if there were, were they of a transient or permanent nature?

Such are the questions that stand at the beginning of this study. It should be noted at the outset that their answers really only approach the wide and complex issues that comprise the historical realities of both epidemic plague and medieval religion. Both, in some sense, are equally multifarious and hard to trace: there are the intricacies of the epidemic itself, its nature, aetiology, the unevenness of its movements, and its effects on local and national communities; medieval religion is the large category in which doctrine, ecclesiastical administration, and the piety of believers somehow meet. This study raises old questions with what I hope are new approaches; they are also meant to be entirely modest ones, observing life in a small diocese during and after the Black Death in order to understand better what happened in the provision of pastoral care and how far-reaching the events of the plague were in relationship to the cure of souls. Thus, by the very nature of the records examined here, we learn more of the clergy and their work in pastoral care than we do of the laity who were the purpose and object of the church's ministries. The question of the plague's effects on religion in its broader dimensions, the life of the laity and the changes that went on in parish communities and worship remain to be answered. But, for the present, I wish to shed as much light as the sources will allow on one important aspect of the larger question.

From the perspective of pastoral care, the medieval diocese was the basic unit of church life, a gathering of parish communities under the spiritual leadership of the bishop whose duties included the guiding of his flock and the training of others to assist him in his wide ministerial duties of preaching, teaching, and blessing. In this book we will observe structures of pastoral care, those institutions, agents, and operations which the medieval church had developed over the previous centuries and came to rely on for achieving its pastoral ends. Though we will observe structures of pastoral care fairly closely here, especially during a time of considerable change, it is important to remember that the human and spiritual activities which they represent are not far behind. The records of the time rarely describe what actually went on in the pastoral relationship between priests and parishioners; they speak rather of what was expected and how expectations were realized or not. By examining these sources and the structures they describe, we are better able to assess the range of impact from the plague and gauge the level of stress laid upon these structures.

While the events that were taking place in other dioceses are acknowledged here from time to time, the focus is on Hereford, its bishops, clergy, and parishioners. This is not done to the exclusion of other places but, rather, for the sake of thoroughness in viewing the experience of one church during this changeful time. Dioceses differed one from another in many respects: in population, settlement, wealth, topography, political significance, and leadership. But the pastoral life of the late medieval church had its many and familiar features that would have been as recognizable to a London merchant as to a plowman from Herefordshire. Though the more precise contours of impact, response, and effect in the time of plague will vary from one place to another, what we observe in a single diocese occurred in broad terms elsewhere. Hereford is one witness to the complex and profound events that took place in the medieval church during the late fourteenth century and this study is an effort to give voice to its testimony.

The second larger question with which this study deals is an old historiographical commonplace that clerical life and discipline declined markedly after the upheavals caused by the plague and that churchmen made concessions in the urgency of the moment by admitting barely-qualified men to holy orders. As a general rule, historians still maintain that if the Black Death did not initiate powerful changes in the attitudes and standards of the parish clergy that lead to a continued decline until the Reformation, it most assuredly contributed to that long-term trend.[15] Certainly, there was a host of factors that influenced the ministry and the priesthood in the fourteenth and fifteenth centuries but the wide social, economic, and religious changes induced by the period of plagues cannot be discounted. Especially given the fact that the epidemics had close spiritual and religious connotations, the relationship between the two phenomena needs to be more carefully examined. In the end, to what extent did the Black Death contribute to the decline of the English parish clergy in the late middle ages?

Chapter One serves as a broad description of the pastoral structures that served Hereford clergy and parishioners during the fourteenth century. These structures represented levels of responsibility and activity with regard to the diocesan leadership and local church life. Chapter Two considers the first strains placed upon those pastoral structures with the plague's arrival and initial effects in the diocese of Hereford. Within weeks of the plague's arrival, Bishop Trillek was faced with scores of vacant benefices, plummeting numbers in clerical candidates, and parish clergy whose resolve to stay in their churches weakened by the day. He responded to the plague as any administrator might: he labored quickly and effectively to shore up structures that had been sorely tested and worked to restore stability and order in his diocese. But as a pastor he relied on his own sacramental ministry, the prayer of the church, and the intercession of the saints, including and especially his predecessor St. Thomas Cantilupe, bishop of Hereford from 1275 to 1282, for the aid which neither Trillek nor any other mortal could effect. Chapter Three follows the long-term effects of the plague in diocesan administration and pastoral care through the remainder of Trillek's pontificate and the reign of his successor Lewis Charlton (1361–1369). The gradual recovery that Trillek had nursed was set back in 1361 by a second outbreak of plague which required Bishop Charlton to lead the diocese with many of the same problems that had challenged his predecessor. Subsequent epidemics and a host of other influences combined to trouble the diocese through the remainder of the century. One of the most challenging responses to all of this lay in the area of clerical recruitment and pastoral provision. Chapter Four is a study of how the sacrament of holy orders was celebrated in Hereford during the half century following the Black Death and what affect diminishing numbers of clerical candidates had on pastoral care in Hereford parishes. The shifting patterns of clerical recruitment and the institutional demands of parishes for clergy forced bishops to face the crisis as best they could. Chapter Five concludes the discussion with a view of clerical life and pastoral care at the century's end and relies mainly on the extensive returns from Bishop Trefnant's visitation of Hereford parishes in 1397.

Because this study is based on a variety of sources, it might be helpful to survey the nature and form of these records in order to understand better the pastoral and religious realities they represented. Since the cure of souls was the result of the coincidence of so many factors — clergy, community, law, property — any study of pastoral care must be based upon an equal variety of historical sources. Priority of place is given to the bishops' registers which included, among the records of diocesan business, decisions and activities that pertained especially to pastoral care.[16] In Hereford the series of bishops' registers begins with St. Thomas Cantilupe's in 1275 and continues with very little interruption to the sixteenth century.[17] Other local records that could shed greater light on particular areas of the diocese — parish registers, churchwardens' accounts and archdeacons's registers — do not exist for Hereford from the fourteenth century. Episcopal court act books survive from 1407 but do not occur in a series until 1455. Most of the materials from the archdeacons' registers are much later than the fourteenth century and no records of the rural deans, except occasional references in the bishops' registers, remain.[18] Thus practically every facet of pastoral care in fourteenth-century Hereford has been found and examined in the episcopal registers. Since these volumes, in both their manuscript and printed forms, serve as the major sources of this study, their contents need to be described in brief.

Although the registers provide the greatest insight into pastoral care in the fourteenth century, the type and quality of their entries regarding parishioners, clergy, and the cure of souls differ from one register to another. A bishop's register was a documentary representation of diocesan government. Thus the entries reflect the bishop's activities in and outside the diocese, and his policies regarding administration of the see and the cure of souls which were, at least in theory, his first concerns. The registrar, the diocesan official responsible for copying and preserving the bishop's records, also influenced to some degree what went into his master's register. A more vigilant and organized scribe was often behind the fuller and more complete register.[19] In character, they are not random samplings of documents, but records of the regular and frequent duties the bishop performed: ordinations, institutions to benefices, licences for non-residence and dispensations of every kind. Letters and memoranda carry up the less usual concerns of a bishop and these often reveal the more particular aspects of diocesan, parochial, and pastoral life in the local church.

The records of the cathedral dean and chapter, though they do not represent the diocese to the extent that the episcopal registers do, are indispensable to a study of this kind. The rights of jurisdiction, which included the disposition of benefices (except cathedral dignities and prebends, which remained in the patronage of the bishop), the collection of dues, the day to day management of the cathedral, and the visitation of churches in the deanery, were jealously guarded by the dean and chapter. The cathedral clergy were busy with many things and the records of their activities survive in great quantity.[20] The most continuous records kept by the cathedral administrators — account rolls, court rolls, rentals, and surveys — had more to do with the running of the cathedral and capitular estates than with the provision of parishes in the deanery. Indeed, most references to the latter appear in an incidental fashion, usually in light of some dispute over the rights of the chapter. One record that combines both facets of chapter administration and local pastoral care is the fascinating series of documents resulting from the lengthy contest between a Hereford vicar and the dean and chapter over mortuary rights. The cause, which was initiated before the dean's own court, moved by appeal to the Court of Arches, and finally resolved at the papal court, had as its primary concern the alienation of mortuary dues from the cathedral.[21]

There were forces outside the diocese as well which, though in a sometimes distant manner, influenced pastoral activities and structures in the Hereford diocese. Much of this influence was a matter of patronage exercised in Hereford benefices by agents of kingdom and church. The Crown presented clerics regularly to churches in the gift of the king and occasionally to benefices whose advowsons had escheated with other properties to the Crown. A great number of these presentations are found in the volumes of calendars of Patent Rolls from 1301 to 1405.[22] The effect of royal patronage can usually be tested in a comparison of these presentations with the institutions to benefices recorded in the bishops' registers. But central records contain other types of references to diocesan clergy and parishioners as well: in the patent letters there are frequent references to such matters as delinquent clerics, royal commissions of "oyer and terminer" and confirmations of church possessions. Other central records which contain information pertaining to the diocese, parishes, and clergy of Hereford include the vast royal correspondence of the Close Rolls and reception and auditing of accounts preserved in the rolls of the Exchequer. The most useful records from the latter are the clerical subsidy rolls for all or parts of the Hereford diocese in 1379 and 1406.[23]

Papal records provide further clues as to the condition of pastoral care in the Hereford diocese. Much of the business represented in petitions to the pope and grants issuing from his chancery had to do with ecclesiastical benefices. And most of these, as we will see, were wealthier cathedral benefices and livings in the gift of the bishop. Very seldom did papal provisions reach the greater number of parishes and chapels in the diocese, largely on account of the low level of interest in these benefices on the part of the usual papal supplicants. Although most of the references to Hereford in the calendars of papal petitions and letters concern provisions, one can find other issues of a religious nature in those records.[24] Clerics petitioned for and received dispensations from illegitimacy and minority of age, two impediments to holy orders. They also petitioned regularly for licenses to hold more than one benefice, or permission to augment the value of the only one they possessed. The laity were numbered among petitions and grants for private altars, personal confessors, the remission of sin at the hour of death, and other graces that pertained to the papal authority.

These are the major sources that inform this study of the effects of the Black Death on pastoral provision in the diocese of Hereford. Before we consider in closer detail what the diocese looked like pastorally, a final word needs to be offered regarding the epidemic itself and how it is regarded in these pages. I do not presume here to enter, much less settle, the debate among medical historians as to the precise nature of the plague which was only later called the Black Death. Witnesses to its course and survivors of its visitation referred to it in general terms as the "great pestilence," the "unprecedented pestilence" and the "great mortality." Later, when subsequent epidemics broke out, fourteenth-century observers referred to the Black Death as the "prima pestilentia" to distinguish it from latter epidemics, much as later generations would number their world wars. Most historians agree that the epidemic was primarily bubonic plague accompanied by its variant and more virulent strains of pneumonic and septicaemic plague, though others have argued for different causes and a different aetiology, including typhus, anthrax, and poisoned food stores.[25] Many, too, have maintained that the plague was really a combination of diseases and ailments including bubonic plague, which when influenced by climatic conditions, rodent and human populations, diet, and hygiene had varying effects from place to place.[26] As fascinating as all these studies are, I am not so much concerned with how the plague occurred but rather that it occurred and that there is enough objective evidence to suggest that its mortal effects were significant. I have attempted to keep a respectful distance on this debate by using those terms which contemporaries employed such as *epidemia* and *pestilentia* to describe the outbreaks of disease, though the customary and usual reference to the plague of 1347–50 as the Black Death is also used throughout. All other incidents of plague are distinguished by the time in which they occurred.

1. The Diocese of Hereford in the Fourteenth Century

When the plague finally reached Hereford in the late summer of 1348, its effects on the religious practices of people were as troubling as they were widespread. Some Christians already had their soul's provision in mind but others were urged in the mandates of bishops and priests to ready themselves against the coming scourge through prayer, penitential acts, and the confession of their sins. While the church maintained that faith in God's mercy was the only true antidote to the pestilence, the institution found it increasingly difficult to provide the very solace it held out to the faithful. All were urged to pray, but priests were needed to take the sacraments to the dying and to bless, bury, and shrive. But priests died in significant numbers along with their people, while some curates fled their churches in fear of the contagion or out of despair. And, yet, the church's challenge in the face of this epidemic was not restricted to the number of priests willing to serve in pastoral cures. Every aspect of local life, all the daily routines, structures, and offices that helped describe the more normative practices of pastoral care and provision were, for a time, unsettled and interrupted.

The aim of this chapter is to identify and describe these various structures assigned to the support of pastoral care in the diocese. Understanding what these structures were and how they operated in more normal times will give us a better sense of how the Black Death placed powerful strains upon them and, to what extent, if any, they underwent change in the period of crisis. The diocese was the basic unit of pastoral care united under the bishop but it was also a complex of relationships, official and personal, having to do with religion, of course, but also with authority, property, and law. The plague's impact on the diocese and its operations was simultaneous, affecting every aspect of local life. But in order to evaluate more clearly how this impact occurred, we must examine in separate fashion those principle structures that made up the larger religious and pastoral framework of the diocese: the diocese itself, the bishop and his assistants, the parishes, their clergy and people, and, lastly, the religious communities.

The Diocese of Hereford and Its Leadership

The diocese of Hereford was the first diocese west of the Severn River, carved out of the ancient Mercian see of Lichfield in the seventh century. Its earliest boundaries had been generally defined by the settlement of the Hecani, a West Saxon tribe, and these markings endured with little change through the medieval period.[1] At least seven counties had boundaries within the medieval diocese of Hereford: Herefordshire in its entirety, the southern half of Shropshire, which comprised the northern portion of the diocese, and smaller parts of Monmouthshire, Worcestershire, Gloucestershire, Radnorshire, and Montgomeryshire. Hereford's longest borders were shared with the dioceses of Worcester and Coventry and Lichfield to the east and north; the Welsh dioceses of Llandaff, St. David's, and Asaph touched its western boundaries.

The diocese was not very large either in land or in population. It was roughly eighty miles from north to south, its northern and eastern boundaries running with the Severn on its long course through the heart of Shropshire, and continuing through the western parts of Worcestershire and Monmouthshire to the south and east. Narrower than it was long, a traveler on horseback could cross the diocese in a couple of days, riding westward from the Malverns near the Worcestershire border to the Black Hills and Wales. Though most of the people in the region spoke English with a West Midlands accent, there were numerous pockets of Welsh-speaking parishioners, particularly in the western reaches of Radnorshire and Montgomeryshire.[2]

The diocese was important militarily and politically with the changing fortunes of England's policies regarding Wales. Since Norman times there had been castles along the borderlands, defending the boundaries and keeping Welsh marauders at bay. Larger and more impressive fortifications were built at Shrewsbury, north of the diocesan border, Ludlow, and Hereford, while smaller castles dotted the landscape to keep the shires in peace. These are mentioned here not only because pastors required some measure of political stability to be about effective work, but because every castle was to some extent a pastoral site with a priest employed to administer the sacraments to the local lord, the garrison, and their families.

The political life of the diocese was bound to effect its leadership. Since the days of the Conqueror, the bishops of Hereford had also been Marcher Lords with special duties of defense attendant on their more usual work as spiritual shepherds. During Owen Glendower's rebellion in the early fif-

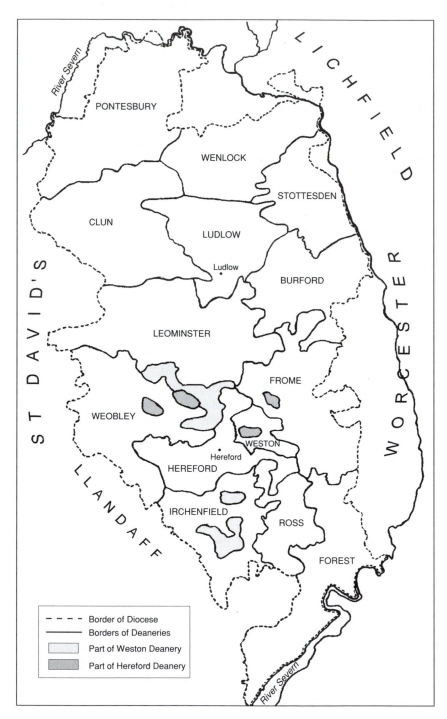

Figure 1.1. The late medieval diocese of Hereford.

teenth century, Bishop Mascall mustered his knights and even his clergy to protect Hereford's borders.[3] Accordingly, the men who became bishops of Hereford were often drawn from prominent local families such as the Charltons, Thomas (1327–1344), and Lewis (1361–1369), who were related to the lords of Powys.

The diocese was sparsely populated, even before the wasting effects of the Black Death checked the long trend of expansion since the twelfth and thirteenth centuries. Population figures for this time are inexact, but, according to poll tax returns from 1377, twenty-five years after the first epidemic plague in the region there were nearly 26,000 people in all Herefordshire and about 15,000 in the northern half of the diocese, the southern half of Shropshire. The same tax returns indicate a population of some eight hundred secular clerics ministering to Hereford parishioners.[4] Most people in the diocese lived in the villages and hamlets of the country, but there were a few noteworthy towns in the diocese: the cathedral city itself, Ludlow, the main political and ecclesiastical center of the northern half of the diocese, and the lesser towns of Leominster, Ledbury, and Ross.

During the fourteenth century there were just under four hundred parish churches and chapels scattered through the diocese and gathered into basic regional units called rural deaneries. These, in turn, comprised the two archdeaconries of the diocese, Hereford, slightly larger with the cathedral city at its center, and Shropshire or Salop to the north with its administrative seat in Ludlow. Hereford Archdeaconry had been divided into seven deaneries including the cathedral deanery which, under the authority of the Dean and Chapter, enjoyed considerable independence from episcopal authority as a peculiar jurisdiction. The other deaneries included Frome, the largest in area, Leominster, which had been the ancient center of the diocese, Ross, Irchenfield, Weston, Weobley, and, at the southern tip of the diocese, the Deanery of the Forest. The Shropshire Archdeaconry had six deaneries: Ludlow, Burford, Clun, Stottesden, Wenlock, and Pontesbury. With the two archdeaconries and the diocese itself, the rural deaneries often took their boundaries from old settlements and religious foundations. For example, Leominster's borders were much the same as the old minster church's boundaries when it had been at the center of missionary territory. Burford, Clun, and Pontesbury up in the north were former minster churches, while Wenlock's borders ran along the old estates of St. Milburga's monastery.[5]

THE BISHOPS OF HEREFORD

Hereford, remote and relatively poor, was not really much of a prize from the perspective of the more ambitious medieval ecclesiastic. If anything, it was a sturdy stepping-stone to a more lucrative and prestigious placement. But for the bishop intent on preaching and guiding the souls of his clergy and parishioners, Hereford provided as great a challenge as any medieval diocese. Certainly, there was an impressive range of talent among the men who presided over the diocese during the fourteenth century.[6] Some were sons of noble houses who had been raised to manage power in one form or another, such as the two Charltons of Powys and William Courtenay (1370–75), whose father was the Earl of Devon. All the bishops of Hereford in the fourteenth century, from that eminent pastor, Richard Swinfield, whose pontificate ended in 1317, to John Trefnant, promoted in 1389, were able administrators. Adam Orleton (1317–27), Thomas Charlton, and John Gilbert (1370–89) had held powerful positions in royal government. John Trefnant (1389–1404) had exercised great influence as a papal auditor before his appointment to Hereford. Most of them were local men: Orleton and the Charltons were from Shropshire, John Trillek (1344–1360) grew up in Worcestershire within easy reach of Hereford's borders. John Gilbert, though born abroad, seems to have had family relations in the diocese.[7] Courtenay and Trefnant were from neighboring regions, Devon and northern Wales respectively, and Swinfield, though he spent most of his life in Hereford, was a Kentish man.

All of these bishops were university graduates: six of them (Swinfield, Orleton, Thomas Charlton, Courtenay, Gilbert, and Trefnant) held doctorates in civil or canon law or theology; John Trillek was a Paris master who had spent some time at Oxford and his successor, Lewis Charlton, had been a distinguished lecturer and chancellor of Oxford.

No doubt, their administrative gifts put them in good standing with their most powerful patrons, the king and pope, who were more often than not of like minds regarding episcopal appointments in fourteenth-century England. But their competence in presiding over papal commissions or seeing to the timely payment of church subsidies to the Crown are not central to this discussion. Rather, we are here concerned with how they functioned as pastors.

No medieval bishop, however worldly or ambitious, could utterly ignore the fact that his power resided in his ecclesiastical station, that he was ordained a priest and consecrated a bishop to govern souls and shepherd them to salvation. There is no question that some bishops did this with more zeal and dedication than others and that some paid only passing attention to their pastoral duties. The diversity among fourteenth-century bishops did not end with their administrative experience or academic training. Some were clearly better pastors than others. Their pastoral role in the diocese was comprehensive to say the least, but it may be divided into two broad areas of episcopal activity: the bishop's personal and sacramental role as a pastor — the duties he himself performed — and the ways he carried out his pastoral leadership through an array of assistants.

A medieval bishop's role as pastor was evident in many of the tasks he performed within his own diocese.[8] As a priest he celebrated the Eucharist regularly and prayed the Divine Office daily, usually in the chapel of one of his manors where he tended to reside. As a bishop he took on special sacramental duties in the celebration of Confirmation and Holy Orders. In the case of the former, there were no set times for the sacrament. Whenever the bishop was in a particular area of the diocese, local curates urged their parishioners to take their children if they had not yet been confirmed to present them to the bishop for his blessing, sometimes granted as he passed along the road.[9] Ordinations were a different matter. Here regularity and well-published announcements of the bishop's intention to ordain were a matter of course. Canon law dictated that a bishop should convene candidates for promotion to orders at least four times a year on the seasonal Ember Days and twice more, on the vigils of Passion Sunday and Easter, if required.[10] This was perhaps the bishop's most important ministry in the pastoral leadership of his extended flock, for at the celebrations of this sacrament he promoted candidates to all ranks of the clergy, from the children who appeared for first tonsure to deacons who had finished their period of apprenticeship and were considered ready for ordination to the priesthood. It was not merely a matter of providing the necessary number of clergy to administer the parishes and chapels of the diocese; the bishop was required to invigilate the process of ordination carefully and to promote only those men who were qualified for the order they sought according to the terms set out in canon law.[11]

The bishop's responsibilites for pastoral placement did not end with ordination. As the overseer of every church benefice in his diocese, he had a special role to play in the appointment of clerics to parishes and pastoral cures. Once nominated by the local patron or the owner of the church advowson, a candidate for a benefice had to appear before the bishop or his delegate and be examined on his abilities to govern a cure. If approved, the newly-instituted cleric was subsequently inducted into the parish at the bishop's formal request, usually to some local official such as the rural dean. On occasion, the bishop might appoint a cleric to a benefice in his own keeping, in which case presentation and institution were conflated into a single act called a collation. One last function of the bishop regarding parochial appointments occurs in cases where the patron of the benefice neglected or was unable to exercise his or her patronal function; if a benefice remained vacant for six months, the advowson lapsed temporarily to the bishop who appointed directly.[12]

Along with his celebration of the sacraments and regulation of pastoral appointments, the bishop had other important spiritual duties to perform in the diocese such as preaching the Gospel and instructing the faithful in matters of doctrine and discipline. In Hereford, the bishop customarily preached and presided in the cathedral on the major solemnities of Christmas, Ash Wednesday, and Easter, as well as important local feasts such as St. Milburga's day (February 23) and, after 1320, the feast of St. Thomas Cantilupe on October 2.[13] But he preached as well when touring his diocese on visitation, at ordinations, and church dedications.[14]

EPISCOPAL ASSISTANTS

Long before the fourteenth century it was apparent that no bishop, not even the most pastorally minded, could acquit all the responsibilities of his office single-handedly. Bishops required larger staffs of administrative and pastoral assistants, secretaries, scribes, and commissaries in order to manage the affairs of the local church. Some of these offices, such as the cathedral dean and the archdeacons, had been around for centuries and though their place in the diocese was assured by weight of custom and reasonable use on the bishop's part, they were positions held for life and could be encumbered by men of less effect and loyalty. Nevertheless, the bishop was wise to rely on them to complete certain tasks and in Hereford some of the most significant leaders in diocesan administration and pastoral care were numbered among these assistants.

The dean assisted in the pastoral life of the diocese chiefly through his role as rector of the cathedral of St. Mary and St. Ethelbert. Though his place in the hierarchical order had been long clarified and distinguished from that of the bishop, his ministry in the cathedral was in its origins an extension of the bishop's work as pastor. The dean had charge of preaching in the cathedral and hearing the confessions of his chapter and, in general, overseeing the liturgical life of the mother church of the diocese. But his responsibilities did not end at the boundaries of the cathedral close. He had authority over the six parishes of the cathedral city and the thirty-one parishes in the deanery of Hereford. It was he, not the bishop, who instituted clerics to those churches under his decanal jurisdiction and with his chapter presided over the principal ecclesiastical court in the deanery.[15] He also visited churches to supervise their administration and invoked ecclesiastical sanctions against malefactors much like the bishop would in his wide jurisdiction.[16]

Like the dean, the archdeacons were important and permanent officers in the administration of the diocese. Their title gave them a place of influence in the cathedal chapter but their real work was among the parish clergy of the archdeaconry.[17] Like the bishop, they exercised their office most fully when they were visiting the parishes and clergy in their territories, an important duty they were to carry out once a year. As the bishop's deputy the archdeacon was an important means for carrying out diocesan policy, and as a "pastor's pastor" much of his work entailed the moral supervision of the local clergy. These duties were meant to bring him close to the everyday realities of parish life and pastoral care. But the archdeaconry of Hereford was the size of a county and Shropshire, though smaller, was still a territory of many parishes and clergy. In order to facilitate the pastoral obligations of the bishop and his archdeacons another episcopal assistant, the rural dean, was necessary for local applications of diocesan policy.

The deans of the thirteen rural deaneries in the diocese completed the chain of command from the bishop through the archdeacon to the parish clergy and chaplains of the diocese.[18] Though their office was a permanent and useful structure in the diocesan framework, deans did not occupy their position for life. It was usually assigned by the bishop to one of the more senior and trustworthy clerics of the local deanery. Their importance to the bishop and the clergy of the deanery has been generally overlooked in medieval church histories. The bishop often based his own policies for a particular region on their acquired familiarity with local circumstances, communities, and clergy. In Hereford, the rural dean was often the bishop's local commissary, appointed to cite individuals to church courts, publish excommunications, induct newly instituted clerics to their benefices, and put criminous clerks into custody until the bishop could see to them himself.[19]

In his own deanery the rural dean was the local authority in all matters which pertained to the cure of souls. He was obliged to inspect the fabric of the churches of his deanery and, if warranted, issue commands for their repair or for the obtaining of vessels and books necessary for the worthy celebration of the sacraments. Even exempt religious houses, when appropriators of parish churches, were expected to answer to him for the condition of their churches.[20] The rural dean was further obliged to supervise the moral behavior of his clergy and gather them in monthly meetings where the bishop's mandates might be read and certain issues pertinent to the local churches discussed. He also acted as local confessor or penitentiary to the clergy and was encouraged to visit them with the last sacraments when they were sick.[21] From the early fourteenth century rural deans were involved in modest probate business, proving wills of testators whose goods totaled less than five pounds in value.

These positions were more or less permanent in the running of the diocese. They were made to be as useful to the bishop as he could render them, but they were not flexible enough to meet the changing demands of episcopal government. These requirements — and they included the delegation of practically every aspect of diocesan rule — were carried up by a second group of episcopal assistants. These officials occupied positions of authority at the grace of the bishop and could be employed or dismissed at will; they also had closer access to the ordinary and to diocesan government and formed a coterie of close advisors and assistants called the episcopal *familia*. The most important of their number was the vicar general who governed the diocese in his master's absence. His was a vital position in that he appointed other administrative officials who helped administer the see.[22] On occasion the customary duties of this deputy were combined with the responsibilities of the *officialis*, the bishop's legal officer. However, in Hereford the judicial activities delegated by the bishop were often interchangeable with the *officialis* and an agent called the commissary general. Other commissaries were appointed on an ad hoc basis for special duties such as sequestering tithes and other revenues or gaining control over testamentary goods. These unappealing appointments often went to rural deans or other local clerics.[23] Other members of the *familia* included the scribes, secretaries, and notaries who kept the administration of the diocese and its records in good form.[24] Chief among these was the registrar, who traveled with the bishop, drafting and saving records of diocesan administration until they were gathered together into the bishop's register at the end of his pontificate.[25]

The Parishes of Hereford

Bishops, deans, and commissaries played occasional and impressive roles, but it was the local curate who exercised the greatest influence over the religious and pastoral life of his parishioners. The extent of pastoral care and its quality were almost entirely his sole responsibility, and a parish prospered or faltered religiously under the guidance of the parish curate. While it is important to consider the range and type of clergy involved in pastoral offices in the diocese of Hereford, it is also necessary to view them in relationship to other critical factors of local pastoral provision: the parishioners gave real shape to the church's expectations regarding pastoral care, not only through their needs for the sacraments and other ministries but through their necessary material support of the cure and the curate. Similarly, the local patron who owned the church advowson functioned in an important way with regard to the pastoral leadership of the parish. Each of these latter two elements will be considered in place after a few general comments about the parish clergy.

The Parish Clergy

The parish clergy were the largest body of clerics in the diocese, outnumbering monastic and conventual clergy who served their own houses and who were usually excluded from direct involvement with the cure of souls. The secular clergy were divided into two large and unequal groups defined by their ecclesiastical status and rank: in some sense the elite of the diocese, the leaders of parishes — rectors and vicars — formed the upper clergy, so-called because they enjoyed the security of a freehold in the benefice they occupied. They were typically better educated and certainly better paid than their more numerous counterparts, the wage-earning clergy, who formed the larger body of the clerical proletariat. There were, of course, clearly defined responsibilities which went with rank and privilege: beneficed clerics were required to be resident in their churches and see to the pastoral provision of the cure, either directly (if they were in priest's orders) or indirectly, in which case they were required to employ a suitable vicar or chaplain. They were also expected to administer the revenues of the church with good stewardship, seeing to the upkeep of the church and the parish house. Under some circumstances the rector of the church was perennially absent from the parish, as in the case of corporate rectors such as religious houses which had appropriated the parish's revenues with the approval of the bishop. Typically, in such a case, a certain portion of the parish income was reserved for the employment of a suitable pastor and the parish "ordained" a vicarage.[26]

Though every parish had but one rector or vicar, depending on its status, there were other clergy attached to the local church who also contributed, perhaps in more direct ways, to the pastoral life of the parish community. Principal among these were the numerous stipendiary clergy, wage-earning priests who got themselves employed by local rectors as assistant clergy. Given the possibility of their employer's occasional leaves, these men often carried out the actual day-to-day running of the parish and the celebration of masses at scandalously low wages. Before the Black Death there had been little change in the annual salary of five marks typical of this post, which had been set as a minimum by the Council of Oxford in 1222.[27] In status, this wage scale put the stipendiary on fairly equal footing, at least financially, with the local plowman.

The stipendiaries were joined by other clerics, often local parishioners who had recently received minor or major orders and were employed at the parish until such a time as they could garner their own living.[28] Depending on his clerical status, this type of assistant could be of great help in the local cure. Deacons could administer some of the sacraments, recite the gospel at mass, and sing liturgical antiphons and canticles; subdeacons read the epistle and, with the acolyte, assisted the priest at the altar. All could be employed for the countless tasks of keeping up the church and the rector's manse, leading processions with thurible or cross, ringing bells in the churchtower, and lighting the curate's way with a candle at night were he called to the bedside of an ill parishioner. The importance of having such assistants in parish churches was often underscored when vicarages were ordained and the revenues of a parish divided according to the priorities of pastoral care. When he ordained a vicarage at Dorstone church in 1331, Bishop Thomas Charlton stipulated that the vicar employ from his portion a cleric who could assist him at the altar and in "other services" required in the church.[29]

Two other types of clerics were often associated with parishes though they were not directly involved in the daily obligations of the cure. These were chantry and guild chaplains. There were clearly more of the former than the latter, as nearly every parish in England by the end of the middle ages had at least one chantry altar established by pious patrons for the daily singing of masses for the dead. Unlike the typical wage-earning chaplain, the chantrist had but a single duty to perform or, at least, one for which he was paid. But by custom he was supposed to join the rector or vicar at the altar for Sunday mass and appear regularly in choir for matins and even-song.[30] Still, with apparently much time on his hands, the chantrist was given the added responsibility quite often of running a parish grammar school, whose provision was often attached to the foundation of chantries in the late fourteenth and fifteenth centuries.[31]

Like the chantrists, guild priests or chaplains formed another small class of clerics whose activities contributed to the wider pastoral life of local communities. Much like the founders of chantries, the men and women who formed guilds based on work or Christian service under the name of a particular saint employed priests to celebrate mass daily for the members of the guild. And, like chantrists, guild priests were expected to assist at the altars of the church where their guild worshipped on a regular basis.

Finally, some local clerics would be occupied as chaplains to a lord or lady, celebrating masses in manor chapels and perhaps providing instruction for the children of the estate. Hereford bishops regularly granted leaves of absence to diocesan clergy for terms as chaplains of private oratories. Richard David, the rector of Neen Solers, was allowed to serve the countess of March for an indefinite period of time; the rector of Abberley was given leave as a chaplain to Prince Lionel for one year, and Petronella de Penbridge was allowed to hire chaplains to serve at oratories on her manors at Newland, Monnington, and Clehonger. In Lady Penbridge's case, as in others where permissions for oratories had been granted, bishops gave their approval so long as these pious activities were not carried out in prejudice to the rights of local parish churches. Bishop Trillek urged Lady Penbridge to leave her oratories on Sundays and solemnities to worship in her own parish.[32] In some cases the petitions came from priests who had their own oratories such as Thomas de Routon, who, too old and feeble to celebrate mass at St. Mary's in Ludlow, asked Bishop Orleton if he could keep to his own altar.[33]

All of these men contributed in some measure to the pastoral life of the parish. Once again, their number and condition varied according to the needs and income of a church. In many Hereford parishes the curate got by with a young cleric from the local village who would serve as a factotum for a small wage. In other places there could actually be small communities of clergy such as the ones who served in the larger and wealthier parishes of Bromyard, Leominster, or Ludlow.

Before we pass from the local clergy to their parishioners and the patron of the advowson, a few words about the preparation of clerics for pastoral service are needed. The requirements for ordination were very basic: a candidate was expected to be sound in mind and body, born of a valid marriage, in possession of enough learning and latinity to pray as his order required, and, in general, free from any impediments, physical and spiritual, that would hinder the free exercise of his ministry.

It was universally recognized that more of his learning as a pastor would occur in the parish itself. Still, how was he to come by the rudiments of an education that would qualify him for ordination or help win him sponsorship for a benefice? Most parish clergy came by their pastoral education through a period of apprenticeship to a curate. Beyond this chancy course of study, a cleric could attend a local grammar school for studies in the trivium. Larger parish churches such as Leominster, Bromyard, and Ross were liklier than others to have adequate provision for a grammar school. Ludlow, mainly through the strong support of its very active and generous Palmers' Guild, had the best parish grammar school in the northern part of the diocese.[34] There were at least seventy-six chantries in the diocese by the end of the fourteenth century, though it must be said that increased association of grammar schools with chantries tended to be a fifteenth-century development in Hereford as elsewhere.[35] Finally, prospective clerics could find some education in the greater religious houses of the diocese such as Wigmore and Wenlock abbeys, or in the neighboring monastic schools at Gloucester and Worcester.[36] Students would find a more advanced curriculum at the cathedral school and a fewer still would be able to study theology or law at Oxford, Cambridge, or Paris.

Having such educational facilities in or outside the diocese met only part of the challenge of providing the foundations of a pastoral education. Opportunity was typically a matter of financial support, which usually meant personal or family wealth or patronage. In fourteenth-century Hereford, clerics could attend local grammar schools *gratis*. Even grammatical and theological studies at the cathedral school were offered free of charge, though provisions for room and board for non-city dwellers was another matter.[37] In fourteenth-century Hereford there were two means of support for basic or advanced education available to junior and senior clerics. The office of *aquabajulus*, or water-bearer, was usually offered to young acolytes or subdeacons as a stipend for their education at a neighboring grammar school. It was thought a worthy investment by the local curate and the parish for a better-educated future pastor. Priests who had missed that earlier opportunity and later found themselves obligated to reside in their parishes as rectors or vicars were able, by the late thirteenth century, to arrange for a term or two at a university under the provisions of the papal decree *Cum ex eo*.[38]

THE PARISHIONERS

The background, character, and learning of the parish clergy were not singular influences on the life of the local church and its provision for pastoral care. The spiritual and caritative requirements of a local community were often met in the rhythm of liturgical seasons and the celebration of feastdays and the church's sacraments. But they also shifted and changed constantly according to the needs of parishioners and the mission of the church. But neither were parishioners motionless subjects in the dynamic life of the local clergy; they contributed directly to the pastoral care of the church in ways already suggested, but were also the essential means of support for that same endeavor.[39] Their contributions to the physical upkeep of the church's fabric, their payment of tithes and whatever free-will gifts they offered to the clergy for their ministries supplied the material basis for most spiritual activities in the parish. Parishioners were also often patrons who had considerable influence on the disposition of a benefice. They could act individually or as a group in providing clerical candidates with titles necessary for ordination or by founding more enduring institutions such as chantries and guild altars.

These activities were indispensable in the practice of medieval religion, but parishioners were not primarily founders of chantries nor even necessarily patrons of the local church. They were members of a local community defined by their participation in the life of the church which included prayer and worship but also material support for the local cure.

By the fourteenth century, local church operations had come to depend on two forms of income from the parish community, tithes, and other offerings, obligatory and free-will. The former were usually collected on special feasts during the church year, at Christmas, Easter, and the feastday of the local church; failure to pay them could draw sanctions from the bishop.[40] These offerings also included mortuary dues, typically in the form of the "second legacy" — usually the deceased's second beast — against the possibility that he or she had neglected to fulfill the seasonal responsibilities of tithing.[41] Though they were not required, free-will offerings formed an indispensable part of the local church's revenues. Unlike tithes, they were not given to the rector for his disposition, but to the minister of a particular service. Stipendiaries were the usual beneficiaries of this form of contribution. Free-will offerings included "confession pennies," altar bread, and other gifts given in kind. Often when a vicarage was ordained, the vicar was owed any money from the publication of banns and weddings (*sponsalia*), dues paid for the churching of women, and for funerals. Priests often served as witnesses to deathbed testaments and when this service was provided it was customary to make some small offering.

Parishioners had other duties of material support to perform as well. All were required to contribute to the maintenance of the church fabric and occasional building projects such as the construction or repair of a bell-tower or a cemetery wall. The lines of responsibility in this respect were not clearly drawn in every case, but custom declared that the rector took care of the church sanctuary and usually everything that went on in that sacred precinct, and that parishioners were given responsibility over the church nave. Depositions at episcopal visitations and court records indicate that arguments over who was required to do what were not rare. But it should also be said that parishioners were not universally remiss in their duties of support for the local cure. Indeed, many were generous in bequests and chantries or the purchase of liturgical vestments, vessels, books, and candles, or in the provision of food and clothing for the poor and sick of the parish.

Though parishioners made these various contributions to the local church in a separate manner, their common regard for the administration of the church and their own particular interests were often safeguarded by the *custos* or churchwarden.[42] As a position in the local administration of parishes, the churchwarden was a common fixture by the latter half of the fourteenth century. He served as the local representative of the parishioners before the rector and other ecclesiastical authorities and was involved mainly with the inspection of the church fabric, the regular upkeep of the church customarily pertaining to the parishioners. He acted on their behalf, as well, in distributing parishioners' offerings to the poor. The church-warden also managed certain funds of the parish such as legacies destined for particular uses in the church. As they managed funds that were not their own, churchwardens were sometimes challenged to render an account of their stewardship to the parishioners they were meant to represent. The people of Llancaut parish accused their churchwarden, Thomas Amney, of unjustly withholding 6 s. and 8 d. from Wilfrid Longhope's legacy. The money that Thomas kept was supposed to be spent on candles raised at the elevation of the Blessed Sacrament during mass.[43]

THE PARISH PATRON

Though parishes were established primarily as settings for the spiritual life of a community, they were never regarded solely in this light. A parish was also a unit of property and a measure of wealth and as long as money was to be a part of the operation, interests other than religious ones were bound to affect the life of the local church. This was apparent in the ways many rectors and vicars regarded their benefice, but it was also undeniably present in the exerise of patronage. The patrons of English parish churches were a diverse group ranging from the heads of wealthy families to religious houses, the local ordinary, and the Crown. In possessing the church advowson, a patron served the parish most directly in the presentation of a prospective incumbent to the bishop, and with this right of presentation came other obligations to act as the legal defender and advocate of all rights pertaining to the parish church.[44] But the patron's role was not exclusively proprietary or merely legal; patronage also involved benefactions to the local church, the expansion and embellishment of its fabric, acts of charity, and continued provisions for the parish church, its clergy, and people.

In most cases the patron's relationship to the church was a matter of temporal administration, but there were limits. The patron was to have no control over the curate's land or the glebe, tithes, oblations, or any other income deriving from the spiritualities of the church. In fact, patrons, often lay persons before the fourteenth century, were forbidden any control over spiritualities and their administration.[45] This clear distinction between spiritual and secular authority was obscured, however, in cases where religious orders appropriated the revenues of a parish church. The involvement of religious administrators in these spiritual revenues opened up the possibility of religious corporations holding both the right of presentation and the management of church revenues, giving them significant powers over the affairs of a parish church.

Like other properties the church advowson could be alienated as well as bequeathed, sold, or given to a religious foundation as a pious benefaction. Ownership of the advowson and the accompanying rights of presentation could be shared by more than one individual. The grant of presentation might alternate from one owner to another, or, in cases where benefices were divided into shares or medieties, the portioners might act in any combination of ways, by turn or as a collective patron in presenting a cleric to the cure. In Hereford, portioners existed in the churches of Bouldon, Bromyard, Burford, Pontesbury, Ledbury, and Castle Holdgate. The revenues of one parish, Stottesden, were divided between six different parties, the parochial vicar, Shrewsbury Abbey, the rector of Corley church, the Dean of the royal chapel at Bridgnorth, the Abbot of Wigmore, and the Precentor of Wenlock Priory. The portioners of Ledbury church shared in the right of presentation on a rotational basis. On occasion a presentor could give up right of presentation for one turn and there are numerous examples in the bishops' registers when the king enjoyed temporary ownership of advowsons pending the inheritance of property or the filling of a vacancy.

The system of church patronage in the fourteenth century was largely divided between the interests of local patrons, what W. A. Pantin called a "native system," and the disposal of ecclesiastical benefices by papal provision.[46] Institutions to Hereford benefices reveal a variety of patrons in the diocese including the bishop himself, the dean and chapter, the king, and a host of religious houses. Even groups of parishioners acted as patrons of benefices, more often by the end of the fourteenth century for guild chapels and chantries. The people of Ledbury parish regularly presented candidates for the service of an altar in their church dedicated to the Blessed Virgin.[47] The bishop could not usually override the rights of the patron unless the pastoral care of the parish in question were to be placed in jeopardy.

The true strength of patronage in the diocese lay not with the bishop but rather with the religious foundations which had accumulated rights of patronage in parish churches. The largest of these religious corporations was the Dean and Chapter of Hereford Cathedral who, by the early sixteenth century, had acquired the advowsons, and revenues of at least thirty-four churches and chapels in the diocese, most of them within the cathedral deanery itself.[48] According to a list of appropriators of Hereford parishes drawn up in 1419, at least half the churches of the diocese were subject to some form of monastic control either in the outright possession of revenues by appropriation, parish advowsons or annual pensions owed them by churches.[49] Some of the largest possessors of parish advowsons were Wigmore Abbey with twenty-one churches, Leominster, Llanthony Prima, and Wenlock with nine each, and Monmouth Priory with seven. The Hospitallers held rights of presentation to seven parish churches and Ledbury Hospital had three under its patronage.

The Crown also possessed extensive patronal rights in the diocese. With other great landowners, the king owned the advowsons of churches which he or his predecessors had founded and regularly presented his clerks to them. He had temporary rights of presentation during the vacancy of a see when the temporalities of the diocese reverted to the Crown and came into similar possessions on the deaths of religious heads and tenants-in-chief. The English king found a particularly lucrative windfall in the confiscation of advowsons of churches owned by French religious houses during the Hundred Years War.[50]

There was an inevitable rivalry between this native system of patronage over English parish churches and the foreign or papal encroachments directed through papal provisions.[51] During the later thirteenth and early fourteenth centuries the popes had developed both theory and practice with regard to direct provision based on the plenitude of power and the right to control in some measure all church properties. But there is little in the registers of papal petitions and letters indicating much interest on the part of popes or impetrants for Hereford parish churches, probably due to the relative poverty of those benefices. During the fourteenth century only four letters of papal provision were made to Hereford parish churches, out of ninety-five made to Hereford clerics in general. The greater number were divided between the more lucrative benefices of cathedral dignities, canonries, and prebends. Yet even in these cases, few royal and papal clerks were much interested in the meager prebends of Hereford. As far as petitions to the pope for the same period, only three of thirty-one requests involving Hereford benefices had to do with parish churches.[52]

Religious Communities and Pastoral Care

When examining the pastoral apparatus of a medieval diocese, we would naturally look to the bishop and his administration and to parish life for the most concrete evidence for pastoral provision. But pastoral care was not exclusively parochial care: religious communities had been the sources of spiritual and material provision for Hereford souls for centuries. They formed another ecclesiastical map within the boundaries of the diocese and because of their influence on pastoral life, we need to acknowledge both their presence and the range of their activities regarding the cure of souls.

THE RELIGIOUS HOUSES OF THE DIOCESE

Every religious foundation, from the great Augustinian house at Wigmore to the small preceptory of the Knights Hospitallers in Garway, had a chapel to which visitors, travelers, and tenants might come for the Eucharist or some other form of pastoral care. Along with the rhythm of monastic prayer, travelers might find hospitality and the poor food within the walls of a monastic house. The houses at Morville up in Shrewsbury and Bromfield in northern Herefordshire were both built near well-traveled roads with this ministry in mind. Leominster Priory had from its foundations given alms to the poor and provision to beggars.[53]

Almost every religious order and charitable foundation was represented in the fourteenth-century diocese of Hereford. There were Benedictine foundations at St. Guthlac's in Hereford, Kilpeck, and Bromfield, all cells of Gloucester Abbey. Other prominent religious houses of Black monks were at Morville in Shropshire and at Leominster. Wenlock was the largest of the Cluniac houses and the Cistercians were at Abbey Dore and Flaxley. Three other Cistercian houses, Buildwas, Grace Dieu, and Tintern, all outside the boundaries of Hereford diocese, nevertheless exerted appreciable influence as patrons of a number of Hereford parishes. Augustinian canons and canonesses had the most houses of any religious order in the diocese. These included Wigmore, Llanthony Prima, Llanthony Secunda, Wormsley, Chirbury, and, in 1346, a new foundation at Flanesford which, on account of the Black Death, was never able to prosper much as a religious community. Small groups of canonesses were at Aconbury and Limebrook. The four mendicant orders had convents in Hereford and Ludlow and there were neighboring friaries in Gloucester which had regular involvement in the Hereford diocese. A number of the friars from these convents were commissioned on occasion as preachers and confessors for the diocese.[54] Hospitallers and other religious helped staff the hospitals and almshouses in the dioceses where travelers, the sick and poor could find comfort for body and soul. There were four places of such care in and around the city of Hereford, with other hospitals in the southern half of the diocese, two at Leominster and one at Ledbury. In the north there were hospitals in Much Wenlock, Cleobury Mortimer, and Ludlow, with a leper house not far from that town. At St. Katherine's in Ledbury, a hospital that functioned under the auspices of the cathedral dean and chapter, chaplains assisted the work of the hospital brethren by caring for the spiritual needs of patients. Endowments following the hospital's foundation had by the mid-fourteenth century provided for three chaplains to serve at chantries in the hospital chapel.[55]

THE CATHEDRAL OF ST. MARY AND ST. ETHELBERT

Among the collegiate churches in the diocese with their sizeable communities of clergy, such as existed at the minster at Ledbury and the royal free chapel at Castle Holdgate, the cathedral at Hereford was by far the most significant. We have already seen how the cathedral dean and the two archdeacons played important roles in the leadership of the cathedral church and the diocese at large. But since the cathedral was so important to the life of the diocese, we need to comment further on its place as a community or college of clergy in the pastoral framework of fourteenth-century Hereford.

The cathedral clergy served as pastors in generally two ways: to the cathedral itself and its environs, as well as to the parishes of the entire cathedral deanery. Their statutes and customs required certain services "for the wellbeing of souls in Hereford"[56] and these often centered around the celebrations of major feasts when the bishop himself would preside. Otherwise, the cathedral clergy themselves officiated at the liturgies of the church. Also, by ancient custom, the cathedral clergy had charge of funeral liturgies for the local community as well as for most of the parishes of the cathedral deanery. As an ancient minster, the cathedral church had offered its churchyard as a burial ground for the members of its far-flung parish. Even as late as the fourteenth century, parishes in the cathedral city along with some that stood a good distance from the town were required to bring the bodies of their dead to the cathedral for prayers followed by burial in the close.

The spiritual labors and overall administration of the cathedral and its parishioners called for a sizeable number of clerics and vicars. By the midtwelfth century the size of the chapter had been fixed at twenty-eight canons, each having his own prebend and a stall in the choir. Unlike monastic cathedrals, the clerics of secular cathedrals were not required to reside in common; their separate houses were located in the cathedral environs. But they were required to be in the cathedral thirty-six weeks of the year.[57] In order to maintain the continuous service of the cathedral, any canon who could not reside was required to employ and support a vicar. There were at least twenty-six of these vicars choral by the early fifteenth century, obliged to attend the services held in the cathedral along with their daily celebrations in chantry chapels, as well as their participation in the intercessory prayers attached to obits, anniversaries, and trentals.[58]

Every member of the chapter had some part to play in the liturgical and pastoral life of the cathedral and its environs, but there were three canons whose pastoral work was central to their offices and who need to be mentioned in greater detail here: the dean, the chancellor and the penitentiary. The dean was the pastor of the cathedral: the church was his to govern along with admitting clerics to churches and chapels in the deanery. An added responsibility was the preparation and examination of clerical candidates for admission or employment in the parish churches of the cathedral deanery. The chancellor's involvement in documentary activities led very early on to his management of all things that pertained to books, their provision, and upkeep. He had special authority over the cathedal school and was charged, among other things, with the appointment of a grammar master to instruct the choristers and students in the fundamentals of an education.[59] Lastly, the penitentiary combined the pastoral role of the dean with the educational duties of the chancellor and became one of the most influential pastoral officers of the chapter. He was considered the bishop's own vicar in the cathedral deanery and exercised his ministry as a confessor to the clergy and people, especially in matters of absolution usually reserved to the bishop. Though he was a special vicar for the bishop in this respect, he was not the only confessor so appointed in the diocese. Bishops regularly named men of high reputation and respect to preach and hear confessions, often through the season of Lent. But they usually served only for a particular term; the cathedral penitentiary held the position for as long as he was a member of the chapter. To help qualify him for this eminently pastoral work, the Hereford cathedral statutes decreed that the penitentiary be educated in Sacred Scripture or canon law and that he preach at specified times to the cathedral community and instruct them in matters of the faith.[60]

There were other ways in which the cathedral clergy and other religious communities helped foster the spiritual life and pastoral care of the diocese. There were even cases of monks, regularly excluded from the *cura animarum* proper, appointed to parish churches and carrying on much as their secular counterparts in neighboring communities. Late in the fourteenth century, the Benedictine monks at St. Guthlac's in the city of Hereford asked for and received papal permission to place one of their own in the vicarage of St. Peter's.[61] A similar arrangement had been worked out at Peterchurch where one of the monks from Great Malvern served as the parish curate. But these were unusual solutions to local problems calling for exceptional measures. Regardless of their rare direct participation in parish life, the regular clergy of Hereford and the many kinds of religious communities that existed there in the fourteenth century played crucial roles in the pastoral care of the diocese.

There has been much left unsaid about the pastoral structures of the Hereford diocese and the ways they supported pastoral care individually and in relationship to one another. But this large sketch has served to underscore one simple fact: that the pastoral life of a diocese in the late middle ages was comprised of more than the relationship between priest and people. To be sure, what went on in the parish churches of the diocese described in the most complete fashion the religious life of the majority of medieval Christians. But no parish stood alone but was, rather, part of a larger religious and legal network characterized by tremendous diversity and tied together by bonds of spiritual community, ecclesiastical authority, and economics. This unity was represented in the office of the bishop and his administration of the diocese and personal ministries as ordinary were the ways in which this unity was put into effect. But often enough for medieval people that unity was an external reality and one that only seldom touched them directly. They were made to understand its importance through ritual and church discipline. But there were stronger forces within the local community itself, forces which were spiritual, social, and economic, that gave real shape to the profound ideas of religion and community. In a very real sense, all of this was meant to work together and it did so to the extent that imperfect institutions can. But it was also true that forces from without could alter the uneasy balances: the patron's support and the bishop's approval of an inept or indifferent pastor, a season of bad harvests, or the burden of taxation in meager times. Any such circumstance would affect pastoral support or provision or religious life in its own particular ways. But epidemic plague — as with any great disaster — would touch every aspect of life and place an unprecedented degree of strain upon these structures of pastoral care, some more than others.

2. The Black Death in Hereford

In October, 1348 Bishop John Trillek received a letter from the bishop of London confirming fears that had been growing in Hereford, as elsewhere, during the previous few months. The letter asked for prayers and processions in the parishes and religious houses throughout the diocese in the hope that the pestilence reported from abroad might be averted.[1] But the plague had already reached England's shores by the time the letter was issued and the very manner in which it finally reached Trillek suggested that the troubles had already begun. At the first news of the plague's arrival, the king ordered Archbishop Stratford to command prayers throughout the province but the prelate's death in late August, 1348 delayed the announcement. The task then fell to the Prior of Canterbury who was charged with the spiritual government of the province during the vacancy. He acted with haste and wrote the late archbishop's nephew, Ralph Stratford, bishop of London, who was also dean of the College of Bishops. By the time the lesser Stratford could act on the request, a full month had passed and the plague had already spread from the Devonshire coast inland to the southern and western counties.

The bishop of Hereford had already heard about the plague, but Stratford's letter gave the prospect even greater urgency and belied the hopes that the Welsh marches might be spared the coming judgment. Other bishops such as Gynewell of Lincoln, Edington of Winchester, Ralph of Shrewsbury in Bath and Wells, and the archbishop of York had issued their own mandates for prayers in anticipation of the king's formal request.[2] Upon receiving the royal letter Trillek made the king's will his own and ordered his archdeacons, the dean of the cathedral, and all religious heads in the diocese to put the mandate into effect. Special masses were to be celebrated in churches throughout Hereford, sermons were to be preached, clergy and people alike were to walk humbly and devoutly in processions twice weekly and commend themselves to works of charity and other pious acts so that the diocese and the kingdom might be spared. Trillek ordered his people to do all these things so "that God, appeased by their prayers, might deliver the English people from these many tribulations, govern them with the help of his grace and, by his ineffable pity, preserve human frailty from pestilences and death."[3]

Hereford was no better prepared than any other diocese in England to receive the advancing plague. In fact it may have been worse off for the hard challenges faced by its parishes and people in the years prior to the Black Death. In 1315 and 1316 Hereford had suffered with other regions from famine brought on by torrential rains, general crop failure and livestock murrains. In the 1320s the turbulence of Edward II's reign and the contentiousness of the Mortimers added other burdens of civil strife and political instability to the communities of the March. Even the national celebrations in the wake of rousing English victories at Crécy and Calais could not lessen for long the burden of taxation required to finance Edward III's costly war with France. In 1346 and 1347, just a few years prior to the plague's arrival in Hereford, the king made repeated attempts to secure advances on the subsidies already granted him by the clergy in convocation, but, for as often as Edward III pushed his requests, the rectors and vicars of Hereford denied them on the basis that their benefices were too meager and poverty was rife in the diocese.[4]

The bishop of Hereford was himself personally affected by the economic vagaries of the times. In the spring of 1346 in the wake of a livestock murrain, Trillek sent only a few proctors to a provincial council in London as too many horses had died in the recent epidemic to provide adequately for a bishop and his retinue. Trillek further excused himself from the council on the plea that the county was too poor for him to secure a loan for travel to London.[5] One year later the king pressed the bishop for a loan of wool which Edward promised would be repaid once Parliament confirmed its grants to the king. Trillek delayed payment of the loan in the face of his own financial problems in Hereford but after some months was able to forward a modest shipment of wool to the king.[6]

Poverty and the king's ill-timed demands were not the only weaknesses afflicting the diocese in the mid-fourteenth century. From the beginning of his pontificate in 1344, Trillek had dedicated himself to reforming a clergy that had grown too slack in discipline and a laity that showed ominously little regard for the rights of the church. Trillek's predecessor, Thomas Charlton (1327–1344), had managed the diocese well enough when he was in Hereford, but his frequent travels on the king's business to Westminster and Ireland had seriously diminished episcopal vigilance.

During his first four years in Hereford and before the plague was to divert his attention to more urgent matters, Trillek spent a good deal of his time touring the diocese on visitation, expediting the cases of criminous clerks, defending clergy and churches against depradations and assaults, and upholding with strict sanctions the rights and liberties of the church of Hereford.[7] He issued several commissions for the transfer of clergy convicted of crimes in the secular courts to his own prison to await ecclesiastical trial.[8] He did not hesitate to remove the vicar of Long Stanton from his benefice for reasons which, though unspecified in the register, had to be necessarily grave. He threatened a chaplain from Bosbury with excommunication for poaching episcopal lands and warned the rector of Hopton Wafer to reside in his benefice or face deprivation. He also issued a stern warning to the assisting clergy of Leominster parish to cease their scandalous disruptions of the Mass and their patent disregard for the divine services.[9]

The bishop was equally concerned with the lives of Hereford parishioners. He threatened with excommunication those who unlawfully witheld the property of the late vicar of Newland, reprimanded the parishioners of Old Radnor who opposed their new rector, required the solution to a violent quarrel between a priest and the parish patron over a chantry in Dorestone church, and excommunicated assailants of priests and destroyers of church property.[10] In 1346 Trillek excommunicated a number of persons who assaulted the parish priest at Stanford during vespers and kept him prisoner there until the king's soldiers were able to free him. Later that same year the bishop ordered the excommunication of individuals who took Ullingswick church by force of arms and occupied its sanctuary, refusing to allow masses to go on.[11]

Clearly, Hereford was not unique in this respect. Other dioceses had to contend with unruly subjects and crimes against the church. But the diocese of Hereford for its relative poverty, its occasionally troubled borders, and years of neglect was a wilder place and its bishop, were he in earnest about correcting and absolving sinnners, accepted a considerable burden of pastoral responsibility. In any case, the condition of the diocese in the mid-1340s did not bode well for the vast challenges that awaited it by the decade's end. Not many days after he published the bishop of London's letter setting preachers and mass-priests to their work in praying against the impending disaster, Trillek issued a sharply-worded mandate to the parish community at Leominster. Two years previously he had reprimanded the stipendiary clergy there for their follies during mass. This time the bishop chastised the entire community for making the sanctuary a place for inappropriate spectacles and plays. Trillek ordered a stop to these *ludi* and urged priests and parishioners alike to set their minds on holier things.[12] By themselves, the plays seem a trivial concern, but Trillek was of the mind that any hindrance to divine worship and the salvation of souls, especially in these threatened times, was too great a matter to overlook.

General Mortality in Hereford Diocese

The threat was finally realized by the spring of 1349 with the first casualties of Hereford clergy. The plague very likely entered Hereford through counties situated along the southern, eastern, and northern boundaries of the diocese, Gloucestershire, Worcestershire, and Staffordshire. From April to the following October, the epidemic raged in the West Midlands, reaching its greatest virulence in the languid summer months of July and August and declining only in the late autumn. During this brief span of time every aspect of life in the diocese was altered to some degree. The usual routines and labors that make up the daily activities of households and communities were interrupted. In some places commerce was suspended until the disease had run its course; people were loath to linger in larger groups, the harvest was delayed and feasts and holy days passed uncelebrated while survivors tended the sick and buried their dead. Many lay dying without the consolation of the church's sacraments; their priests had died of the sickness or had fled in fear of the contagion. Clerics who did remain in their cures found their pastoral tasks severely multiplied, their visitations to the dying and their presiding at funerals only perfunctory at times. There were likely more burials of infants than christenings in these months, and the joys of the wedding feast were replaced by more somber funeral ceremonies. There was also the pastoral challenge of coping with the malaise that set into parish communities in the midst of the epidemic, an unbounded anxiety over what further destruction the plague might exact before it was fully spent. There were the seemingly contrary images of God's vengeance against a sinful race and the preacher's adjuration to confessing sins to a God of mercy. In years after, pastors would also need to contend with the enduring bitterness of survivors who marveled less at the wrath of God and more at the impotence of the church and its ministers to placate God.

Precisely how God's wrath was visited upon the people of Hereford is impossible to know. As with any epidemic, this plague's effects were uneven and some communities suffered considerably more than others. With the exception of a few incidental references, our knowledge of mortality rates among the people of the diocese is sketchy and impressionistic. We know rather more about the pastors than their parishioners during the plague, and figures derived from records of institutions to vacant benefices may suggest a larger pattern of mortality beyond that of the higher clergy. But if the few references we have to deaths among Hereford tenants and parishioners are any indication of what happened elsewhere in the diocese, the rate of sickness and death must have been great.

This was certainly the case in the parishes of Frome deanery which shared its eastern border with Worcester and which became one of the main routes into Hereford for the plague. In the four episcopal manors of Bosbury, Colwall, Coddington, and Cradley, all located along the border, as many as 158 tenants were reported to have died during the plague.[13] The impact on the life of these manors and parishes must have been considerable. Even by 1352 three of the four manors, excepting Coddington, were hard places to work and live. Bishop Trillek had to intervene that year on account of the complaints that he had received from his laborers that they feared for their lives and were kept from their work by marauders and criminals.[14]

The northern part of the deanery fared just as badly. The neighboring parishes of Great and Little Collington had been burdened by poverty before the plague, but after 1349 there had been such a loss of life among the parishioners and their clergy that the patron of Collington represented the survivors in a petition to consolidate the two parishes. Trillek received their petition in April, 1352, which stated that the plague had so diminished the populations of both parishes, had rendered the land sterile, and caused such enduring poverty that there was scarcely income to support one priest, much less two for the care of the churches. The bishop acceded to their request.[15] Further north, in Ludlow deanery within the boundaries of Stanton Lacy parish, neighbors described the township of Yeye as having been depopulated during the course of the plague. A final reference to the township occurs in 1350 where the place is described simply as ruinous.[16] Just beyond the boundaries of Wenlock deanery and within Coventry and Lichfield diocese, the parish of Kenley was wiped out by the pestilence and by 1363 the tenants of Boomcraft had either died or left the township and no one was there to cultivate its lands.[17]

The country parishes were not the only ones hard hit by the epidemic; denser populations in villages and towns were often more vulnerable to infection and disease. Work on the new chapter house near the cathedral was halted as a result of the plague and would be resumed only years later when the canons had recovered some of their financial losses and laborers could again be hired for the work.[18] People were naturally hesitant to gather in large numbers for fear of contagion. But survival depended not only on avoiding the plague but in the continued commerce of food supplies and other daily provisions. To aid in the effort the city's leaders moved the market from the center of Hereford just north of the cathedral to a point about a mile to the west beyond the city walls and, it was hoped, beyond the threat of contamination.[19] The move may have encouraged trade but offered little protection from the pestilence. In a court case begun in the early 1360s, it was reported that mass-burials had taken place at St. Peter's church in Hereford and one parishioner remembered seeing up to twenty bodies buried from the church on a single day.[20] The other parishes of the city suffered as well: during the plague parishioners in Hereford appealed to the cathedral clergy to offer pastoral assistance in the absence of their own parish clergy who had died during the plague. But the chapter was hard pressed itself to manage the affairs of the cathedral as well as make up for the loss of parish priests and chaplains in the city. Nearly a third of the canons died during the plague and there must have been similar losses among the vicars choral.[21]

Neither were the religious houses of the diocese spared during the epidemic. At the Augustinian priory of Llanthony in Gloucestershire, only four of the thirty canons survived the plague. Barely two years later those who were left begged Bishop Trillek to give them the revenues from nearby Awre church in order to offset the great losses suffered during the recent pestilence.[22] Further south in the diocese another Augustinian house, Flanesford Priory, suffered great setbacks as a result of the plague. Founded only three years before the Black Death, the house barely had time to establish itself and assume the stature intended for it. Judging from the size of Flanesford's refectory, the house was meant to hold at least thirteen canons but after the plague it is doubtful that the priory ever had more than two or three religious living there.[23] In 1352 the Benedictines of Wenlock Abbey in the northern part of the diocese were given a royal pardon of 200 marks on account of the loss of tenants and the great poverty of the house.[24] The monks of Leominster were unable to work their lands as they once had and in 1355 were granted a similar pardon for arrears owed to the king; that same year the women at Limebrook, not far from Leominster, were granted a licence of mortmain "out of compassion for the great poverty and indigence at the present time."[25] Many of the smaller houses such as Limebrook were generally poor even in prosperous times, but the deaths of religious who administered the houses and contributed to the life of the community combined with the deaths or departure of tenants added far greater burdens than usual in the course of the plague.

Clerical Mortality in the Diocese

From the grim perspective of general mortality, the death of one cleric weighed no more than the loss of any other individual in the community. But with respect to the spiritual well-being of a parish, losses among the pastors only heightened the level of despair. There are numerous references to the losses among priests and other clerics, but most of these occur in the large and anonymous reports of mortality found in official correspondence from churchmen or in the generalized comments of chroniclers. Though we can never know precisely how many clerics died during the course of this plague, there are clues in the official records of the time — institutions to vacant benefices and clerical ordinations — that indicate the swiftness and widespread nature of the changes taking place within the clerical population of the diocese.[26] But even here these figures occupy the lower ranges of the likely rates of mortality in 1349 and this for several reasons. First, they include only the higher or beneficed clergy; the larger body of the clerical proletariat — the stipendiary chaplains and apprentice clerics who were part of the parish community — are never mentioned. Second, we are lacking institution records for the most populous region in the diocese, the deanery of Hereford. Since these parishes were under the jurisdiction of the cathedral dean and his records of institution do not survive, our assessment of clerical mortality, even among the higher clergy, is accordingly hampered. Third, not all the institutions that took place in the diocese were always faithfully entered in Trillek's register. The bishop's registrar was usually careful to enter all institutions in his master's records, but some might be missed. During the plague when more parish churches changed hands than at any other time in the diocese's history, it is not surprising that we find the odd lapse in record keeping. For example, Philip Ilger, a canon of the cathedral and a close advisor to John Trillek, was instituted to Eastnor, church in Frome deanery on July 1, 1348 on the death of the previous rector William de Marcle. One week later, Ilger exchanged benefices with John de Middleton who accordingly became rector of Eastnor. But in September of 1350, William de Withington was instituted to the same church on the death of a man named Stephen de Eastnor though there is no record in Trillek's register that Stephen was ever instituted. This case — and there are others — is particularly interesting as the timing of the vacancies and institutions indicates that Stephen died sometime between the summer of 1348 and the fall of 1350. There are twelve other incumbents who disappeared from the records of institution during 1349 and who fail to show up in other possible circumstances such as resignation from their churches or exchanges of benefices with other clerics.[27] A second case bears mentioning: in late November, 1354 Bishop Trillek wrote the king about the benefice of Montgomery which was in the gift of the crown. The bishop noted that a certain Robert de Wynnesbury had occupied the benefice until his death during the pestilence. He was succeeded at Montgomery by John de Hopton whom the Prince of Wales had presented to the church on October 2, 1349. Robert had been presented to the church in 1340, though his institution was never recorded in Thomas Charlton's register.[28] These cases merely illustrate that records of institution are not perfect and that they represent only a portion — though a considerable one — of the churches that fell vacant during the plague year.

Of the more than three hundred ecclesiastical benefices in the diocese, over half of them lost their curate during the year the plague swept through Hereford. Some were through resignation, others through exchange. But most of the vacancies that occurred in 1349 were due to the death of the previous incumbent.

When viewed against the number of institutions that occurred in more typical years, the degree of change in Hereford parishes during the plague is all the more striking. During the first three years of John Trillek's pontificate only a small number of churches in the diocese changed hands through the death, resignation, or exchange of the previous incumbent (Table 2.1). Of the seventeen institutions which occurred between 1345 and 1347, only two were death vacancies. Three clerics resigned their benefices while another three exchanged their churches for others. There were a further nine institutions during this period but the record does not indicate why.

In 1348 the figures began to change. The total number of vacancies was almost double what it had been the previous year and, of those eleven institutions, four were attributed to death (though two involve the same cleric), four to exchange and the remaining three unspecified. The first death-vacancy for 1348 was at the end of June, when William de Marcle died and left the church of Eastnor vacant. William was the rector of the church and was expected to be resident in his cure. But there were excep-

TABLE 2.1   Institutions to Hereford Benefices, 1344–1360

Year	Total institutions	Causes of vacancy			
		Death	Resignation	Exchange	Not given
1345	5	1	0	2	2
1346	6	0	2	1	3
1347	6	1	1	0	4
1348	11	4	0	4	3
1349	160	56	12	4	88
1350	45	7	12	8	18
1351	25	3	6	3	13
1352	26	1	3	9	13
1353	18	11	0	0	7
1354	10	1	3	3	3
1355	23	4	7	6	6
1356	13	2	2	3	6
1357	22	3	4	12	3
1358	7	0	5	0	2
1359	18	5	7	4	2
1360	7	4	1	1	1

tions to this requirement and though no record of dispensation or leave is to be found in Trillek's register, William may have been elsewhere in England at the time and may even have died of the plague. By the summer of 1348 the epidemic had not yet moved into Hereford but toward the year's end deaths among the clergy began to increase. In early October the rector of English Bicknor died and in December Walter Carles, a cathedral canon and rector of Cradley, died as well. No one can be certain that these two priests died from the plague, but as both English Bicknor and Cradley are in the southeast corner of the diocese, the area where the plague made its first appearance in Hereford, they may have been the first clerics of the diocese to succumb to the pestilence.

If doubts about the impact of the disease still lingered in 1348, they had disappeared by the summer of the following year. In 1349 the number of institutions in the diocese, excluding the cathedral deanery, soared to 160, more than five times the total of the previous four years combined. At least a third of these vacancies (56) occurred with the death of the incumbent; twelve more were attributed to resignation and four to exchange. But more than half the institutions made during the plague year are entered in

Trillek's register without any specific reference to how they became vacant. The possible reasons behind this surprising statistic will be considered more carefully below. In 1350, after the epidemic had moved north and west beyond Hereford's boundaries, the rate of change in benefices remained far higher than usual. There were forty-five vacancies that year, seven of which had occurred through the deaths of their incumbents. Numbers of resignations were still as high as they had been during the plague year and exchanges of benefices, though still small in relationship to the overall picture, doubled from 1349. Changes in the administration of benefices continued at a higher rate than usual for the remainder of Trillek's pontificate and only in the last years of his reign did the numbers finally fall to levels reminiscent of the years before the plague.

The disparity in figures for institutions in Hereford over the course of Trillek's sixteen-year pontificate indicates in broad strokes the sudden and extensive changes borne by the diocese in a narrow span of time. The dramatic flux in vacant benefices and subsequent institutions reveals as well the stark differences from the relatively stable years before 1349 and the changeful times that followed. The diocese was small and changes in benefices happened within a relatively narrow range. There were rarely more than a dozen changes annually in the administration of benefices through Thomas Charlton's reign and in the first few years of Trillek's pontificate. Yet in a single year a little less than half of all Hereford benefices changed hands. More clerics resigned their benefices in that one year than in any other year previous. Some of the changes which had begun in 1348 and increased rapidly in 1349 continued through most of the following decade. Benefices continued to fall vacant at a higher than normal rate; some of these were attributed to the deaths of incumbents, though fewer to resignation after 1350, while the numbers of unspecified vacancies remained exceptionally high for some years after the plague.

If we consider only those figures that fall with confidence under the category of death-vacancies, we can see that of the more than 160 benefices that fell vacant during 1349 only 56 of these—15 percent of the total number of benefices in the diocese—lost their incumbents to the plague. Even this figure is not insignificant when we consider the subsequent effects these deaths had on the administration of individual parishes and the leadership of the diocese. But the figure is also far lower than the probable mortality rate among Hereford beneficed clerics. Making up for the loss in this category is the equally impressive figure of institutions for which we have no stated cause of vacancy. Over half of the plague-year institutions

(88: 160) fall into this puzzling category. Strictly speaking, we cannot assign these vacancies to the death of the previous incumbent as there is no certainty that the curate had in fact died. It can also be argued that not every report of death in the diocese during 1349 was necessarily a death due to the plague. But given the overall profile of vacancies and institutions in Hereford and the extreme fluctuations that coincided with the epidemic, it is difficult not to see these uncertain vacancies as having been the result of the deaths of incumbents who died during the course of the epidemic.

This sort of statement cannot be made without offering some reasonable defense. There are at least two reasons why this large number of unspecified vacancies occur in Trillek's register during this critical year. One is that the bishop's registrar was hard-pressed to keep up with his master's usual business, much less the extraordinary rate of change in Hereford benefices, and may have neglected to record every aspect of an institution to a benefice. We have already seen that the registrar missed some institutions that, we know from other references, actually took place. But we do better to look for a reason behind this large number of non-specific vacancies in the procedure surrounding the institution itself. It may be recalled that the normal procedure was intitiated by the presentation of a candidate for a benefice. The official response was an inquest usually comprised of beneficed clergy from the area who would look into the circumstances of the presentation. Was the benefice in fact vacant? If so, what was the cause of the vacancy? Who was the previous incumbent and who held the right of presentation? If all was satisfactory, the bishop made his own examination of the candidate and instituted him to the benefice. Subsequently, the new incumbent was given full administration of the benefice at his installation.

It should come as no surprise that these inquests, along with other typical functions of administration, were greatly impeded during the time of plague. It would have been a challenging effort on the part of local authorities to organize such inquests for immediate and effective consideration of reported vacancies, not only because rectors and vicars hesitated to assemble for fear of infection, but also because benefices had fallen vacant in such great numbers that organized inquests were simply infeasible. Though it was usual to have as much information as an inquest could offer, it was only essential to know that a church was vacant and in need of a rector or vicar, less so who the previous incumbent was or how he came to vacate his benefice. The bishop no doubt relied on the sworn testimonies of the patron and presentee before he instituted to a benefice, but he could expect little more given the difficult times. During the early part of the year, before the plague had made much of an inroad into the diocese, the inquests, their summaries, and entry into the register followed a typical pattern. But by the spring when more benefices fell vacant than at any time previous, there was a proportionate rise in unspecified vacancies. The greatest number of these vacancies occurs in the later months of the summer when the plague was at its height in the diocese, when institutions were taking place at an alarming rate and when juries of local clerics could be convened only with difficulty.

Discerning the cause behind these vacancies is made more difficult by the fact that the identity of the previous incumbent is also missing from the records. But in most cases this information can be retrieved from the last institution to the benefice and in none of the eighty-eight unspecified vacancies can the previous incumbent be found elsewhere in the diocese or listed among the beneficed clergy after 1349. This fact weakens the possibility that many of these vacancies could have occurred as a result of unregistered resignations or exchanges. It is possible that some of these benefices were abandoned by their curates, a scandal reported by other contemporary sources. But Trillek's register contains no references at all to this sort of activity. He directed his concerns for clerical residence not at the incumbents but at the stipendiaries who had less reason to tolerate their meager stipends and to seek better employment elsewhere.[29] It is far more likely that Hereford institutions continued to be vacated as a result of the deaths of previous incumbents during August and September when the plague was still active in the diocese. As inquests were harder to organize and their information less complete than in less frantic times, the registrar was unable to note in every case the cause of vacancy. He could record only what he knew and in eighty-eight of the institutions carried out during 1349 this information was restricted to the names of the benefice, the patron, the presentee, and the date of the institution.

The overall numbers for 1349 are impressive for the sudden and profound changes they reflect in the diocese during that year and in the years immediately following. But what can they tell of the impact these changes exerted on the churches and clergy of Hereford during and after the plague? We can observe something of the local effect by analyzing the institutions according to more specific categories such as the time they occurred, their location in the diocese, and the identity of the incumbents. Regarding dates, it must be remembered that the time the vacancy occurred and the day the institution was held were not the same. When clerics died during the plague, some length of time passed before their successors were officially instituted by the bishop. It is impossible to pinpoint the date of

TABLE 2.2   Institutions to Hereford Benefices, 1349

Year	Institutions	Death	Resignation	Exchange	Not given
			Causes of vacancy		
January	1	1	0	0	0
February	4	3	1	0	0
March	8	6	0	1	1
April	10	8	1	0	1
May	11	6	0	0	5
June	14	9	1	0	4
July	37	19	5	2	11
August	30	2	0	0	28
September	18	0	0	0	18
October	11	0	0	0	11
November	11	0	1	1	9
December	4	1	3	0	0

death; some benefices were recovered almost at once depending upon the swiftness of the patron, the availability of a worthy incumbent, and the availability of the bishop or his delegate to examine the nominee and approve his induction. There were other churches in the diocese that remained vacant without benefit of these customary interventions and their vacancies endured until the bishop had been notified. Still, he could not act to fill the vacancy before the patron had made presentation, unless six months had elapsed since the vacancy occurred. Consequently, dates of institution should not be confused with dates of vacancy and the chronicle of "plague benefices" which follows only suggests the pattern of death and replacement in Hereford churches during 1349.

In Table 2.2 all Hereford institutions for 1349 have been set out by month and cause of vacancy. The progress of plague becomes more evident when we consider the increase, rise, and decline in the numbers of vacancies and institutions during the plague year. In January, 1349 there was but one institution and it was to a vicarage at Westbury. The following month, however, brought four new institutions, one of which involved the resignation of John de Leigh from Bredenbury. The remaining three were in response to the deaths of the vicars of Bacton, Ross, and Linton. Two points need to be made here: all four deaths in January and February of 1349 were of priests and vicars whose pastoral involvement and personal residence in the parishes were requirements of their position as vicars. Second, three of the four deaths occurred in the deaneries of Ross and Forest, that border the southeast corner of the diocese. It was from there and the neighboring counties of Worcestershire and Gloucesterhire that the plague first entered the diocese of Hereford. The fourth vicar, Richard de Dore, died at Bacton in Weobley deanery, further west but still in the southern portion of the diocese.

By March the total number of institutions for the diocese had doubled, including those that had fallen vacant through death. One exchange had occurred involving the parish of Knill and the cause of one vacancy went unaccounted for. Among the dead were three rectors (Ganarew, English Bicknor, and Hope Mansel), two vicars (Felton and Ross), and one of the chantry chaplains at Ledbury church. Both English Bicknor and Ross vicarage had lost incumbents twice in as many years. Judging by the sequence of vacancy and institution, the plague was moving north in the diocese, though still clinging to the eastern borders. Most of the parishes where clergy had died thus far were in the three deaneries in the eastern and southern parts of the diocese, which formed a crescent from Irchenfield in the south to Ross and Frome in the north and east.

The increase in vacancies continued through April with eight deaths and one resignation. Included among the dead were Thomas de Astley, a canon whose house in the cathedral precinct was given to the bishop's brother, Thomas Trillek. Another canon took Trillek's former house, now vacant by resignation. The rectors of three parishes had died as well, among them the rector of Great Collington which was to suffer so greatly from the plague. Richard de Ketford, who had been instituted as vicar of Westbury in January, 1349, died little more than four months later. The vicars of Llanrothal, Woolstaston, and Badger also died and were replaced during the month of April. The plague must have taken a firm hold on the southeastern part of the diocese since five of the eight deaths that April were confined to Irchenfield (1), Ross (1), and Forest (3) deaneries.

In May there was a slight leveling off with only one more institution than had taken place in April. There were two fewer deaths than the month previous, no resignations or exchanges, but a full five cases of unspecified vacancies. The rectors of Awre, Tasley, and Knill and the vicars of Weston and Bishop's Frome were all dead by the end of the month. Most of the vacancies continued to occur in the southeastern part of the diocese. Exceptions included Weston Beggard, toward the center of the diocese in Weston deanery and, to the far west, Knill parish, which would be particularly hard-hit by the plague. When we consider all institutions, including those for which no cause was mentioned, the vacancies now begin to move further north in the diocese. There were two in Burford deanery in the southern part of Shropshire, and one in Stottesden during the month of May.

The toll in lives continued unabated in June and through the summer months, causing the greatest rate of mortality in July and August. Of the fifteen institutions in June, ten were required because their incumbents had died. The larger number of death-vacancies occurred, as usual, in the border deaneries. There were three deaths in Frome (Bosbury, Avenbury, and Evesbatch) and two in Irchenfield (Peterstow and Kentchurch). By this time the plague had reached the city of Hereford, with the deaths of two canons, Thomas de Staunton and the chancellor John de Ambresbury. By the end of the month, some beneficed clergy had died in every deanery in the southern half of the diocese while the vacancy figures were just beginning to rise in the northern deaneries of Wenlock, Burford, and Clun.

July was the worst month for the diocese during the plague. The highest number of deaths recorded for the year occurred at this time. Of the nineteen death-vacancies, two had opened up with the death of one man, Richard de Sidenhale, cathedral canon, portioner in Holdgate, and rector of Staunton. Among the dead were a further eleven rectors and seven vicars. Five clerics were permitted exchanges of benefices and two resigned. This month also witnessed a larger number of institutions with unspecified causes, a situation which was to increase sharply in August and continue over the next two months. By early August every deanery in the diocese had reported the death of at least one beneficed cleric and the vacancy of his benefice.

The figures for August, September, and October are curious given the trends that had been established since late spring. We know from other sources that the epidemic had not abated in Hereford and surrounding dioceses and, in fact, was not to end until the late fall. Nevertheless, we find only two references to incumbents' deaths among the thirty August institutions in Trillek's register; the remaining twenty-eight offer no cause for the vacancy. No deaths were recorded for the months of September and October nor were there any officially noted resignations or exchanges. And yet we know from another reference in Trillek's register that one of the October institutions did in fact follow on the death of the previous incumbent. This case and its bearing on conclusions for clerical mortality in Hereford during the plague will be discussed in greater detail below. For the present, the only significant change in the records of institution for these two months was the fact that more vacancies had occurred in the northern archdeaconry than previous, suggesting that the disease took a northerly path through the diocese.

The trend in high numbers of unspecified causes continued through November. There was one resignation and one exchange: William de Foye stepped down as vicar of Kentchurch and Walter Elvedon, former archdeacon of Sudbury, became cathedral precentor by an exchange with Thomas de Winchester. This extraordinary year in the history of the diocese ended very much as it had begun. In December there were four new institutions, only one of which was caused by the death of an incumbent. John Golafre, who had been rector of Little Marcle in Frome deanery for only five years, died and was replaced by Richard Oweyn. The rectors of Glazely, Upton Cresset, and the vicar of Stoke Bliss all resigned their benefices that same month.

By the early months of 1350 there were hopeful signs of recovery or, at least, its beginnings. The bishop was less burdened with institutions than the previous year and those which he oversaw did not as often carry the grim news of the deaths of Hereford clergy. Still, the number of institutions was higher than usual and the cause of nearly half the forty-five vacancies went unrecorded that year.

In the aftermath of the plague, the diocese was left to mourn the deaths of many, not least of whom were the rectors and vicars of Hereford churches. We know of fifty-six deaths among these pastors and church administrators and can surmise from the evidence cited above that the death toll was far greater than the institution records will allow. It could be argued that some of these men acted as mere managers of the parish, inclined to practice a care for revenues more than souls and that their deaths, though disruptive to parochial administration at one level, did not much influence the pastoral provision of the church. This, of course, is hard to determine, but it is only likely in those fewer cases when the rector, such as a cathedral canon, was bound to be occupied elsewhere. In most cases, the death of the incumbent had a direct bearing on the local cure, on the celebration of masses, visitations to the sick, burials of the dead, and comfort to the poor.

This was even more the case when chaplains, whose primary role was pastoral assistance to the curate, died during the course of the plague. We have no records such as institution lists to go by with regard to their fate

TABLE 2.3   Ordinations of Hereford Secular Clerics, 1349–1350

Date	Season	Order				Total
		A	S	D	P	
1349/03/07	2	75	55	29	30	189
03/28	Passion	52	33	51	28	164
04/11	Easter	6	19	30	35	90
06/0609/19	3	21	25	18	31	95
12/19	4	21	25	17	14	77
1350/02/20	1	15	18	17	19	69
03/13	2	15	22	17	19	73
03/21	Passion	13	13	21	15	62
05/22	Easter	2	2	7	17	28
09/18	3	13	12	14	12	51
12/18	4	9	13	13	16	51
	1	15	4	6	7	32

during this bleak year, but the ordination records in the bishop's register will indicate a decline among the wider body of clergy beyond those who served as incumbents.

There is every indication in the first years of Trillek's pontificate that ordination levels were high, continuing the trend that had predominated in Hereford and other English dioceses in the first quarter of the fourteenth century.[30] Between 1345 and 1348 the bishop ordained on the average about 130 acolytes and 70 priests each year. From 1349 to 1352 the annual number of acolytes had slipped to eighty-five while the priests actually increased to eighty-one. This was probably a function of the demand for more priests to fill the many vacancies that had occurred throughout the diocese; it also represents the large number of ordinands in the first months of 1349 before the plague had reached Hereford. After the spring of that year, numbers in both groups decreased markedly, initiating a long-term decline that would continue for the rest of the century.[31] In Table 2.3 the numbers of Hereford secular clerics ordained to the orders of acolyte, subdeacon, deacon, and priest are given for each ordination held in the diocese in the years 1349 and 1350. In the column marked 'Season' the numbers correspond to the four seasonal or Ember Saturdays when ordination ceremonies were usually held. The first of these days (1), from the point of view of the church calendar, was the third Sunday in Advent; 2, 3

TABLE 2.4   Attrition Rates from Diaconate to Priesthood Ordinations, 1348–1349

Date	Deacons	Priests	Attrition (percent)
1348/09/20	21	17	19
12/20	22	18	18
1349/03/07	18	16	11
03/28	51	38	26
04/11	22	10	55
06/06	18	10	45
09/19	16	16	0

and 4 being respectively the first Sunday in Lent, the Saturday after Pentecost and the Saturday following the Feast of the Exaltation of the Holy Cross on September 14.[32] Ordinations could also be celebrated on the vigils of Passion Sunday and Easter.

These figures only suggest the presence of plague mortality as a factor of change in the clerical candidate pool during this period, but the image is sharper when we consider the progress of individuals from one order to another during the plague year. As has already been mentioned, the number of acoyltes was not always a clear indication of how many subdeacons, deacons, or priests would follow. Many factors might intervene along the way which would delay or alter careers. But this was less likely to occur in the relatively short time between ordination to the diaconate and priesthood, when most deacons were on a well-marked path to the presbyterate.

At the seven ordinations held between September of 1348 and September of 1349, 168 men were ordained to the diaconate for the Hereford diocese. Of these, 125 appear subsequently as priest-ordinands but forty-three deacons are missing from later lists. Though it is true some may have sought ordination to priesthood elsewhere for any number of reasons, none of the forty-three appear as recipients of the necessary letters dimissory in Trillek's register. Once again, there is no certainty that these deacons died during the plague, but the coincidence of the arrival of the epidemic and higher rates of attrition more than suggests that mortality was the critical factor.

As the data in Table 2.4 indicate, the rate of attrition between diaconate and priesthood at ordinations held in late 1348 and early 1349 was relatively low. Even the 26 percent rate in late March was not extraordinary for any single ordination. But by mid-April, when ordination figures in general began to drop in the diocese, more than half of the deacons listed at that ordination failed to appear in any subsequent list in Trillek's register. Though somewhat less drastic in June, the 45 percent rate of attrition was still remarkably high, indicating at the very least that fewer men were being ordained to the priesthood than the diocese needed at this crucial time. By September, when the plague was waning in Hereford, so too was the fallout from the diaconate and all sixteen deacons ordained at the cathedral on September 19 were later admitted to priest's orders.

While rates of attrition are not synonymous with rates of mortality among clerics, it is hard not to see the plague at work in these changes. By the time a man had reached the order of deacon he had committed himself to celibacy, on occasion had already been instituted to a benefice or saw the prospect of one in the future, had exercised other ministries in his local church, and was fairly definite in his resolve to continue to priest's orders. Thus, deacons had little reason not to be ordained to the priesthood unless some grave impediment were discovered after their ordination to the diaconate, or they decided to seek ordination elsewhere, or to abandon their clerical careers altogether. Given the mood of the times and the fear that was naturally attached to ministering to the sick and dying, this latter possibility, although extreme, should not be dismissed. And neither should the likely deaths of men who, though aspiring to priest's orders, died prematurely in the season of plague.

These analyses of institution and ordination records indicate critical changes within the clerical body and pastoral workforce of the diocese of Hereford during the Black Death. Conservatively, between 38 percent and 40 percent of all beneficed clergy died during the plague year and though the evidence for mortality among the wider body of clergy is scant, the downward trends in recruitment and the simultaneous rise in rates of attrition point to similar, perhaps even greater, losses among the non-beneficed clergy as well. Indeed, rectors and vicars were more certain of a stable income and tended to be better housed and fed than their poorer wage-earning brothers. If mortality was so extensive among the beneficed clergy, it must have been equally so or greater among those whose livelihoods depended upon direct service to parish communities, many of which had been laid low by the plague. As impressive as such figures might be, they do not indicate what sort of effects the deaths of clerics had on pastoral care. It is at this point that we must turn to the effects of clerical mortality on the running of the diocese and the administration of its parishes.

The leadership of Hereford diocese was almost always drawn from the body of cathedral clergy; either bishops had learned to depend on the able and learned men who occupied canonries and prebends at the cathedral or, when they brought with them close associates from other places, they found ways of assigning them stalls in the cathedral choir and positions of responsibility in diocesan administration. The general effects of the plague on the cathedral have only been alluded to. From a closer examination of assorted records, we know that at least eight canons of the cathedral died during the plague year. Six of them had been university graduates and had offered their talents and abilities to the cathedral and the diocese in different capacities. Walter Carles, Adam Orelton's old friend and advisor and later commissary for John Trillek, died during the plague, though he was away from Hereford at the time. Thomas de Astley, a distinguished civil lawyer and also a friend of Orelton's, died before late April 1349. Another veteran of diocesan administration, the highly influential Richard de Sidenhale, had served as Thomas Charlton's commissary general and *officialis*. His pastoral instincts had been put to good use in the 1330s when he was archdeacon of Shropshire and Bishop Trillek saw in him a trusted advisor when he gave him several important commissions early in his reign. The old administrator resigned his dignities in 1348 to live out the rest of his life as rector of Staunton on Wye, where he died shortly after in July, 1349. Another distinguished member of the chapter, John de Ambresbury, had begun a promising career as chancellor and head of the cathedral school in 1345, but died as well in the summer of 1349. John Abraham, who served as cathedral subdean, rector of Peterstow, and judge for Trillek in matrimonial causes, died as well in June, 1349. In the mass pence rolls of the time, accounts kept of payments to members of the chapter who attended cathedral services, three prebendaries dropped from the list of participants. Thomas de Staunton, John de Orleton, and Richard Passmer all died between the summer of 1349 and the spring of 1350.[33]

Though the cathedral clergy played an important role in the leadership of the diocese from its center, there were far more rectors and vicars of parish churches whose deaths during the plague had a more proximate affect on the religious lives of parishioners. Among their number were the high-born, like the rector of Badger chapel whose father was the lord of Beckbury, or those whose influence was felt at the center of the diocese, like the vicar of Ledbury who was a cleric in the bishop's household. The rectors of Awre, Pembridge, and Little Marcle had all obtained licenses for study and had received an education from the support of their parishioners for sounder administration and the cure of souls. All three were numbered among the dead in Hereford.

There were many others who had neither been distinguished by birth or learning, or even noteworthy service to their bishop, but who had established a place in the leadership of their own parishes. Even those whose occupations and careers took them from their churches were required to provide the cure with worthy and able men; the death of an absentee rector might at the very least initiate a period of disruption in the adminstration of the parish while the curate's death forced parishioners to seek what solace they could in the sacraments from another priest, perhaps in a neighboring parish or a nearby monastery. The death of the local curate was a hardship endured by many parishes; but there were also a number of churches in the diocese that suffered repeated vacancies. Between 1349 and 1351 nearly half of the parishes in the diocese had lost their incumbents; a full third of these had been vacant twice in the same three-year period and most had fallen vacant through the death of the rector or vicar. Three times in 1349 the parishioners of Bosbury had lost their vicar. Henry Boter, who had been instituted to the church in 1325, was dead by late May, 1349. His successor, John de Herwynton, died a little over a month after his institution on June 6. The parishioners struggled through two of the worst weeks of the plague before John's successor, Richard de Brugge, was instituted to Bosbury on July 21. There is no record of how he departed the parish later that summer, but by late September a new vicar, Philip le Smith—the fourth in five months—was instituted to Bosbury.[34]

Something very similar happened in Ross, south of Frome deanery, where Bosbury is located. John de Henley had been instituted to the vicarage in the spring of 1340. Early in 1349 Thomas le Mercer succeeded to the church on John's death. A little over a month later Thomas was dead and had been replaced by a new vicar, Adam de Berrington. Adam's fate is unknown but by May 13, 1349 Ross had a new vicar, John le Yonge.[35] In Kentchurch in the southernmost deanery of the diocese, Irchenfield, four rectors held the benefice in three years. William de Foye was instituted there on the death of his predecessor in June 1349. By November the rectory was vacant again but, this time, by William's resignation. Richard de Ewyas kept the church until a year later when he exchanged it for another. However, the same Richard returned to Kentchurch where he died before April, 1351.[36]

The small rectory of Knill in Leominster deanery in the western part of the diocese was vacant no less than five times in eight years. Roger de Carlisle, instituted to the church in February, 1342, was dead by the spring of 1349. His successor, Hugh le Brut, succeeded him on March 19 and remained there until his death in May. John de Bateron obtained the church at the end of May but was dead sometime before July 4 when Richard le Merchs became rector. By the end of August Richard was gone, presumably yet another victim of the plague. All in all, Knill church had five rectors in six months; the man who followed Richard as rector there, Philip de Russchook, gave the church some measure of stability by remaining there until his resignation from the cure in the fall of 1359.[37] Finally, in the northern reaches of the diocese the church of Westbury in Pontesbury deanery suffered from repeated vacancies around the year of the Black Death. Philip de Landow had been vicar there since his institution in 1341. After his death in 1348, he was followed by Richard de Ketford who was dead by the end of April.[38]

Pastoral Challenges and the Bishop's First Response

In the midst of the plague, when neither John Trillek nor anyone else could see a time when the mortality would lift and the diocese begin to recover, there were hard challenges with regard to pastoral provision. A large number of Hereford priests and clerical candidates had already died, leaving parishes with fewer clergy and in some cases bereft entirely of pastoral ministers. Still, there were survivors: people who needed to bury their dead and needed all the more in this time of unprecedented mortality the consolation of the church's sacraments and the ritual actions that signaled the passing of a soul from this world to the next. Thus Trillek's greatest challenges in the turbulent summer of 1349 and the months that followed were to maintain some order in the diocese and to provide in any way he could pastors for the churches of Hereford.

The bishop was limited in what he could do to shore up the pastoral workforce of his diocese. Most of the churches were in the hands of monastic rectors and lay patrons and the crown possessed numerous advowsons in the diocese. Their presentation to the vacant benefice was an essential first step in the procedure that brought a new rector or vicar to a church. But the bishop could oversee this procedure with a careful eye, expedite presentations of candidates to vacant churches without excessive compromise of the acceptable standards of the time, and seize the opportunity to fill the vacancy by lapse as was his right and duty were the patron to fail in his. The bishop, too, was a great patron in the diocese and could deal immediately with the vacant churches and dignities in his own gift. As the ordinary minister of the sacrament of Orders he could encourage any able men who had survived the plague to seek admission to the clerical and pastoral life of the diocese by conferring the sacrament whenever possible. It was also within his power to enforce the church's laws on clerical residence and the right administration of churches. These were only some of the more significant ways a bishop could deal with the sudden crisis brought on by the plague. But above all else, it was essential that he be available to the clergy and people of his diocese, available to administer, institute, and adjudicate, to preach, decide, and ordain.

The bishop's itinerary for 1349 can be reconstructed from a number of sources, chief among which are the dating clauses of episcopal memoranda and letters in the register as well as the dates and places noted in the headings of ordination lists. Throughout his administration of the see it was rare that the bishop resided for long in his palace at Hereford. Rather, he administered the diocese from any one of his episcopal manors and some he surely favored over others. The plague year was no exception to this usual procedure; indeed, it was much in the bishop's mind to sustain as much normalcy in his work as these unsettling times would allow. In the early months of 1349, January through March, Trillek stayed at his manors in Bosbury, close to the eastern border of the diocese, and Sugwas, his estate a few miles north of the cathedral city. He left Sugwas only once in March to celebrate ordinations at St. Michael's, Ledbury on the 27th. From mid-April to the end of May he was in Gloucestershire at his favorite manor of Prestbury, some ten miles east of his own diocese. During the following month, after the first effects of plague began to be felt in Hereford, the bishop began to move more frequently. He returned to the diocese on June 6 to hold ordinations at Burghill, a few miles west of Sugwas manor. The remainder of the month was spent at Sugwas and at the palace in Hereford where Trillek held fifteen institutions to vacant benefices.

The city was no place to linger during the pestilence and in early July the bishop sought the familiar and safer confines of his manor at Prestbury where he remained through the month, administering the diocese from the Worcestershire countryside. It is impossible to tell what Trillek's motives were for this, but the imputation of cowardice in the face of a grave challenge is too facile. Trillek had chosen the path of pragmatism over heroism; every indication was that the plague was mounting in his diocese and reports of death must have reached him daily. The numbers of institutions already held suggested that many more would be needed before the epidemic had run its course. If the bishop was to continue the critical work of replacing beneficed clergy, he had to be found and found at once. To travel through the diocese in this desperate hour may have been consoling to some but it would have added to the jeopardy already faced by Trillek and his assistants, and leadership of the diocese would have been in greater peril. Thus he remained at Prestbury and there numerous clerics sought him out; in July the bishop instituted thirty-seven clerics to Hereford benefices, most of which had fallen vacant through death.

At the end of July Trillek returned to his own diocese. He was at Bosbury on August 2 to institute the new rector of Tedstone but spent most of the month in his manor at Whitbourne, close to the Worcester border. Bishop Wulstan had died from the plague on August 6 and Trillek would be called upon by the prior and chapter of Worcester to assist the church there in the ordinations of clergy and other episcopal duties during the vacancy.[39] Trillek's work in both dioceses was evident through August when he divided his time between his manors at Prestbury, Whitbourne, and Sugwas. Still, he managed to be found often enough to institute thirty clerics to vacant benefices. For most of September he was at Sugwas, very near the cathedral where he journeyed on the 19th for ordinations. It seems he remained at Sugwas for most of the fall, perhaps assessing with his household the terrible plague that had recently passed from the borders of his diocese and dealing as best he could with the scandalous trial of his archdeacon in Salop, Henry de Shipton, as an accessory to murder. From Sugwas in November he wrote a letter to the king regarding the status of a prebend, and in December traveled the short distance to Ledbury where he celebrated his last ordination in this troubled year.

It is to Trillek's credit that there was as much stability in the diocese as the records of his labors indicate. Though he shared to some extent the burden of institutions to benefices with his most trusted commissaries, Trillek devoted much of his time to the task of personally examining candidates for churches and dignities in his diocese. His registrar noted in the records of institution those occasions when Trillek himself instituted to a benefice (*dominus admissit*) and when a subordinate acted on the bishop's behalf (*admissus fuit*). At the very least, 160 benefices had been vacant in a single year, some of them several times within a matter of weeks and months. Though Trillek could scarcely devote the time and care reviewing the applications of presentees which more normal periods allowed, all of these institutions were carried out and recorded with as much diligence as circumstances could allow. He promptly filled churches in his own gift and instituted men to canons' residences, prebendal portions, and cathedral dignities with dispatch, all with an effort to sustain the churches, people, and clergy of his diocese in the midst of this cataclysm.

The institution of clerics to vacant churches was not the sole means of shoring up the diocese in these critical days. Trillek needed to equip churches with the clergy they needed and so he turned much of his attention during the plague year to ordinations. The bishop distinguished himself in this respect, admitting more than 1,000 youths to the order of acolyte and some 700 men to the priesthood for Hereford alone during his pontificate. He ordained a futher 1100 regular and secular priests from his and other dioceses. These extraordinary figures resulted from a host of factors, not least of which was the great mortality among clergy in 1349. Like any other bishop, Trillek was limited in the things he could do to increase the field of candidates for Holy Orders. Perhaps he leaned on his archdeacons, who played a special role in the preparation of candidates, to encourage as many men as they could to apply for orders. But it could also be a dangerous strategy were unsuitable candidates rushed through the ordination scrutinies and allowed to pass unchecked into the clerical ranks, all on account of the urgent need for parish priests. What Trillek could do with respect to clerical recruitment was to hold as many ordinations as possible and to take advantage of the interest in Holy Orders that motivated these large numbers of candidates to receive the sacrament.

Ordinations were held at regular times during the year on the four seasonal Ember Saturdays. Were it required, a bishop could confer the sacrament on the vigils of Passion Sunday and Easter. Beyond this a bishop might hold small, private ordinations for one or two clerics in his manor chapel but for anything that amounted to a public gathering the bishop had to receive papal permission.[40]

Trillek evidently took seriously his obligations as minister of the sacrament of Holy Orders. Not only did he work diligently to provide clergy for churches in his own diocese, but his reputation as a resident bishop circulated widely enough that hundreds of candidates came to him from other dioceses to receive the sacrament. As we shall see in the next chapter, Trillek did not hesitate to require those priests who had been ordained for service in the diocese to remain in their churches, administering the sacraments and leading their people in prayer. His strategies of frequent ordinations, the personal residence of his clergy, and a sustained vigilance over the parishes and their curates were some of the most effective policies in his administration of the diocese in the years following the plague.

It is easier to observe and understand how, when faced with the administrative and pastoral crises generated by the plague, John Trillek answered those challenges with whatever talents he possessed as a leader and shepherd. His steadfast residence in the diocese during these difficult times, his quick actions in attempting to keep priests in their places, and tireless celebration of the sacrament of Holy Order to promote new curates to assist in the increased pastoral labor were all characteristic of the man as he appears in official acts recorded in his register. But there was more in his response to the spiritual challenge provoked by the widescale mortality and disruption. Trillek had as well a reputation in his diocese for being a man of prayer and great faith. When, after his death in 1360, he was buried in the cathedral choir, the brass that decorated his tomb described him as "gratus, prudens, pius" and he had occasion to demonstrate those spiritual characteristics during the plague. While at Prestbury in July, 1349, he asked permission of his fellow bishop, Wulstan de Bransford, to consecrate altars in his manor chapel. The bishop of Worcester was generous in his recognition of the extraordinary needs of the time. Trillek was permitted to consecrate "two or three, four, five or six or however many votive altars" he deemed necessary.[41] During those months that he ruled the diocese from Prestbury, not all of Trillek's energies were devoted to administrative challenges. He and his household clerics were singing Requiem masses and praying for the dead of Hereford.

In a similar vein, though with greater consequences for the religious history of the diocese and the English church, Trillek saw in the moment of the plague an urgent reason to complete the shrine to his saintly predecessor, Thomas Cantilupe, and implore the aid of heaven against the epidemic. When he became bishop of Hereford in 1344 preparations had already begun on St. Thomas's shrine in the north transept of the cathedral. Pilgrims had come from all over England to honor the memory of that great bishop and Hereford, at least for a while in the early 1300s, had been one of the most popular religious sites in the kingdom. For his own part, Bishop Trillek had invested time, energy, and resources in the embellishment of Cantilupe's new tomb and planned a fitting ceremony that would mark the translation of the saint's relics in due course. The outbreak of plague in the diocese in 1349 brought a new urgency to this occasion. The people of Hereford took refuge in the firm belief that their saint would help them in the time of plague and implored him to "calm the tumult of the times, drive out the dread infection and lift from them the burden of the pestilence."[42] The bishop and the dean decided that the translation must go forward and the shrine brought to a quick completion. Thus, in October, 1349 in the wake of the great mortality, Trillek issued a mandate to the archdeacons and religious heads of the diocese notifying them of his intention to solemnly translate the bones of St. Thomas Cantilupe on Sunday, October 25, a few weeks after his feastday. Trillek also urged the people to fast and pray in anticipation of this important event in the history of the church of Hereford. It was the bishop's hope that the occasion would recall a similar event in England's history when the relics of another St. Thomas were taken to their new shrine, "after which all things prospered."[43]

Though Cantilupe's worthy successor, John Trillek, had labored hard in finding ways to guide his church through a period of unprecedented turbulence and hardship, it is perhaps this picture of devotion and prayer that is most appropriate in understanding the pastoral challenges of the time. Trillek had done what he could to keep the fold from utter ruin and, on October 25, with King Edward III, the lords of church and realm, and the people of Hereford gathered in the church dedicated to the Blessed Virgin and St. Ethelbert, the bishop consigned into the hands of that formidable saint the protection of his church in time of plague.

3. Diocesan and Parochial Administration After the Black Death

It seemed to many in Hereford that St. Thomas had listened to their prayers, for it was not long after the solemn translation of his relics that the plague began to abate in the diocese and elsewhere. There were now fewer vacancies being reported from Hereford parishes and fewer deaths of clerics noted in Trillek's register of institutions. Less, too, the sounds of mourning that had been heard almost every day—the ringing of the passing bell, funeral dirges, and the shuffling sounds of mourners in processions from the homes of parishioners to the churchyard.

By late February, 1350 reports that the disease was leaving England were common enough that the king issued a decree on the 23rd calling for prayers of thanksgiving to the Almighty that the dreadful judgment had been lifted. Bishop Trillek, who received the mandate in Ledbury where he had celebrated ordinations on February 20, indicated in his return letter that he would comply with the king's wishes.[1] Still, the intent of the mandate must have seemed incongruous, arriving as it did near the middle of Lent; it was also true, whatever enthusiasm the Crown could muster, that it was hard to summon a new public mood in England with memories of recent tragedies still fresh in the minds of most survivors. To be sure, people had desperately searched for signs of the plague's end during its too-long course and preachers had urged their flocks to sustain a Christian hope that God's favor would be restored. Almost at once when the plague began to lift, survivors sought to recover things that had been lost: new relationships were forged to replace the bonds of family and neighbor severed by the recent death; some would cling to the customary as a defense against the flux that moved all about, while others would realize new opportunities and set aside, with no little consequence, the ways of the past. But however we describe the long process of recovery which began when the calamity ended, its beginnings were slow and often somewhat aimless while much grieving and healing yet remained.

The impressions the plague left in people's minds are difficult to assess, but we err in imagining a quick return to normalcy, though such was the firm desire of most. People would continue to wonder at the calamity that had recently been visited upon the world. Not long after the plague had ended and perhaps not far from Hereford, one Midlands writer confessed his own preoccupation with the ruin experienced in the recent pestilence. In a piece entitled "The Three Messengers of Death," he stated that

> Man's life is but brief; young and old, rich and poor, fall before Death. His messengers are Disasters, Sickness, and Old Age. Disasters chance to all as a thief in the night; woe to him to whom unshriven they come. Sickness comes openly, and in God's courteous warning; when ill—we love God—but we soon forget; we should pray for sickness. Old Age is like a man kept out of his lord's gate by a porter; though one live to be four-score, one's life is woeful, all must die; all should fear who pass a churchyard, where in poor-hall lie the bodies full of maggots. Earthly life is as nothing to eternity. In Hell a man shall weep more than all the water in the earth—alms, masses, and prayers shall not avail him. Heaven is for those who serve God.[2]

Though the writer does not mention the pestilence specifically, its presence is all about the piece. The author was after all witness to Death's first messengers, Disaster and Sickness, in the plague that had just visited the land. He comments on the great changes that have occurred, enough to regard Old Age as a curse. People must think on death, for in meditating on its swiftness and its caprice, one is led to repentance and the prospect of eternal salvation. Unshriven in life, one is beyond hope in death and no number of masses sung for such a one will lift the condemnation.

It is impossible to view accurately the slow process of recovery in the diocese of Hereford after the Black Death without considering this point of view. As we shall see, from the perspective of administration, John Trillek and his successor, Lewis Charlton, applied their considerable talents maintaining stability in the diocese during and following the great plague. The evidence of their registers indicates as much. But we cannot ignore the possibilities too that able administration was joined with pastoral vigilance through times that seemed most uncertain. The rule of the diocese had been challenged in more devastating ways than anyone could recall. The recent affliction had been without precedent, and Trillek and Charlton looked in vain for guidance from the acts of their venerable predecessors. As we have seen, in the moment of the crisis Bishop Trillek's immediate response was to keep the diocese and its pastoral operations in as much order as his wits and the law could provide. But in some sense the real challenges were yet to come once the violent changes caused by the plague had begun to subside.

The royal summons for thanksgiving and jubilation were at odds with the sobering fact that the bishop now had to guide those of his subjects who survived through a world that was much changed.

Trillek's plans for recovery, if we may even attribute such far-ranging vision to the man, were that routine business should go on as much after the plague as before; he maintained cordial and cooperative relations with the king and with ecclesiastical authorities within and beyond Hereford. His efforts to sustain the parishes and provide them with adequate numbers of clergy during the plague year continued as a matter of diocesan policy in the bishop's concern over institutions to vacant benefices and regular ordination ceremonies. Lastly, his vigilance in the diocese and his interests in safeguarding the slow progress realized in the years following the plague were evident in his expectations of the clergy regarding the cure of souls. The recovery patiently guided in these and similar policies would be checked violently in the early 1360s when the plague erupted anew. It was for Trillek's successor, Lewis Charlton, to guide his flock through equally perilous times.

The Diocese in the Decade Following the Black Death

The epidemic had made an already taxing labor even more difficult for John Trillek. During the months when the epidemic raged in Hereford, he acquitted the extraordinary tasks that had fallen to him as a result of the upheaval. He had instituted more clerics to vacant benefices in a few months than he had done in all the previous years of his pontificate combined. Ordinations for the plague year were the highest they had been since the beginning of the century. The bishop executed emergency measures regarding clerical stability and residence in the churches, but along with all these activities, Trillek carried on with whatever routine business occurred in these exceptional days. Though the critical point of the epidemic had passed, the bishop continued in the same manner of administration through the years immediately following the plague. On February 20, only a few days before he received the king's mandate for thanksgiving liturgies, Trillek had presided at an ordination ceremony in Ledbury where 262 men from Hereford and other dioceses were promoted to all orders. He stayed there a further three weeks when nearly as many men appeared for ordinations on March 13.[3] Trillek then went to his manor at Prestbury where he ordained a sizeable number of Worcester clerics on behalf of the new bishop, John

Thoresby. He remained at the manor through the remainder of the year, leaving it only a few times for business in Leominster and at the cathedral, or for ordinations, as he did in Burghill in May and Ledbury again the following September.[4]

Though he showed no indications of being ambitious for higher rank in the church, Trillek was not the type of prelate to shun responsibilities. But he did distinguish between what was pertinent and immediate to his care, and what should be taken up by other able hands. In May, 1350 he declined from accepting a papal commission to judge a quarrel between the nuns of Waterbeach and their sister house at Denny, turning the task over to churchmen who included the trustworthy John de Ewe, Treasurer of Hereford Cathedral and a seasoned bureaucrat.[5] He had never been anxious to attend parliaments and showed the same detachment when summoned by the king to the Hilary parliament early in 1351. Trillek begged to be excused on reasons of ill health and sent delegates to represent himself and the church of Hereford. He did the same when the archbishop called him to a provincial council in London in early May of the same year.[6] Even when he was not sick Trillek preferred to stay home and occupy himself with the administration of his diocese and the repair of structures recently put under great strain.

Primary among these structures and requiring the bishop's personal attention were the parishes, clergy, and people of Hereford. Thus, late in the spring of 1353, Trillek organized a visitation of the entire diocese. His register does not detail what he found on his visitation of the northern deaneries, but whatever crimes he uncovered, he judged them serious enough to order local deans to publish his sanctions against certain disturbers of the peace. Trillek marked out especially fomentors of discord and perjurers against the king's justice, in particular forgerers of wills who had taken advantage of the recent chaos to acquire and dispose of property as they wished.[7] Bishops were usually anxious to defend the testamentary rights of their people and the goods that might otherwise be lost to the church. But in these years following the plague when the ownership of property was a frequent subject of argument and litigation, the abuse of inheritance rights was as great as the bishop's fear of deprivation.

The pastoral work of religious communities, either in the direct service of hospitals and almshouses, or indirectly, as with religious appropriators of parish churches, were also of particular concern to Trillek during this visitation. He warned the *custos* of St. Katherine's Hospital in Ledbury to correct and reform the excessive behavior of his brothers and to see to it that their lives were more in keeping with their high calling.[8] The White Ladies of Brewood, though very poor, appeared before the bishop and admitted that it was their responsibility to provide a chaplain for Bold church which they had appropriated.[9] The Prior of Moreville, a small daughter house of Shrewsbury Abbey, was under the same duty to provide a curate for Astley chapel nearby.[10] The abbot of Gloucester was less cooperative with Trillek over the visitation of his abbey's daughter house, Bromfield Priory, and engaged the bishop in a dispute that took three years to resolve.[11] In a related incident, the parishioners of Leinthall Chapel won their case against the vicar of Wigmore who, they asserted, was obliged to hire a chaplain to celebrate mass at the smaller church on Sundays, Wednesdays, Fridays, and feast days.[12]

By Michaelmas, the visitation proper had ended and Trillek was back at his manor at Whitbourne where he appointed William de Wroth his commissary general to judge those cases that required the more patient consideration of the bishop's courts. Trillek never underestimated the value of personal visitation to the parishes and religious houses of the diocese. Three years later, in January 1356, he was at Churcham where he received with some satisfaction the letters of possession and title from the abbot of Gloucester to all properties the abbey possessed in Hereford. The following October Trillek was at Lindridge church in Burford deanery, resolving a dispute as to who possessed the revenues of the church and its dependent chapels of Pensax and Knighton.[13]

It was not always from neglect, benign or otherwise, that religious appropriators and rectors failed to provide sufficient clergy for the pastoral care of their churches. Surely the system of church appropriations was abused and the fair management of a parish church's revenues was reduced to the greed of the proprietor. This was one of the central matters opened up at visitations and Trillek showed himself to be the sort of bishop who enforced the terms of the appropriation. But in the years immediately following the Black Death, he also demonstrated a flexibility in his judgments, aware of the changes that had troubled local economies and smaller landowners. In early October, 1351, he honored the petition of the monks at Llanthony Priory near Gloucester to appropriate the revenues of the parish church of Awre, so impoverished had the monastery become on account of the plague and other disasters of the time.[14] In the summer of 1352 he permitted the monks at Brecon to lease their church revenues at Bodenham for five years.[15] Behind the grant was the hope that the church's revenues could be administered to greater effect by others than the monks and so help ease the burden of debt in which Brecon and other houses had found themselves. Again, there were dangers of abuse here as farmers of benefices, when unwatched, could cut corners at the expense of the very purpose of the church, the pastoral needs of the community. But Trillek had to keep what vigilance he could in this respect. Later, in 1356 he would make similar grants to the monks at St. Peter's, Gloucester for the church of Much Cowarne and the nuns of Aconbury for Wolferlow, and, in 1358, to the Prior of Ewyas for the revenues of Foy church.[16]

To judge fairly between a rector's or patron's interests in local church administration and the pastoral health of a parish was not always an easy matter to negotiate, but Trillek regularly showed himself as much in favor of the parishioners and clergy as he was of local church leadership. In the case of Great and Little Collington already commented upon, the bishop recognized at once the legitimate plea of the patron, Ralph de Yeddefin, and the parishioners to unite the two churches formally on account of the devastation brought on by the plague.[17] In 1355 the vicar of Pyon maintained that his income was too mean to sustain his work and the labors of his ministries there and asked the bishop that his portion of the church revenues be augmented. Trillek referred the case to his commissary and its outcome is not known; but for the fact that no further appeal was made, it seems likely that the bishop's judgment was ultimately for the vicar.[18] In the fall of 1357, after having visited the deanery of Leominster, the bishop took note of the poor conditions in which the vicar of Eardisland had been living. The church house was so tightly hedged that the poor vicar hadn't room enough to walk in prayer or land enough to plant a garden to grow leeks, vegetables, and other herbs. On his own initiative, Trillek informed the abbot and convent of Lyre, appropriators of Eardisland, that he was giving the vicar an added portion of land out of the rectorial glebe, that his life and work might be adequately supported.[19]

The early 1350s were troubled enough by the difficulties that emerged in the wake of the Black Death, so Edward III's request for a clerical subsidy for his war efforts in 1352 could hardly have been welcomed by the parish clergy and bishop of Hereford. At the summer parliament that year, king and clergy negotiated for the subsidy and for certain royal concessions to clerical rights, especially as they pertained to civil trials.[20] But the king got his way and by October had sent mandates to the bishops for the appointment of collectors of the clerical tenth promised. Trillek's was dated October 20 and a few weeks later he commissioned the Prior and Convent of St. Guthlac's in Hereford to serve as the royal collectors.[21] By the following summer, when Trillek was on visitation in the diocese, he observed such poverty in some of his parishes that he wrote to the Chancellor of the Exchequer certifying that ten churches in the deaneries of Stottesden, Pontesbury, and Irchenfield, some of the poorer regions of the diocese, were all so insufficiently endowed that they should be exempt from the biennial tenth.[22]

It must have been difficult for Trillek to enforce blindly the will of the king in this regard. There were legitimate excuses on grounds of poverty and the bishop, too, had to make sure that his clergy were not backing out of an assessment that they themselves had agreed to. In November, 1357 the king, upset at the refusal of some Hereford clergy to pay the tenth as promised, ordered the bishop to sequestrate the goods of certain churches until their debts had been acquitted. The vicar of Alberbury and the rector of Much Marcle were particularly opposed to the idea of paying the tenth and their revenues were duly sequestrated by the bishop early the following year.[23] Trillek had to beg off from sequestrating the goods of other clerics, he told the king, at least until the following fall when the first harvests were in. Until that time, New Radnor and Hanwood joined the list of the churches that avoided the tenth.[24] So would more prominent persons such as Thomas Hakeluit, the cathedral chancellor, and the Abbot of Dore, both of whom were cited by the king as being excessively tardy in their payments.[25] It was inevitable in some cases that obstinacy would turn to violence. In October, 1360, the king ordered Trillek to force William, a Hereford priest and vicar of Dilwyn, to appear before the Exchequer on charges of assault and battery against a Chancery official named Nicholas Goldene. Goldene claimed that the vicar not only assaulted him but made off from Dilwyn parish with twenty marks worth of goods and chattel.[26]

The vicar's alleged rough behavior with the Chancellor's servant was as much a concern for Trillek as his refusal to pay the subsidy. Trillek made sure in the unsettled years that followed the plague to continue his policies of clerical reform established in the first months of his pontificate. But in many ways reform had to wait for stability to return to the parishes of Hereford. What Trillek had foremost in mind during the plague and in the years immediately following was the provision of priests to Hereford churches through the sacrament of ordination and the episcopal act of institution to benefices.

John Trillek knew that the most important function of his own pastoral ministry was the promotion of men to Holy Orders. In his first years as bishop of Hereford he celebrated the sacrament at most of the usual times, holding an average of two ordination ceremonies each year from 1345 to 1348, each of considerable size. As was often the case with other bishops, Trillek held smaller ceremonies, usually of ten or less candidates, in his manor chapels on the two vigils of Passion Sunday and Easter. But by the spring of 1349, with the rise in clerical deaths and the resulting threat to the pastoral care of Hereford parishes, the bishop had to increase the number of annual ordinations held in the diocese. During the plague year and for the three years following, Trillek conferred the sacrament at every possible opportunity. The results of his labors in the early spring must have seemed encouraging. At the two ordinations he celebrated during March, 1349, before the plague took a firm hold on the diocese, Trillek ordained some 470 clerics to all orders, 353 of whom were from his own diocese and thirty-five of them priests. After the Easter Vigil ordinations on April 11, a decline in the annual number of candidates would begin and endure with little significant change through the next half century. The reasons behind these changes in clerical recruitment is the subject for the following chapter, but it needs to be said here that if Hereford experienced a decline in candidates for the clergy in the years immediately following the Black Death, it was not for want of ordination ceremonies celebrated by the bishop.[27] From 1349 to 1352 Trillek celebrated the sacrament six times a year, and continued for the next three years to hold ordinations at a frequency greater than usual. It was during the last five years of his pontificate that his resolve in this respect began to wane, but not so much through his own weariness as the fact that smaller and smaller numbers of candidates were appearing before him for ordination at the scheduled celebrations.

Trillek was right to conclude that the more often ordinations were held in the diocese, the better was the chance at keeping recruitment levels high or at least normal. There was another reason behind the frequency of these celebrations: the path from acolyte to priesthood was accordingly shortened and ordinands were able to be put into parishes as priests all the more quickly. There were safeguards against moving too rapidly, however. Candidates were prohibited from receiving more than one order at the same ceremony and church law decreed that a decent period of time should lapse before the cleric was promoted to the next order.[28] Still, what was considered decent was generally determined by the bishop when he fixed the date for the next ordination ceremony. One also needs to recall that though a bishop might celebrate the sacrament on any of the established times throughout the year, he was not obliged to do so. He set his schedule according to the circumstances of his own itinerary and the need for ordinations in the diocese. That Trillek held as many ordinations as he did during and immediately following the plague up to the mid-1350s indicates a new and more vigorous strategy for recruitment, precipitated by the plague. Candidates were moved through the ranks of orders with unusual speed: one cleric, William de Newnton, was ordained an acolyte on March 28, 1349, promoted to subdeacon on April 11, deacon the following June, and a priest on September 14, all in less than six months.[29] Even more unusual was the ordination of John de Hulle to the orders of acolyte and subdeacon at the same ceremony on April 11, 1349. By late August he had already been priested and instituted to the vicarage of Eye.[30] In other years Trillek ordained large groups of acolytes and subdeacons with the realistic confidence that many would move on to priest's orders in their own time. During the plague and immediately following, no number of minor clerics would have been able to assist the church in the sacramental ministry so desperately needed in the parishes. It was of paramount importance that Trillek provide as many priests to Hereford parishes as possible.

Trillek further aided the process of recruitment and ordination by celebrating Holy Orders at regular and accessible sites in the diocese. Sometimes, as when on visitation, the bishop arranged for celebrations at the chapel of the episcopal manor where he was staying or in one of the larger churches in the vicinity. During 1349 he held three of the six larger ordinations at the cathedral or just outside the city. The other three ordinations were held in the eastern part of the diocese at Bosbury and Ledbury in Frome deanery, within easy reach of his residence at Prestbury. St. Michael's church in Ledbury was the preferred site for ordinations in 1351 not only for of its great size (it had once been called Hereford's premier parish) but because there were increasing numbers of candidates coming to Trillek for the sacrament from their parishes in the neighboring dioceses of Worcester and Coventry and Lichfield. In the two years following the plague, Trillek actually ordained twice as many men from other dioceses as he did Hereford clerics. Twice in 1352 Trillek was commissioned by Bishop Thoresby to celebrate orders in the Worcester diocese and on both occasions the bishop of Hereford let it be known that any of his own clerics who wished to be ordained could find him at Cheltenham in Gloucestershire. Sixty Hereford clerics, regular and secular, made the journey to Cheltenham, some ten miles east of the Hereford border. For the remainder of the year, ordinations were celebrated either at Hereford Cathedral, in the bishop's palace nearby, or at Bromyard, again not far from the Worcester border. In fact, after ordination activities began to slow in the mid-1350s, Trillek continued to favor churches and manor chapels in the eastern parts of his diocese or in the cathedral city, possibly because of the better-traveled roads between Hereford and Worcester and to avoid the wilder and less accessible parts of the diocese in the north and west.

The most effective means of enhancing clerical recruitment for a medieval bishop such as Trillek was to hold ordinations frequently and in an accessible manner, two things which he undoubtedly achieved. There was one further measure of episcopal control in this process, though it rarely involved sizeable numbers of new recruits. This was the bishop's prerogative in seeking dispensations for men otherwise barred from receiving the sacrament of orders, usually with impediments of illegitimate birth or minority of age. During and immediately following the Black Death, a number of prelates appealed to the pope for permission to ordain such men, so dire was the need for priests in their dioceses and religious houses.[31] Trillek joined these appeals in October, 1349 when he asked that six of his clerics be dispensed from illegitimacy in order to be ordained. Once ordained, he had it in mind that they be admitted at once to a pastoral cure, but he went on in the petition to ask that each be given further permission to hold an additional benefice.[32] It is also likely that he took advantage of a collective petition made on behalf of the bishops of the province of Canterbury by Archbishop Simon Islip in the fall of 1349. Islip assured the pope that no prelate in his province had been able to find sufficient numbers of "priests to celebrate the divine services and minister in parishes and other churches on account of the epidemic which has raged and rages still in England."[33] It was for this reason of clerical scarcity that Islip asked for himself and each of his suffragans permission to dispense from minority of age up to twenty men who had not yet reached the minimum age requirement of twenty-four years for priesthood.

Trillek's petition for the six young men to be ordained to the priesthood and admitted to benefices suggests another critical step in the bishop's attempts to solve the pastoral crisis of his diocese. Earlier in the century and certainly before, it was not unusual that a cleric be instituted as rector of a benefice with a cure of souls who was yet in minor orders and not ordained a priest. Canon law provided that the rector secure priest's orders within a specific period of time from his institution.[34] Meanwhile, the rector had to employ a parochial vicar who would see to the pastoral needs of the parish community.[35] When Thomas Charlton was bishop in the 1330s and early 1340s, some 24 clerics in the diocese were ordained to the priesthood after they had already been instituted to Hereford parish churches. Trillek ordained 37 benefice clerics to the priesthood, but nearly half of these were ordained at one of the ordinations in 1349 and 1350, when the bishop was urgently finding ways to place and keep priests in parishes. Trillek was faced with decreasing numbers, both in benefices and in the larger clerical pro-letariat, and though he was forced by circumstances to institute some minor clerics to incumbencies, he was equally careful that these clerics should advance to the priesthood as soon as possible.

Though the worst of the plague was over in Hereford by the winter of 1349/50, Trillek continued his policies regarding institutions to vacant livings for the remainder of his pontificate. Certainly, he faced nothing in the after years of the plague like the spate of institutions carried out in 1349 but he was insistant in remaining in the diocese and accessible to ordinands and presentees alike in his efforts to reestablish some pastoral equilibrium. Much as he had done during the plague year, he continued to fill churches promptly, especially those that were in his own gift and over which he had immediate control such as canons' residences, prebendal portions and cathedral dignities and the churches on his own estates. After the plague and through the remainder of his pontificate, he instituted larger numbers of clerics to vacant benefices than in any of his earlier years. By 1350 the number of vacancies had dropped almost as steeply as it had jumped the previous year (Table 3.1). He instituted only forty-five clerics to livings that year — still considerable given the averages from earlier years — and fewer every year after until 1358 and 1360 when the numbers were finally compa-rable to what they had been in the stabler days before the plague.

There was one final aspect to Trillek's efforts at providing priests to the parishes of Hereford during and after the momentous changes of the Black Death, and this was perhaps his most difficult challenge. Not only had he to ordain and institute men to pastoral cures, but he had to keep them there. The issue of clerical residency was not so problematic among the beneficed clergy; rectors and vicars were expected among their primary duties to live in the benefice to which they had been instituted. There were some excep-tions, of course, and Trillek had to be clear on what would be allowed and what would not. A more difficult problem, however, lay with the stipendi-ary clergy who, though clearly important in the pastoral administration of the parish, did not feel so bound to the local church as their employers.

A beneficed cleric could apply to his bishop for a leave from his church for a variety of reasons, usually because important work took him else-where, or he wished to go on pilgrimage or spend a term or two at a university under the terms set out in the papal decretal *Cum ex eo*.[36] John

TABLE 3.1   Institutions and Presentations to Hereford Benefices, 1345–1360

Year	Institutions	Presentations
1345	5	7
1346	6	10
1347	6	10
1348	11	6
1349	**160**	**41**
1350	45	5
1351	22	6
1352	25	7
1353	18	1
1354	10	4
1355	25	5
1356	12	4
1357	22	6
1358	7	3
1359	18	8
1360	7	5

Trillek inherited a generally liberal policy from his predecessors regarding study leaves and he himself was a supporter of opportunities for clerical education. In 1346 Bishop Trillek permitted six of his clerics to leave their benefices in order to study. Two years later he granted a further eleven absences, most of which were academic leaves. But in 1349 he allowed only four clerics to leave their benefices; one occurred in mid-August and the remaining three in late October and December after the diocese had re-gained some relative calm. Only one of these leaves was given for purposes of study and this was a grant to young John le Ferrour, who was appointed portioner of Burford as an acolyte. The remaining three clerics were allowed to serve in attendance to a local noble or an ecclesiastic.[37] There were some fluctuations in the numbers of leaves granted for the remainder of Trillek's reign. For instance, the bishop was more liberal in this matter in 1351 when seven clerics went off to study and another to serve Lady Constance at Kingston. But the larger numbers of leaves, study and otherwise, typical of earlier years were not as readily supported after the Black Death. There were very likely not anywhere near the number of requests in the straited times following the plague; the fewer grants of leaves in the 1350s may have reflected as much the diminished interests of clerics to leave their benefices as the bishop's new determination to keep his priests in their churches. Also, were *Cum ex eo* to be strictly interpreted, only clerics short of ordination to the priesthood were permitted study leaves. With the bishop more concerned about pacing clerics through the ranks, there were fewer acolytes and subdeacons as heads of parochial benefices.

Clerics could leave benefices for other reasons such as resignation due to ill health or old age. They might also leave one benefice to take up another in the practice of exchanges. Among the 399 institutions to benefices recorded in the Trillek register from 1344 to 1360, 65 were from resignations, but almost half of these occurred in 1349 and 1350. Although the precise reasons for the resignations are never specified, it is clear that none of these occurred due to exchanges. While the bishop was striving to maintain as much stability as he could in the parishes by discouraging unnecessary movement, he nonetheless recognized that certain of his rectors and vicars were no longer able to carry on the administration of their churches. In previous years when the number of available clerics was greater, the bishop was able to appoint coadjutors to assist incumbents who were feeble and infirmed, allowing the rector to retain possession of his church. But all of this changed with the plague. Local clerics could no longer rely on usual procedures in this respect and many were faced with new and hard-met challenges, including the devaluation of properties and a drop in income, pastoral demands that taxed and overshot the strength of some clerics, and the diminished availability of priests in the diocese who might assist. Though, no doubt, Trillek attempted to halt unnecessary resignations, there was often little he could do other than attempt to fill the benefice as quickly as possible once it fell vacant.

He had more control in the matter of exchanges. Though the practice of leaving one benefice to go to another had not reached the level of abuse that it would later in the century, Trillek did not seem to favor the practice much. Between 1345 and 1347 he approved only seventeen exchanges in his diocese. In 1348 and 1349 he allowed only four for each year and in 1350 only one exchange took place.[38] Later in 1354 he allowed up to six exchanges but this was the exception rather than the rule for the remainder of the decade.

Regulation of his higher clergy was an important feature of Trillek's administration of the diocese. After all, the rectors and vicars were the local leaders of the parish communities and their steady placement and service in their cures was of critical concern for the bishop. But Trillek's real challenges in pastoral stability came not from the higher clergy but from the chaplains and wage-earning clergy who played a crucial role in pastoral care. In the stronger days of clerical recruitment, when there were nearly more clergy than churches to employ them, the competition for placements was oftentimes keen. Even poorer parishes could afford a stipendiary, though perhaps not one of impressive qualities, given the mean wage he worked for. This situation, too, had changed after the Black Death. The need for clergy was more pressing than it had ever been but the old bonds of association between these assistant clergy and their parishes had weakened considerably with a changed economy. With the upheavals caused by the plague, these clerics were likelier than others to leave their churches for better employment in a much-improved market.

This conflict of old loyalties and new opportunties was shared by those who labored in other fields. Surviving tenants had found their work in greater demand after the plague than at any time previous in human memory. At the same time, landowners were hard-pressed to retain their tenants under outdated terms and agreements. The challenge posed by this rapid change in attitude to the established structures of economy and society was too great to leave unattended. Thus on June 18, 1349, after the first effects of the plague had begun to threaten the economic order of the kingdom, Edward III and his Council issued the Ordinance of Laborers, which attempted to freeze the earnable wages of tenants and keep laborers where they had been, in wages and in service, in the days before the epidemic.[39] In order to make this decree the more effective, it was published as usual through the lords of the realm, spiritual and secular.

Trillek received the ordinance days after it was issued and moved swiftly to apply its terms of wage restriction and tenure to his own laborers. But the bishop took further advantage of the spirit of the king's mandate by ordering all the wage-earning clerics in his diocese to keep to their churches and accept the fees to which they had been accustomed before the plague. Trillek issued his own mandate covering the king's ordinance to the dean of Hereford Cathedral as well as to the archdeacons of Hereford and Shropshire, commanding them to admonish "each and every stipendiary cleric dwelling in [their] jurisdiction that under penalty of suspension and interdict, they are not to require excessive charges for their services" to the faithful.[40] The swiftness of Trillek's action illustrates how clearly the bishop recognized the threat to stability in his diocese at about the same time the plague was mounting in intensity within Hereford's borders. The bishop could ill-afford to lose a single cleric when so many of his priests and parishioners were dying and when the need for pastors was so urgent.

Trillek's letter is significant as well for the fact that it anticipated by almost a year the policy that would be announced through the province of Canterbury in Archbishop Islip's famous mandate, *Effrenata*. This decree was more explicit than Trillek's on the matter of clerical wages and it carried the full weight of metropolitan authority. It would be reissued on two further occasions and was to influence prospects for clerical employment in the English church for years to come.[41] But Trillek did not wait for provincial policies to be set in this matter. Some of his tenants had already moved from their established places of service and others were doubtless threatening to do the same and the bishop as a prominent landholder in the diocese was well aware of how the continued weakening of custom and structure would only add to the instability created by the plague. Furthermore, he took the opportunity to require the same steadiness of his priests as soon as he had a law that would defend him in this course.

There are two final aspects of Trillek's administration of the parishes and their clergy that merit comment, both having to do with transgression and forgiveness. When he came to the diocese in 1344 he knew that much of his energy would be taken up with keeping unruly clergy in line, and his register gives us every indication that he took the charge of clerical discipline seriously. Whether or not Trillek had more on his hands in this regard after the plague than before is uncertain. The business probably varied less in kind than in volume. The most controversial case involving any of his clergy occurred in the fall of 1349 when Trillek had to face the scandal of an archdeacon charged as an accessory to murder. Henry de Shipton, the ambitious archdeacon of Shropshire who would play a role many thought villainous in the last days of John Trillek's life, had been accused of aiding in the murder of John Ace of Ludlow. In October 1349 Trillek received a writ from the king forbidding him to hear the case and to allow the dispute to be settled first in the king's courts. The archdeacon responded by issuing countercharges of defamation against a certain John of Evesham, rector of Ludlow, whom Henry maintained coerced some of the jurors, the rector's tenants, to find him guilty.[42]

But for the most part Trillek was bothered by less sensational clerical crimes in the years following the Black Death. The episcopal prisons in Hereford and Ross were rarely empty for long, but their inhabitants were usually there on charges of theft and minor assault charges. In November, 1354, Trillek commissioned his *officialis* William de Wroth to make the necessary inquisitions in two cases of criminous clerks. Richard Aglyon of Ledbury had been charged and convicted of stealing a cow and a calf. John Hales, another cleric of the diocese, was convicted of robbing William de

Gorewell in Fownhope park of 4s and 8p and a set of beads. Trillek ordered his official to free the two men from prison if the inquisitions — usually a matter of purgation on the testimony of good character — resulted in their favor.[43]

Transgression that could not be purged so easily was a matter for confession; Trillek was aware of this and provided confessors for his clergy and people as needed. He relied on the work of his own rectors and vicars, the *proprii sacerdotes* of Hereford parishioners, to absolve penitents in the usual course of the celebration of that sacrament. But there were occasions as well when he appointed confessors for the diocese, local penitentiaries who were to assist parish priests in this important sacramental ministry. At the beginning of Advent in 1346 the bishop appointed three Dominican friars from the Hereford convent to preach and hear confessions, but this was the only time before the plague that Trillek had judged it necessary to arrange for special confessors in the diocese.[44] There is no record of his appointing confessors during the time of the plague. Doubtless, Trillek was challenged enough to keep his parish clergy in place and the mendicant houses were undergoing their own trials during the epidemic. But after the plague had left the diocese, the bishop renewed his commissions of penitentiaries to work all or parts of the diocese. While he was at Prestbury in 1351 he licensed six Dominicans to travel to parishes all over the diocese and hear confessions. Other like commissions followed during the next several years with Dominicans being joined by two Austin and eleven Franciscan friars.[45] However, in September, 1355, only a few weeks after he had commissioned a group of Austin friars as confessors, Trillek suddenly reversed this policy and issued a mandate to all the pastors in the diocese informing them that all such licenses recently issued were revoked. No names were included in the mandate as entered in the register nor were any specific reasons given for the bishop's dramatic decision.[46] The licenses specified no particular term for the confessors and since 1351 there could have been as many as twenty-seven friars moving through the diocese hearing confessions. Perhaps Trillek's confidence in some of the mendicants needed to be reassessed in the midst of great changes that were occurring elsewhere in his diocese; perhaps, too, Trillek had to consider the growing animosity between mendicants and secular clerics on matters of preaching, hearing confessions, and the general, if unsubstantiated, fears that parish revenues could be further lost in economically depressed times. Whatever the reasons behind the bishop's act in 1355, the matter had been adequately addressed by Lent the following year when Trillek appointed three Dominicans to preach and shrive. For the remainder of his pontificate, Trillek's confidence in the mendicants in this pastoral work did not wane. Licenses were granted for every year until 1358 and every region of the diocese had assigned confessors. No reason is given, but no licenses for confessions were given to Franciscans after the controversy of 1355.[47]

By 1358 the energies of the bishop had begun to wane. The volume of business recorded in his register indicated a slackened pace in comparison with the wide range of episcopal business in the 1340s and early 1350s. The one significant exception to this retiring tendency was the number of ordinations Trillek continued to celebrate, in spite of their diminishing effect. In September, 1358 he celebrated the sacrament at his manor chapel in Whitbourne, the first ordination to take place in sixteen months. Business for the following year was similarly thin; beyond the five ordinations at Whitbourne and Bishop's Castle, Trillek concerned himself with usual matters from the king, including an inquiry into the status of Brosely chapel and the seemingly incessant demands for unpaid clerical subsidies.[48] He received a summons to Parliament in the spring of 1360 and appointed collectors for the tenth in May. The rest of the year he spent in relative quiet at his manor in Sugwas, a few miles north of the cathedral where he held two small ordinations, one in early April and his last on May 30.[49] By this time the bishop had become incapacitated in body as well as in mind and his last months were a pathetic comedy played out between the scheming archdeacon of Shropshire, Henry de Shipton, and the Cathedral Dean, Trillek's own brother Thomas, fighting over possession of the bishop's body and whatever influence remained in his hands. Henry de Shipton had the bishop placed under guard at Bishop's Castle, governing the diocese in his name. The Dean and Chapter protested the indignity to the king and on the eve of royal intervention into the matter the bishop was said to have regained his senses sufficiently to execute the duties of his office. But if there had been any change it was passing.[50] The bishop died at Sugwas on November 30, 1360 and was buried in the cathedral choir where an elegant memorial brass fittingly described this shepherd of Hereford as *gratus, prudens, pius*.[51]

Trillek had been a good steward of his diocese during some of the most turbulent and bewildering years in the history of the see. He brought native intelligence and genuine determination to his post and had learned well under the mentorship of his powerful uncle, Adam Orleton. As bishop he had accepted responsibility for the spiritual well-being of souls placed in his care and took seriously his duties to find able men to assist him in this large task. Even in the best of times that was a hard challenge. But the plague of 1349 had taxed his diocese, its clergy, and the bishop's own energies to meet the demands which grew daily. Nevertheless, Trillek sought every opportunity to regain the balances lost through death, sickness, and spiritual malaise. He oversaw numerous institutions to vacant benefices, admitted hundreds of Hereford men to Holy Orders, considered more carefully than usual any situation that might leave a church without a resident incumbent, and applied every sanction available to keep stipendiary clergy in the service of their churches. Of course, none of this was done single-handedly; Trillek had to rely on capable advisors to influence and effect sound policies in the diocese during, and especially following, the plague. The cathedral dean and canons who occupied the higher dignities of the chapter, the archdeacons of Hereford and Shropshire, their officials, rural deans, and a host of other commissaries were all pressed into service to meet the crisis and work for whatever solutions could be found. They shared in the pastoral and administrative labors required in these changeful times, but they did so under the able command of John Trillek.

Lewis Charlton (1361–1369) and the Second Plague

The animosities and divisions that had burdened the final months of Trillek's pontificate had an adverse affect on the cathedral chapter which was troubled with factionalism during the vacancy after his death. The canons of the cathedral had received the king's leave in mid-December to elect Trillek's successor but the election was stalled over a split in chapter loyalties. Half supported John Barnet, the impressive Archdeacon of London, while the rest sided with Lewis Charlton, a cathedral canon, an Oxford scholar and a kinsman of Trillek's predecessor, Thomas Charlton.[52] By early October, 1361, Charlton had won the election, was papally provided to the see and received his temporalities from the king in mid-November.[53]

It was John Trillek's good fortune that after his strenuous work in post-plague Hereford he did not live to see the fresh outbreak of plague that began in the summer of 1361 and lasted to the following May.[54] Contemporaries labeled it the "pestilentia puerorum" for the toll it took on the young who had been born since the first epidemic and had acquired no immunity against the plague.[55] Since this pestilence was most virulent in Hereford during the vacancy, much is lost from the same kind of diocesan records that helped chronicle the plague during the Trillek years. If records of institution were kept by the vicars general appointed during the vacancy they do not survive and there are no records of ordinations being held in the diocese in 1361 to help determine attrition rates from one clerical rank to another.[56] But there are other references to suggest that this plague had a ruinous effect on the diocese. Once again Edward III suspended all royal assemblies, including the courts, from early May, 1361 to late June; only two days before the courts were to resume their business, the king once again ordered them closed until the octave of Michaelmas.[57] At about the same time in Hereford, Adam Trewlove, close friend and advisor to Bishop Trillek and spiritual vicar of the diocese during the vacancy, adjourned the church's courts in Hereford "on account of the pestilence raging there at the time." The court's business was not resumed until the middle of September when the plague began to abate.[58]

By November, Bishop Charlton was getting his administrative house in order. Adam Esgar, a veteran canon of the cathedral chapter, was joined by the bishop's kinsman William de Charlton and Philip de la More to serve as vicars general until the bishop's arrival.[59] Charlton did not actually take up residence in his diocese until late 1361 or early in the new year; he held his first ordination celebration at Bromyard church on March 12, 1362.[60]

Lewis Charlton came to Hereford in inauspicious times. The second epidemic had frustrated the slow progress begun under John Trillek, but Charlton gave every indication that he would continue the policies of his predecessor. The two men were alike in many ways: both were from local families, both had powerful uncles who sponsored their ecclesiastical careers, both were scholars, and both devoted pastors content to stay in the diocese and lead it effectively.

Not long after Lewis Charlton took up his responsibilities in Hereford he made a visitation of his new diocese, perhaps for many of the same reasons that Trillek visited the parishes in the aftermath of the first plague. In May, 1363, he sent a letter of citation to the dean of Frome, ordering him to cite the clergy and people of the deanery in preparation for the bishop's arrival and inquiries. All clerics were admonished to appear before the bishop at an appointed place and to bring with them letters of title from ordination and all certificates of institution. For their part, parishioners were to elect a handful of worthy jurors who would offer sworn testimony regarding the moral and physical condition of their parish.[61] Charlton had to deal with certain devastating results of the recent outbreak of plague. In a scene reminiscent of what Trillek had to do in the merging of Great and Little Collington parishes, Charlton listened to the appeals of parishioners from Puddleston and Whyle. As at Collington, these people claimed that their parishes had been so impoverished by the recent epidemic that they barely had enough to support a single priest in his cure much less two. In response to the appeal, Charlton formally united the two parishes.[62]

Other parishes suffered as well from the plague of 1361. The vicar of Dewchurch begged that his portion be increased, so poor had his church become since the last plague. Charlton prevailed upon the rector of Dewchurch, Kilpeck Priory, to reapportion the revenues they had under their control and give the vicar his due.[63] Alberbury vicarage, which had been poor even in good times and whose vicar had provoked the king's ire for failure to pay the tenth when Trillek was bishop, was suffering from even greater poverty in the 1360s. The vicar, Thomas de Moneford, told the bishop that the appropriators of the church's revenues, Alberbury Priory, took too much and gave too little and that he was not able to support himself or the work he was obliged to do at the parish. The priory was asked to take less for the benefit of the church's vicar.[64]

Poverty was one thing, but the scarcity of clergy to serve Hereford parishes was a problem that continued well into Lewis Charlton's pontificate. His own household had been affected by the recent epidemic; in 1363 he petitioned the pope to acquire additional chaplains for his retinue, "there being a lack of of clerks by reasons of the pestilence."[65] For the diocese at large, Charlton committed himself to the same practical course Trillek had chosen in the priest-scarce times of the 1350s. On his arrival in Hereford in 1362, Charlton began ordinations in earnest. His first celebration of the sacrament in March of that year was a promising harvest; 149 clerics were ordained to all ranks, half of them from Hereford and destined for parishes in the diocese. Charlton did not wait for the next Ember Saturday in spring as he might, but held ordinations on the two vigils of Passion Sunday and Easter. These were atypically large ordinations — 131 clerics in total. All three may have been influenced by the fact that no ordinations had been held in the diocese during the lengthy vacancy.[66] And yet not a single year passed in Charlton's pontificate when he did not hold at least three ordinations annually. Indeed, in 1366 he celebrated the sacrament on five separate occasions, and six times each year between 1367 and 1369.[67] Like Trillek before him, Charlton chose larger churches and more readily accessible sites; he favored Bromyard, the cathedral, Whitbourne, Bosbury, and Ledbury. But for all his efforts, the numbers ordained could compare even with the smaller groups Trillek ordained in the troubled 1350s. In fact, if anything, clerical recruitment during Charlton's pontificate showed the same diminishing trend that had marked the last years of John Trillek's reign.

A final note of comparison between the two bishops leading a diocese in the afteryears of a devastating plague can be found in the areas of clerical crimes and the appointments of diocesan confessors. During Charlton's pontificate, violence erupted in the sanctuary of the Benedictine priory in Hereford, St. Guthlac's. In the late summer of 1366 the bishop, who was at Whitbourne at the time, commissioned the bishop of Llandaff to reconcile the church where blood had been shed.[68] In April, 1367 another commissary acted on the bishop's behalf in cases involving clerical misconduct. The dean of Leominster was ordered to receive and commit to the bishop's prison clerics convicted of felonies in the king's courts and there to await the bishop's inquests and sanctions should they be required.[69]

Like Trillek before him, Charlton used confessors and penitentiaries in the diocese but not as liberally as his predecessor. His appointments came long after the plague of 1361 and suggested that need was not so urgent as Trillek had judged it in the early 1350s. In March, 1367 Charlton gave the vicar of Ledbury a year's license to hear confessions and grant absolution to parishioners, including cases usually reserved to the bishop. In the winter of 1368 Charlton made a similar appointment, charging the vicar of Pool to hear the confessions of Welsh parishioners in the diocese.[70] In August of that year he named John de Shrivenham, a local Dominican friar, a diocesan penitentiary and gave John Milton, another Dominican, a similar appointment the following year.[71] But in the late 1360s Charlton encountered similar kinds of problems regarding the licensing of confessors as his predecessor had in the 1350s. At the beginning of Lent in 1369, the bishop informed his archdeacons that, owing to grave irregularities recently brought to light in the hearing of confessions, he was licensing only certain confessors for work in the diocese until Pentecost. He did not wish to jeopardize souls in need of absolution with untrained and ill-suited confessors especially during this important penitential season. There were men moving through the diocese passing themselves off as penitentiaries who had received no official license from the bishop for this ministry. There were even reports of *ignoti*, strangers who may not have even been in priest's orders, attempting to hear the confessions of Hereford parishioners.[72]

Religious and Economic Discord Following the Black Death

With all that was required of both bishops in the years of upheaval and change following both epidemics, each had to watch out for and resolve irregularities that emerged in the discord that events of such magnitude often create. One of the more sustained difficulties of the post-plague church was the confusion that sometimes prevailed, at least for awhile, in social and legal structures such as customary authority, obligation, and patronage. The epidemics were wholly disruptive for some local communities and the crisis of widespread sickness and mortality and its attendant calamities provoked immediate responses that did not always conform to custom and convention. The tensions that existed in the post-plague economy between landowners and laborers is one dramatic example of this. But there were other areas of daily life where old tensions broke into fresh antagonism and the struggles for change.

One such conflict broke out in Hereford in the aftermath of the plague of 1361 and turned on a legal dispute between the cathedral chapter and a local parish vicar over burial rights and funerary dues. A summary of the case is enough to demonstrate the additional strains of repeated epidemic plague on the local structures of pastoral care. On July 30, 1362, Roger Syde, vicar of St. Peter's, was formally charged by the Dean and Chapter with holding funeral services in his church to the prejudice of the rights of the cathedral chapter.[73] The charges were based on an ancient custom jealously guarded by the cathedral chapter that maintained that all parishioners who died within the bounds of the old minster — which amounted to most of the cathedral deanery — were to be brought to the cathedral, given their final obsequies, and buried in the close. In the past, some parishioners had attempted to obviate the old custom, usually claiming that traveling with corpses to the cathedral was an unnecessary burden and a costly one as well, but the cathedral, usually backed by the bishop, repeatedly affirmed its ancient rights. Bishops Swinfield and Orleton had supported the chapter against parishioners who violated this custom in the early fourteenth century, and John Trillek threatened violators with excommunication and even, on one occasion, ordered the exhumation and reburial of the bodies of certain parishioners improperly interred at Allensmore.[74]

What gave the case of Roger Syde and the burials at St. Peter's a more urgent and troubling sense was the fact that the improper burials had taken place during the recent outbreak of plague in the city. Their impropriety lay in the fact that Roger held the funerals at St. Peter's and buried his parishioners in the close directly, failing to bring the bodies to the cathedral for final blessings. What the cathedral incurred with every such burial was not only an indignity regarding its time-honored dues, but also the loss of revenues in voluntary oblations and the purchase of candles set around the bier. It might have been a small matter in the case of one or two improper burials, but the number of recent plague victims buried from St. Peter's in this manner elevated the chapter's concern to the level of a financial crisis. In fact, from the depositions of St. Peter's parishioners given before the court, the practice was going on at the parish long before Roger Syde and the plague of 1361 had come there. Celia Wenlock, in her eighties and called *illiterata* in the court record, remembered back to the *prima pestilentia* when twenty parishioners had been buried from St. Peter's in a single day and 120 from that parish during the course of the plague. Fellow parishioners Benedict Smith and Thomas le Forbes supported Celia's testimony and updated the record by stating that forty members of St. Peter's had been buried from the church during the recent plague of 1361.[75]

It is a point of frustration in these records that the plaintiff's case is far clearer than the defendant's. It is uncertain, at least on the surface of the documents, how Roger defended himself against the charges. According to parishioners' depositions, members of St. Peter's had been buried directly in the cathedral cemetery before Roger's time and this, judging from the silence of the records, had gone uncontested. It seems likely that the chapter had been too preoccupied with its own affairs following two plagues to pursue the matter immediately. Another point in Roger's favor was the impression that, though unconventional, what he was doing was pastorally expedient, not only regarding the swiftness of the burials required during the course of an epidemic but as an easing of the burdens of the survivors. In fact, one has to wonder how the cathedral chapter could have hoped to carry out all the burials it claimed by custom. St. Peter's was but one parish in the city and others no doubt were expected to bring their dead to the cathedral.

In any case, Roger could not hope to have his case heard impartially in the cathedral's own court, so he appealed to the Archbishop of Canterbury. Accordingly, London prohibited the case from being heard in Hereford, but the cathedral chapter, angry at its losses and Roger's appeal, proceeded nonetheless to fine the parish vicar the startling sum of 22 pounds in lost revenues. By this time Roger's case had been buoyed with support from his own parishioners and fellow clerics in the city of Hereford. One local priest, William Marchaunt, even stood in as Roger's proctor before the courts. Both Roger and William refused to appear before the cathedral chapter in spite of repeated summons to pay the fine. Meanwhile, the Court of Arches sent commissaries in the late summer of 1363 to Hereford to receive the depositions of local witnesses. It was on this occasion that Celia Wenlock and her fellow parishioners gave their sworn testimonies. The case was then moved to London where it languished in delays. Frustrated by the lack of progress, Roger, perhaps in an act of desperation, appealed to the king for justice, winning another prohibition against continued ecclesiastical procedure in the case until royal authorities had determined the Crown's interests in the matter. Roger gained little from the prohibition which was subsequently withdrawn. Just as the Court of Arches was to rule against Roger and order him to pay the fine demanded by the cathedral — by this time the dispute had gone on for nearly four years — the vicar appealed to the papal court for justice. Before the archbishop's court could enforce its judgment, trial of the case was prohibited yet again until the appeal to the pope had been heard. Back in Hereford the chapter was not impressed and proceeded to press its claim against Roger. The vicar was duly summoned to appear for his sentencing in March, 1366 and when he refused, the chapter formally confiscated his benefice, no doubt with the dual intention of ridding a bothersome priest from the deanery and taking from the parish's revenues the sum of the cathedral's losses. The act was hard to defend and when challenged the chapter introduced yet another factor in the case related to the recent plague. The cathedral claimed that Roger had been improperly instituted to St. Peter's in the first place, that he had been given the church hastily and without due process after the plague had taken the former vicar and left the parish without a curate.[76]

By this time Roger was unwilling to give up his claims against the cathedral and both parties had to set out sometime before 1367 for Avignon. The dispute, which had already lasted for more than five years, was to suffer further delays in the changing world of papal politics and the transferral of the pope's court from Avignon to Viterbo to Rome. In 1370 the case had moved through the lists and was ready to be heard, but it was hampered by yet another delay, this one stemming from the death of Urban V. It would not be considered until 1376. For some part of that frustrating period — the records are not clear as to why — Roger spent nearly half a year in the cell of an Italian prison. His fortunes changed, however, in the late summer of 1376 when the papal auditor Nicholas of Cremona judged the case and ruled finally in Roger's favor. The parish priest was vindicated in his rights to bury parishioners from his own church and to accept on his own any offering which might accrue from such ministry. The Dean and Chapter of Hereford, having followed this case as vigilantly as Roger, not only lost their original claims agains the vicar but were ordered to pay an additional 500 florins in court costs. They appealed Nicholas's sentence each year from 1378 to 1380, though without overturning the judgment. Urban VI himself confirmed Roger's victory in the case and issued a letter protecting the priest's rights dated April 9, 1379. At the pope's request, the young English king, Richard II, added his own confirmation and support to the pope's rescript.

Despite the impressive support he had won in Rome and in Westminster, Roger's home was in Hereford and some mutually agreeable arrangement had to be worked out with the Dean and Chapter. A commission representing both parties' interests, comprised of four canons from the cathedral and four parishioners from St. Peter's, reached a compromise. In the future parishioners could choose to be buried as their ancestors were from the cathedral or from St. Peter's. In the latter cases, no claims would be made by the chapter against offerings given to St. Peter's. But the chapter had one requirement: when the bodies of parishioners were brought to the cathedral close for burial, wherever their funerals had been, the mourners would make a nominal offering of candles to the chapter.

Thus, eighteen years, three popes, and at least 500 florins later, the chapter had but candle ends to claim as the result of this prolonged and costly dispute. What is interesting about this case is not only its outcome but the fact that considerable resources, personal and financial, had to be available to the litigants over the long haul. Loans had to be arranged along the way to employ proctors, staffs of clerks and secretaries, and to finance transportation of personnel and materials. Clearly the case challenged the finances of the cathedral chapter, especially following on the economically damaging events of two plagues. But not long into the case the canons must have determined that they would pursue the matter as long as money and nerve would last, for it was now more than the loss of a few pounds worth of funeral tapers and oblations; other parishes in the deanery under the same convention of burying their parishioners from the cathedral were watching the case closely and lending support to the vicar of St. Peter's. After other priests in the cathedral city stood up in defense of Roger, the personal support which he was glad to receive had to continue in the form of material aid; otherwise he could not have pursued the case for as long as he did from Hereford to Rome. He must have been a man of extraordinary stamina brought on by a determination to see justice done or, less flatteringly, out of desperation to retain his livelihood in Hereford. But by the time he had returned to his small vicarage near the cathedral, this parish priest from remote Hereford had been witness to some of the most remarkable events and personalities of his age. He had survived two epidemics, had traveled across France during a renewed outbreak of war between that country and England, he had arrived in Avignon in Gregory XI's last plodding days before the papacy's return to Rome, and, once there, had encountered the Great Schism of 1378 firsthand and come under the protection of the volatile Urban VI.

In all it may seem a minor drama set on a vast stage. But it was not so to Roger Syde and the people of St. Peter's parish, nor was it to the cathedral chapter who, after all of this, merit some sympathy for merely wishing to do what other leaders had done during the plagues of 1349 and 1361, and that is to restore their own world to order. But taken from another perspective, the dispute was symptomatic of more critical issues facing the post-plague church. In the old days parishioners in the cathedral deanery obeyed the customs of their city and with rare exception duly buried their dead from the cathedral. But in the 1350s and 1360s when plague and hardship had severely augmented their burdens as citizens and parishioners, the people grew all the more weary and far less patient with customs that now seemed excessive and outmoded. The plague of 1361 may have been even more ruinous on some levels than the first plague. Parishioners had survived the great scourge of 1349 and had begun the long and difficult process of recovery in their own families, communities, and parishes. The second great outbreak of the disease was a blow delivered against an already weary populace and made more tragic by the fact that the very old and the very young were the unresisting victims of this plague. For the parishioners of St. Peter's to deliver to the cathedral clergy for burial the bodies of families, friends, and neighbors was a moment of strangeness in an otherwise highly personal ritual and something more than they or their vicar were willing any longer to accept.

In the end we do not know Lewis Charlton's opinion on the case, whether he supported the cathedral chapter in this matter as his pre-decessors had done or saw merit in the actions of the parish priest. The bishop died long before the dispute was ended, but surely he and every other churchman in the diocese discussed the issues surrounding the case and wondered together at the changes taking place. But the bishop had other matters to attend to and was probably relieved that the quarrel between Roger de Syde and the cathedral was not one of them.

Lewis Charlton died in 1369, twenty years after the plague first came to Hereford, and in the course of those two tumultuous decades had followed his predecessor in the patient and beleaguering effort of rebuilding the diocese. Hereford parishes had endured two epidemics in twenty years, numerous parishioners and their clergy had died, every family had been affected in some way by the epidemics, and every survivor had become sadly familiar with the rites of Christian burial. The diocese would continue to experience incidents of plague through the rest of the century and into the next, though none would be as great in its ruin as was the first pestilence. Meanwhile, Hereford shepherds would apply their skills in varying degrees of zeal and effect in shoring up the parishes of their diocese, but the critical challenge that every bishop after John Trillek faced in this century was the provision of adequate men, in number and in quality, to the pastoral cures of Hereford parishes.

4. Clerical Recruitment and Pastoral Provision

Like his predecessor, William Courtenay succeeded as bishop of Hereford after a vacancy which lasted about the length of yet another outbreak of plague in the diocese. Lewis Charlton had died on May 23, 1369 and the cause of his death is not given in any of the records of the event. He may have died from the very pestilence that troubled his diocese in the spring and summer of that year.[1] On August 17, 1369 Pope Urban V provided the 28-year-old Courtenay, having already granted the young priest the needed dispensation from minority. It would be nearly another year before the new bishop set foot in his diocese, thereby prolonging the time during which Hereford was without a resident bishop.[2] It was during this same period that Hereford was afflicted with another outbreak of plague. Its effects on the diocese are not immediately observeable, not only because the new bishop was somewhat leisurely in his pace toward Hereford, but because Courtenay's slim register tells little of the diocese during the early 1370s or what sort of work he did as its bishop. Perhaps it was partially owing to the fact that he longed for his home in Exeter; for the better part of his first two years as the bishop of Hereford, Courtenay stayed in Devon, having placed the leadership of his own diocese in the hands of vicars general.[3] It was ironic that the first ordinations celebrated by the bishop were in Exeter, mostly for Exeter men as a favor to the local ordinary, Courtenay's friend and mentor Thomas Brantingham.[4] Not surprisingly, Courtenay did not remain long bishop of Hereford. Indeed, he probably found his five years as bishop there an overly lengthy apprenticeship for a keenly intelligent and ambitious young ecclesiastic. He had few close friends among the cathedral chapter and doubtlessly missed the company he had grown fond of in Devon, Oxford, and London. After that warm welcome by the cathedral canons in August, 1370, the new bishop's preferences for being elsewhere were ominously evident.

It is perhaps too easy to criticize the novice bishop for not paying sufficient attention to poor Hereford. It required much those days. By the

1370s the long and accumulative effects of plague and the host of economic, social, and spiritual anxieties that came with it had tried the diocese severely. But none of this was unique to Hereford; some of the changes in the church, initiated or accelerated by the recent epidemics, were beginning to settle into the ecclesiastical and religious landscape everywhere. The most significant change perhaps, and one that would have extended repercussions in pastoral provision and the religious life of the people, was in the area of clerical recruitment.

Certainly, bishops were limited in what they could do to influence the size of the clerical population. Still, they possessed certain crucial measures of control such as the number of annual celebrations of the sacrament they were willing to hold, and modifying, to the extent that they could, the kinds of men they were willing to admit to the clerical ranks. Dispensations could be had for nearly every impediment, but it was up to the bishop to pursue this strategy. But even bishops zealous in this ministry, like Trillek and Lewis Charlton, could not stem the tide of certain larger trends affecting the diocese and the English Church in the decades following the plague. The pastoral leadership of Hereford had to adjust to certain new changes. For example, there were simply fewer men around to ordain and many of those that were were less inclined now to pursue a life of ministry in the church. Parish churches which had once been poor livings in decent times were not likely to improve in the years following the Black Death. It had been difficult enough for bishops to keep wage-earning priests in their parishes and it would prove equally, if not more challenging, to recruit fresh blood especially to the poorer churches. The post-plague economy was a changeful one but not always in the direction of poverty. Depopulation led to labor shortages, which led to new opportunities, and young men who might once have pursued a life of ministry in the church were increasingly drawn to the prospects of new fortunes in other vineyards. Finally, the latter half of the fourteenth century was not a golden age for the institutional church. Though religion continued to prove vital in the lives of most people, there was a disinclination to the traditional aspects of the Church's mission evidenced in the diminishing interest in priestly and religious life, and also in the rise of anti-clericalism. The effects of these changes included the simple fact that the clerical population had been severely reduced by the Black Death and subsequent plagues and would not recover to the levels it had once enjoyed in the early 1300s until, perhaps, the late fifteenth and early sixteenth centuries.[5] We have already seen how the plague had an immediate effect on clerical recruitment and placement in the diocese of

Hereford. We have also seen that the bishops of Hereford attempted to shore up those dramatic changes in the ways traditionally available, as through ordination and institutions to vacant benefices. In this chapter we will be concerned more with the longer-term changes in the diocese and how clerical recruitment and provision to the parishes of Hereford were persistent challenges for the pastoral leadership of the see.

Clerical recruitment in the fourteenth-century church was a complicated process, not complicated in the liturgical and canonical sense of requirements and rituals from one level of order to another, but in the host of factors, within and outside of medieval society, that influenced the changing profile of the clerical population. These factors included the particular incentive of a man to pursue a life or a career in the church; we know better the ambitious than we do the pastorally zealous, but there were places for both and the many who stood in between. Another factor was patronage. Every candidate for major orders needed some form of support that might come as a solemn statement of worth (meaning employability) or as a benefice in hand. As we shall see, the forms of patronage associated with ordination were to undergo important changes in the decades following the Black Death. A third factor was the canonical examination required of every clerical candidate and it stood either as a shut door or an open gate, with the bishop or his examiners as the guards. It was their responsibility to select and dismiss candidates according to traditional forms and basic canonical requirements. But they could interpret these standards rather widely and thereby influence the number of clerics for the diocese. A final factor for clerical recruitment — one to which we have already alluded — was the frequency of ordination ceremonies performed by the bishop.[6] Whatever factors influenced the size of the clerical pool, men could only be promoted to Orders when the bishop decided to exercise this important ministry.

How these factors and others were at work in clerical recruitment in the late medieval church can be pieced together through a careful analysis of the extensive ordination lists contained in the English bishops' registers. The names of candidates are there, divided by rank of order sought — typically acolyte through priesthood — and their status within the ecclesiastical community, whether for instance they were seculars destined for service to the diocese, or regulars from the many religious houses of Hereford. Compilers of these lists also made sure to distinguish which candidates were for the secular clergy of Hereford and which had traveled from other dioceses. These lists also note the title or statement of patronage that every candidate brought to the ordination, religious clerics being ordained to the title of the poverty of their own house. The lists also record the place and time of the ordination and who was the presiding celebrant. Putting all of this together, we can obtain a fairly accurate reading of diocesan clerical recruitment, but also of frequency and places where the sacrament was celebrated and some ideas of how candidates were supported to ordination and placed in Hereford parishes afterwards.

Patterns of Clerical Recruitment in Fourteenth-Century Hereford

It is not enough merely to count the numbers of clerics ordained at a given ceremony and conclude that all these ordinands had some direct affect on diocesan clerical recruitment or pastoral care. In the analyses of the ordination lists that follow, I have arranged figures and interpretations according to the clerical categories set out in the lists themselves. First of all, the particular rank of the cleric would have had some bearing on his pastoral effectiveness in the diocese. Numbers of acolytes indicated important trends for recruitment but they would not have exerted the same pastoral influence as deacons or priests. Second, regular clerics would have had some distant effect perhaps on the running of Hereford parishes or, more accurately, the management of their finances through the increasingly popular measure of monastic appropriations. The friars would have been excepted from even this. In any case, their numbers do not influence much the pastoral leadership of the diocese. Lastly, the important distinction between secular clerics ordained for the diocese of Hereford and those who had traveled to the diocese for ordination is upheld here in the statistical analyses. Though some of the latter no doubt sought employment in the diocese upon their ordination, it was not a matter of course that every *ignotus*, even with the proper official credentials, was an immigrant to the diocese.[7]

With as much information as these lists generate, there are a number of ways of viewing the data.[8] Figures drawn from ordinations over the better part of the fourteenth century will tell in a blunt way the story of recruitment in the diocese following the critical years of the plague. The period begins in 1328 with the first ordinations of Bishop Thomas Charlton and ends in 1404, the year Bishop Trefnant died.[9] But in order to understand the figures better and to consider the various factors that influenced recruitment, the larger period of the century has been subdivided into three lesser

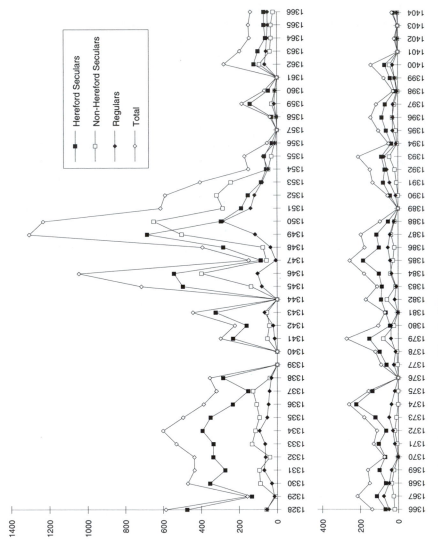

Figure 4.1. Clerical recruitment in Hereford Diocese, 1328–1404.

periods, each having some important reference to the Black Death. Period I (1328–1344) covers Thomas Charlton's pontificate and offers a somewhat typical view of recruitment in the decades before the Black Death. Period II (1345–69) spans the period of the Black Death during John Trillek's pontificate, and the second plague of 1361 up to the end of Lewis Charlton's reign. The last period (1370–1404) takes up the remainder of the century and reveals the long-term effects of the plague on the clerical population and pastoral provision in Hereford diocese. These years cover the pontificates of William Courtenay, John Gilbert, and John Trefnant.

The numbers in Figure 4.1 reflect the annual totals of ordinations in the three main groups of clerical candidates: seculars from Hereford, those from other dioceses, and members of religious houses. Annual totals are also represented in order to give a larger impression of recruitment trends in general. It is important to note that these figures are inclusive of all ranks of orders from acolyte to priest and since they are totals by year and not by ordination, oftentimes the same men will be represented more than once in a given year as they passed from one order to another. Thus, the real purpose of this chart is to show volume in ordination activity each year from 1328 to 1404 and to illustrate general trends in clerical recruitment during that time.

In Period I, the correspondence between the number of Hereford secular ordinands and the larger total of men ordained by Thomas Charlton is a fairly close one; indeed, most of the men ordained during those years were secular clerics from the Hereford diocese. Other normal patterns are illustrated as well: candidates from other dioceses and members of religious houses appear with customary irregularity. There were too many factors that dictated why a cleric would come to Hereford for ordination: perhaps there was a vacancy in his home diocese, or the bishop was away during one of the seasonal celebrations of the sacrament. He might have been in Hereford as a student at the cathedral school or as a servant to a local lord, ecclesiastical or lay. None of these factors influence this field of ordinands in any predictable way. Equally less predictable are the numbers of canons, monks, and friars who were ordained for their houses based on modest local needs for confessors and mass-sayers.

During the first few years of Period II these trends among the three groups remained generally the same. Non-Hereford seculars comprised about a fifth of the clergy ordained in 1345, while regular ordinands numbered less than one-tenth of the total. For reasons which are not entirely clear, this pattern changed dramatically in 1346 when non-Hereford seculars formed 40 percent of the total though regular ordinands remained about the same from the previous year. Numbers for all three groups fell rapidly in 1347, but this was not for want of ordination ceremonies in the diocese, as Trillek celebrated the sacrament on four separate occasions that year. The bishop may have chosen not to augment the number of celebrations given the low numbers that were appearing before him. He held his last ordination for 1347 as early as March 30 and was not to hold another until mid-April, 1348.[10] The change may have resulted from the temporary depletion of the general pool of candidates following the exceptionally high numbers for the previous year. In 1348 something of the usual pattern from the 1330s was regained, with Hereford seculars comprising a full 74 percent of the annual total; non-Hereford seculars numbered about one-fifth of the total with regulars at one-tenth. But the usual pattern was short-lived. With the quick changes in population effected by the Black Death, there were phenomenal rises in all three categories to meet the vacancies which had occurred on a large scale in churches and religious houses. But it is interesting to note when these changes occur in the ordination lists. In 1349, when the plague was at its height in Hereford, Trillek ordained over 1200 men to orders for his diocese, neighboring churches, and religious houses. Although Hereford seculars were largely responsible for these extraordinarily high numbers, they comprised only a little more than half (55 percent) of all ordained that year. Seculars from outside the diocese comprised 35 percent of the total. Regular clerics, though increasing considerably from the previous year, had not yet shown in numbers the devastating effects of the plague on religious communities. This was to come during the following year when the patterns of calmer times disappeared in those unsettled months. In 1350, for the first time in the century, the bishop of Hereford ordained more men from outside his own diocese than within. Fifty-three percent of all the men ordained that year in Hereford were from outside the diocese, most of them coming from Worcester during the vacancy that occured after Bishop Wulstan's death in early August, 1349.[11] Candidates from religious houses doubled and tripled in every rank of order from 1349 to 1350; in fact, their increase during 1350 is proportionately the most dramatic of the three groups considered.

Totals for all three groups fell in 1351 with the larger numbers of ordinands coming from outside the diocese (319), in contrast with those from Hereford (155). Regular clerics fell from their 1349 totals in about the same proportion as they had risen in 1350, but the general trend for the next several years was one of overall decline. More men came from outside the diocese for ordination in 1352, but their number continued to fall afterward and at a steeper rate than either Hereford seculars or regular clerics. The latter two declined in number from 1351 to 1354 but, unlike clerics from outside the diocese who continued to dwindle, rose again briefly in 1355, keeping surprisingly close to one another in volume. No ordinations are recorded in the Trillek register for 1357 but totals for the following year after ordinations were resumed in the diocese were much what they had been in 1356. The large numbers of only ten years previous were a distant memory: the total number of secular clerics ordained for the diocese in 1358 was only 30 and this, perhaps, after a full year when no ordinations were held in Hereford. There were only four clerics from other dioceses, and three monks from Wormsely and Abbey Dore ordained that year. In 1359 the number of Hereford seculars rose again sharply with 142 ordained to all ranks; but the increase was short-lived, as the numbers of recruits fell once more in 1360, the year Bishop Trillek died.

The absence of ordination records for the vacancy which extended from Trillek's death in December 1360 through most of the following year frustrates this analysis at a critical juncture, for it was during this time that Hereford and most of England suffered from the second outbreak of plague in a little over a decade. In any case, Lewis Charlton's first ordinations represented something of a recovery from his predecessor's last years, though this was probably a matter of ordaining men who had not only survived the 1361 plague but had also waited through the vacancy. Though the annual numbers of ordinands were far lower than they had been in the years before the Black Death, the diocese experienced a period of relative calm in recruitment during the 1360s. Increases which occur in the overall totals for Charlton's pontificate, most notably in 1367, are influenced by the ordinations of Hereford clergy rather than by ordinands from outside the diocese. On average there were 88 Hereford clerics per annum during Charlton's pontificate, as against an annual average of 37 seculars from other dioceses for the same period. At the same time the annual averages for regular ordinands during the 1360s were significantly higher at 55 than they had been during the Trillek years (24 per annum). In fact, after 1362 the trend of higher numbers of extra-diocesan ordinands and fewer regulars — typical of the pre-1349 figures — is reversed.

The trend towards fewer numbers in all three groups, but with no-where near the wild fluctuations that had occurred through the 1350s, continued through Period III, from 1370 to 1404. Typical of this time were higher numbers of candidates from Hereford against fewer candidates from outside the diocese or from religious houses. This more traditional pattern had re-emerged in the 1360s under Lewis Charlton and was sustained with minor variations through the remainder of the century. When fluctuation occurred to any appreciable extent, it was among candidates from other dioceses and religious communities, but this was also typical for more normal times (see figures for Period I). Fewer clerics were traveling to Hereford with letters dimissory to be ordained by bishops Courtenay, Gilbert, and Trefnant. Monks, canons, and friars appeared in relatively higher numbers during the mid-1380s and early 1390s, followed their counterparts among the Hereford secular clergy rather closely from 1392 to 1394, but dropped off considerably during the final years of the century.

These figures for clerical recruitment for the better part of a century are impressive in their own right and, in spite of their non-specific features, warrant a few conclusions. The second quarter of the fourteenth century began with large numbers of annual recruits to Holy Orders in Hereford diocese. There were marked declines between 1335 and 1337 but a general righting of the usually high figures returned in 1343 and 1345. There was also a sizeable disparity during this period between the number of Hereford ordinands and candidates from other dioceses and religious houses. Clearly, Hereford men intent on pastoral service in the diocese dominated the ordination groups. But during the period of the Black Death normal patterns in recruitment were replaced with wild fluctuations. It is also true that most of the candidates John Trillek promoted to orders between 1350 and 1354 were not from his own diocese and cannot be considered as having had any direct or appreciable affect on clerical recruitment or pastoral provision for the Hereford diocese. During the same period, religious houses, whose need for priests was neither very great nor subject to much change in normal times, sent more men than they had ever done before to the bishop for ordination. While non-Hereford seculars and religious clerics rose in number at annual ordinations immediately after the Black Death, numbers of Hereford candidates fell sharply after 1349 and continued to do so until there were slight recoveries in numbers in 1355 and 1359. For the remainder of the century the annual totals of each group would continue to decline in number and would never regain the high annual averages witnessed in the years before the Black Death. Though overall numbers would be smaller, the three groups of ordinands would at least achieve similar proportions in relationship to one another in the last quarter of the century, reminiscent of the pre-plague years.

Having observed the changing features of all three groups, it is important now to consider what impact these trends had on pastoral provision in the Hereford diocese and to do so we must look more closely at those figures for Hereford ordinands. Since the emphasis here is on entrance into the clerical life — indicative of general recruitment trends — and eventual service in Hereford parishes, the figures are limited to the orders of aco-lyte — the first order recorded in the ordination lists — and priesthood.

Clerical recruitment during Thomas Charlton's pontificate (Figure 4.2) was characterized by large acolyte groups at almost every ordination. There were occasionally sharp fluctuations in the numbers of ordinands occurring between 1328 and 1329, then again from 1330 to 1331. But this was a reasonable change in the pattern of recruitment as it reflected the temporary depletion of the pool of candidates eligible by age to receive the order of acolyte.

A year when a crowd of youths appeared for ordination as acolytes was likely to be followed by a year of fewer ordinands, until younger aspirants reached the canonical age of fourteen. Another reason for the high number of acolytes may be a break in the seasonal celebrations of Holy Orders. From 1338 to 1339, when Thomas Charlton was in service to the king as Chancellor of Ireland, no ordinations were recorded as having taken place in Hereford. Although a suffragan may have been appointed by the bishop or one of his vicars to ordain in Charlton's place, there are no references to any such commission in Charlton's register. Neither are there records for any more letters dimissory than usual.[12] In spite of these fluctuations, the number of acoyltes remained high through the 1330s and early 1340s. In his seventeen years as bishop of Hereford, Charlton ordained a little under 1500 candidates to the order of acolyte for his diocese alone. Annually, the average number of acolytes was 106 and even with the normal rates of attrition one might expect to occur between acoylte and priesthood, this large group served as a dependable pool for future Hereford priests for the remainder of this period.

This strength was born out in the similarly high numbers of men ordained to the priesthood in the diocese each year. During his first year as bishop, Thomas Charlton ordained 59 priests for Hereford. The annual total dropped the following year much as it had in the acolyte group, but by 1330 the numbers were up to 42 again and continued to climb for the next three years. Between 1334 and 1343 some fluctuations occur, but none that are exceptional. Again, the bishop was not available for ordinations in 1338 and 1339, but these factors notwithstanding, Bishop Charlton ordained 736 men to the priesthood for his diocese during the seventeen years that he was

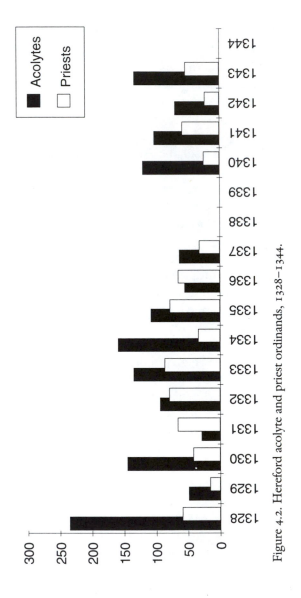

Figure 4.2. Hereford acolyte and priest ordinands, 1328–1344.

bishop of Hereford with an annual average of 52, a confident figure for the needs of the diocese.

During the pontificates of John Trillek and Lewis Charlton, the first two and greatest periods of epidemic plague effected considerable and widespread change in levels of recruitment for Hereford clergy. The striking aspects of this change are evident in the differences between Figure 4.2 and Figure 4.3. During the years when John Trillek was bishop, exceptionally high annual totals for both acolyte and priest groups were matched with new lows for the century from 1350 to 1356. With respect to ordinations, Trillek's pontificate had begun in much the same way as his predecessor's: there were 222 acolytes ordained for the diocese in 1345, creating a sizeable pool for future priests. The numbers were still considerably high the following year when 150 youths were presented to the bishop for the same order. Thus, for the first five years of Trillek's pontificate there was an annual average of 144 acolytes ordained for Hereford, a comfortable margin above the 110 ordained per year in the first quinquennium of Thomas Charlton's reign. But the numbers were drastically reduced in the years following the Black Death. Between 1349 and 1354 the annual average was less than half of what it had been in the earlier years of Trillek's pontificate. No ordinations were held in 1357, a possible result of the new lows to which recruitment had fallen in 1356: nine acolytes and two priests for the entire diocese. There was something of a recovery in 1359 but it hardly encouraged upward trends in recruitment, as figures fell once again in 1360. Ordinations were not held again in the diocese until 1362, after the year-long vacancy following Trillek's death, but the first showed signs a little more encouraging, with 44 new acolytes. The diocese had had this many acolytes in a year only once before in the previous ten-year period and that was in 1359 with 49 acolytes.

Not surprisingly, the patterns in priest-ordinations followed similar trends as established in acolyte groups. Record numbers marked the first years of Trillek's pontificate: 156 deacons were ordained to the priesthood for Hereford in 1346. This number would be surpassed only once in the century and that would be in 1349, before the plague had made its way through the West Midlands. After the Black Death, the annual number of men ordained to the priesthood was cut in half, and then halved again. There were only 86 priests ordained for the diocese in 1350, and 43 during the following year. After remaining somewhat steady at 40 and 32 for 1353 and 1354 respectively, the numbers once again fell at a rapid rate. In the five-year period between 1354 and 1358 Trillek ordained 37 men to the priest-

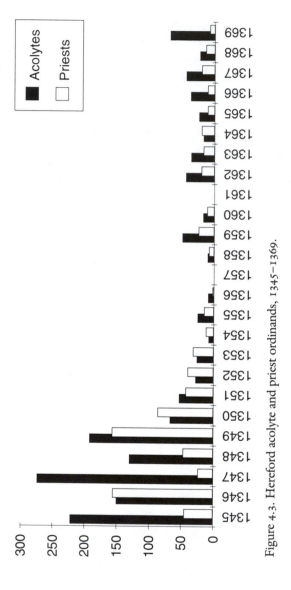

Figure 4.3. Hereford acolyte and priest ordinands, 1345–1369.

hood, a dim reflection of those record ordinations reached in the earlier years of his pontificate. Again, there was an increased stability in annual totals for priest-ordinations under Lewis Charlton, but the slight recovery in 1364 and 1367 with 20 priests for each year did little to offset the meager years of 1365, 1366, and 1369.

If the ordinations carried out by Lewis Charlton in the 1360s marked a period of renewed stability in diocesan recruitment, this trend was continued and improved upon during the administration of the see by William Courtenay. In his short pontificate, annual averages for all orders in the diocese for secular clerics had risen to 131 per year. Larger acolyte groups had made this overall increase possible. But attrition must have been significant as priests continued to be ordained in small numbers, with the noteworthy exception of the ordinations of 1374, when 64 men were priested in the diocese in comparison with the meager 17 from the year before (Figure 4.4). But it was the largest annual total of Hereford priests ordained since 1350, the likely benefit of larger numbers of acolytes in the late 1360s and early 1370s. Subsequent and comparatively large groups of acolytes were ordained in 1381 (52), 1385 (55), and again in 1387 (58). But the numbers were still not as high as they had been in the first half of the decade. There had been an annual average of 41 acolytes in Courtenay's pontificate (1370–75), compared to 31 for the first six years of Gilbert's administration (1376–80). This average was improved upon in the latter six years of Gilbert's reign (37 per year) but the trend in recruitment at this level was less than it had been in a long time and would continue on this course for the remainder of the century. The long and gradual decline in the recruitment of secular clergy in the Hereford diocese continued through the Trefnant years to the beginning of the fifteenth century. By that time, incoming acolytes and prospective curates had fallen in number from previous years, with an average of 15 acolytes and 10 priests each year. These average figures dropped significantly not only because of the proportionate decrease in numbers of candidates but also because of the extraordinary slump in ordination activity during the last four years of Bishop Trefnant's pontificate. There were no ordinations recorded for the year 1401 and of the eight ordinations held by Trefnant or the bishop of Dunkeld, who acted in his stead during 1403 and 1404, only the three which took place in 1400 were of any appreciable size.[13] In the three years which followed, before the first ordination was held during Bishop Mascall's reign late in 1404, only 14 clerics were listed among Hereford ordinands: one acolyte, three subdeacons, nine deacons, and a single priest. It was only with the December, 1404

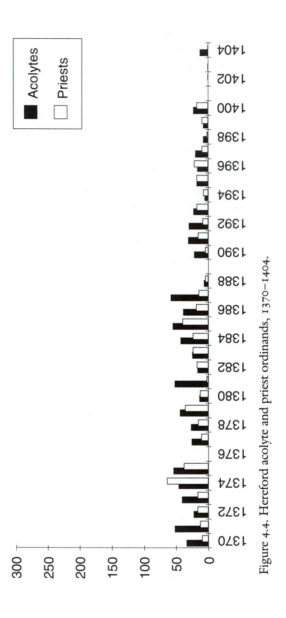

Figure 4.4. Hereford acolyte and priest ordinands, 1370–1404.

ordination at Hereford Cathedral that a larger number of Hereford ordinands appeared before the bishop. But even here there were only 24 clerics received for the diocese, including thirteen acolytes and one priest.[14]

Factors Behind the Changes

As impressive as the above statistics are in illustrating the long downward trend in the Hereford clerical population after the Black Death, other questions need to be asked of the figures. For instance, was the plague alone or directly responsible for the large demographic shifts that occurred in the second half of the fourteenth century? If not, what other forces impinged upon clerical recruitment? The effects of plague have already been suggested, though a few more words need to be said about population changes and the size of candidate pools after the epidemic. But other factors such as the economy, the various incentives that would bring young men to consider the priesthood and the pastoral life, and the role of the bishop as the celebrant of the sacrament and the final arbiter of the worthiness of candidates have all to be explored before we have a clearer understanding of clerical recruitment after the Black Death.

The numbers of men available to meet the pastoral and institutional needs of churches and communities varied according to the larger factors of settlement, marriage, and childbirth. Through the thirteenth and early fourteenth centuries in England, as elsewhere in Europe, there was a steady growth in the general population. Precisely when this period of growth began or how severely it was checked before the Black Death remains a matter of some debate among demographers.[15] But barring the temporary negative effects brought on by the famine of 1315–16, the years from 1322 to 1348 can be seen as a time when the population was still on the rise.[16] These years, it may be noted, coincide with Period I in the statistical commentary above, namely the pontificate of Thomas Charlton (1327 to 1344) and the first years of John Trillek's reign, when the annual averages for Hereford ordinands were the highest for the century. The correspondence between changes in the general and clerical populations continues, of course, during the period of epidemic plague in the middle of the century. But these changes, which occurred rapidly during the 1350s, reflect the immediate effects of mortality among the clergy and current candidates for orders. The prolonged decline in clerical recruitment was also influenced by long-term changes in the wider population. Though both men and women succumbed to the ravages of epidemic disease, there was often a higher mortality rate among the male population and the consequent affects on marriages and birth rates would continue to exert influences on demography long after an epidemic had passed.[17]

Recovery in the population was slowed by these and other factors as post-plague generations continued to dwindle in size. According to statistics gleaned from the *Inquisitiones post mortem*, after 1350 the average number of births steadily declined against the number of deaths, resulting in a negative replacement rate for the first time in the century. This pattern would continue into the middle of the fifteenth century, when the gradual recovery in the population began to reverse the post-plague trend.[18]

Changes in the economy also affected patterns of recruitment among the clergy. But as with shifts in the population, economic changes occurred on many levels and with uneven effect.[19] Once again, in very general terms, we may observe the influence of economic incentive on changing patterns in clerical recruitment. During the period of population growth in the first half of the fourteenth century, there was a concommitant increase in the competition for livings. Sons of larger families may have looked increasingly to the church and to clerical life for an improved economic and social status. But with the sudden decrease in the population and the fall in prices followed by demands for increased wages, new opportunities were likely to appeal to men whose employment choices had been more restricted in earlier days.[20]

An added factor of dissuasion was that at about the same time that new economic opportunities were drawing potential clerics to other livings, there were determined efforts by the Crown and the church to limit clerical wages in order to regain something of the stability lost during the great mortality.[21] In Hereford, Bishop Trillek had acted at once to implement the wage restrictions outlined in the king's ordinance and the statute subsequently issued by Parliament in 1350, along with related policies governing the clergy mandated by Archbishop Islip in his decree *Effrenata culpabilitas*. This latter decree, issued on May 28, 1350, required that the wages of stipendiary clerics be frozen at five marks, the minimum set by the Council of Oxford in 1222.[22] The requirement, though conservative, was not as outlandish as it may seem; a living of five marks annually was not regarded as lucrative by any means, but neither was it unheard of among stipendiaries in the years before the Black Death.[23] Islip had to publish the decree again in 1362 after the second epidemic prompted another wave of clerical departures from parish churches. In 1378 Islip's successor, Simon Sudbury, whose financial policies for the realm would win him few friends among laborers, renewed the old restrictions on clerical wages in his version of *Effrenata*.[24]

The re-issuing of this document suggests several things. First, the hard times experienced by the church in the years immediately following the Black Death were long-lived and there had been too little recovery in the economy to allow for a more fluid market in clerical wages. Furthermore, churchmen like Islip, Sudbury, and even Trillek enforced policies regarding clerical wages that were patently old-fashioned and ignored the changing economy of the post-plague world. Clearly, an administrator's desire for order and stability was at work here and there were sharply stated concerns as well about clerical greed and worldliness. But there was something more. The upper clergy tended to regard the lower clergy much in the same way as landowners had traditionally regarded tenants. The latter were always attempting to take advantage of their masters. To be sure, stereotypes were at work in the opposite direction as well. But the estate records indicate, as A. E. Levett found for St. Albans, and Edmund Fryde for the dioceses of Worcester and Coventry and Lichfield, that the plague did not usually elicit great acts of charity from ecclesiastical landlords or government authorities in regard to their tenants.[25] Changes which had already occurred and further ones which threatened the economic and social status quo were met with restrictions of every kind. How they could be enforced continued to challenge the strengths of leadership and the resourcefulness of workers. One of the effects from all of this was that the disparity that had long existed between the higher and lower clergy had only grown wider. As prelates attempted to stay any measurable increase in the wages of parish clergy, benefices were all the more attractive though still, to many, inaccessible. The crassness of an open market for spiritual services was, in some sense, inevitable in this economic conflict between ecclesiastical authorities and the yeomanry of pastoral care. It should come as no surprise then that *Effrenata* had to be reissued twice after its first declaration, for its demands had gone relatively unattended to. Archbishop Sudbury had to concede that some changes had occurred in the church in the previous three decades, and in 1378 he budged slightly when he raised the wage ceiling to eight instead of five marks per year. Still, the archbishop could not refrain from echoing the stern chastisment of his predecessor when he snapped at "the greed of priests who sold their labor for excessive wages which they squandered on voluptuous living."[26]

Such conservative wage policies, though perhaps sound church management, could not but discourage some from entering the clerical life. Whatever advantages salaried clerics were taking of the still changing economy, the beneficed clergy were often little better off. They were subject to the same market forces that resulted in the devaluation of other lands. Even Langland was sympathetic enough to point this out when he wrote "Parsons and parish priests complain to their bishops that their parish has been poor since the pestilence time."[27]

When the cycle of epidemic, mortality, and the ensuing economic and social instability is seen as having occurred not merely once in the fourteenth century, but seven times between 1349 and 1400, long-term trends of reduction in clerical recruitment are easier to understand.[28] Not only did the larger factors of population and economy play a considerable part in clerical recruitment. The critical factors of personal desire, vocation, and ambition were also at work here as they always are; but because they were so individual to medieval ordinands, they are less discernable. Different periods in the church's history have prompted different motives for clerical aspirants to the pastoral life, and the post-plague church had its own set of challenges and appeals.

Attraction to the priestly life was especially problematic in the decades following the Black Death. Not only were there fewer potential candidates in comparison with pre-plague populations, but in the latter half of the fourteenth century there was a growing disillusioment with the institutional church and the clerical life. There were a number of reasons for this malaise: many survivors of the epidemics had grown despondent over the church's apparent impotence before the curse that had hung over their homes and families. Though some priests had demonstrated great faith and courage in the face of the plague, survivors had watched others quit their churches and their pastoral responsibilities. The wearying effects of plague and the growing discouragement of believers contributed to the growing anti-clerical climate in the decades following the Black Death. The same sort of clerical greed that prelates like Sudbury condemned, parishioners also found worthy of criticism. Men of lesser quality than some parishioners could remember in their old priests were coming into the parishes with little skill and less devotion; some were presiding at the Eucharist as often as or less than they were involved in some quick money-making scheme.[29] Attitudes toward the institutional church and its ministers did not improve with the long schism that split the church in the final decades of the fourteenth century. Though the repercussions from Avignon, Rome, and

Pisa did not often reach the far-flung parishes of Hereford, it was unlikely that those lay people who knew about the scandal in which the papacy was enmeshed could expect better from their local shepherds. The social activism of clerics like John Ball in the late 1370s and early 1380s, though perhaps heroic to the poor and disenfranchised, was a further source of confusion regarding priestly identity. And Wycliffe's sharp criticism of the hierarchy and ordained ministry at around the same time made many question the viability of the priesthood in these changing times.

Thus, the size and composition of the clerical work force in any diocese in the fourteenth century was the result of a number of social, economic, and religious factors, and no single influence can have determined the course of clerical recruitment. There is no doubt that the Black Death and subsequent outbreaks of epidemic plague were controlling factors in the size of the population which served as the basis for all social groups, including the clergy. But there were other influences at work in society which may have been distant echoes of the "momentary" disruptions of plague. Decisions regarding one's situation in life were often something of a luxury in the middle ages, but when they were required, factors of personal desire, economy, and patronage all played critical roles. The prospect of employment, satisfaction, and the prospects of success in one's placement contributed to the broad range of incentives which led men to consider the clerical life over that of the soldier, artisan, laborer, or merchant.

I have noted in the preceding discussion that clerical recruitment in the diocese of Hereford was profoundly influenced by large external forces, such as the population decline and social and economic changes following the Black Death. But two important factors remain that warrant brief attention, both having to do with episcopal controls at ordination. The first was the combined effect that frequency and accessibility of site had on the potential number of new recruits; the second, serving as a screening mechanism of suitable candidates for Orders, was the canonical examination duly performed at every ordination which, among other things, helped set limits on the quality and number of those ordained.

We know from the ordination lists of the Hereford registers that the bishops of that diocese in the fourteenth century were generally faithful to their ministry as celebrants of the sacrament of Holy Orders. There were 243 separate ordination ceremonies during the period covered in this discussion; 29 of these had little bearing on recruitment for Hereford, to the extent that they occurred in other dioceses and included no Hereford men, or were ordinations to First Tonsure, ceremonies only rarely noted in the Hereford registers.[30] These latter 29 have been excluded from the summary on frequency and site that follows.

The vast majority of ordinations held in fourteenth-century Hereford were celebrated by bishops of that diocese. It was rare that foreign or neighboring bishops had to be invited into the diocese to ordain on behalf of the local ordinary.[31] There were some years when no ordinations took place, but these, too, were rare, and vacancies in the see or other forms of absence did not last so long that they called for emergency measures. In sum, the bishops of Hereford from Thomas Charlton, who began his ordinations in 1328, to John Trefnant who last ordained in 1404, all acquitted their responsibilities in this regard with regularity.

Bishops were expected to hold ordinations at least four times a year on the Ember Saturdays in each season. If warranted, they could ordain, as many did, on the vigils of Passion Sunday and Easter. To do more would require papal dispensation. But there were no petitions to the pope for extraordinary celebrations of the sacrament, even during the years when the plague made its most disastrous inroads into the clerical population. John Trillek evidently felt that six ordination ceremonies a year were adequate to handle the initially large numbers that were appearing for ordination in the years preceding the Black Death. If anything, the diminishing numbers of candidates in the half-century following the plague required far less than the usual four annual ordinations. Still, these seasonal celebrations continued to be the rule rather than the exception for much of the century.

Along with assuring regular celebrations of the sacraments, the bishops of Hereford tended to locate the ordinations at larger and generally accessible sites. Thomas Charlton and William Courtenay tended to favor the cathedral, while John Trillek and Lewis Charlton held numerous ordinations at Ledbury church, a large parish situated about twelve miles east of the cathedral city. But it was Bromyard that proved the most popular place for ordinations in fourteenth-century Hereford. Its parish church of St. Peter's was spacious enough to accommodate the larger groups of ordinands, and its location in the east-central part of the diocese made it a fairly easy reach from the larger towns in eastern Herefordshire and western Worcestershire.

The regularity of celebration and the relatively easy access of the preferred sites mentioned above enhanced recruitment, though we must be careful not to exaggerate the determining nature of these factors. But one aspect of ordination that was purposefully determinative was the ordination scrutiny required by canon law.[32] The examination was never meant to be a rigorous affair, but it was certainly to be taken seriously. Examiners looked for rudimentary learning, though it was oftentimes more promise than achievement that preoccupied their scrutinies. Of equal concern were moral and physical impediments which could limit the candidate's abilities to function in his order, or threaten his ministry and the Church with scandal. Still, the overall qualifications were seemingly unspectacular: candidates who had satisfied the basic requirements of learning, sufficient age, and legitimate birth were usually passed on for reception of the sacrament.[33] But one final determining factor at the scrutiny had to do with the ordination title. Every candidate for subdeacon and above had to present one to the examiners and the title might take any number of forms—the sworn testimony of persons of good reputation, family income, or a benefice—so long as it indicated that the candidate would not be unemployed or, at least, unsupported against the prospect that he could not find paid work in his ministry. This particular aspect of the examination procedure is the subject of the final section of this chapter. All that need be said here is that there are no indications in the Hereford registers or their ordination lists that the examination was indifferently performed or that many exceptions to the norms set down in canon law for ordination ever occurred. If anything, the ordination scrutiny continued to limit the number of men who might otherwise come into Holy Orders and increase the levels of recruitment.

Clerical Patronage and Placement in the Late Fourteenth Century

In some sense, the figures available on the clerical population in the diocese of Hereford and the internal and external factors that contributed to larger or smaller numbers of annual ordinations tell only half the story. What must be asked now is what influence recruitment had on the actual placement of newly ordained clerics in Hereford parish churches. This is a critical aspect of pastoral provision and needs to concern us in the final pages of this chapter.

The relationship between ordination and placement was suggested, if not precisely spelled out, in the statement of title mentioned above. Since the title was essentially a statement of personal worth or material support, it often indicated who was supporting the candidate (his family, the local ordinary, or a religious house) and, on occasion, where the cleric was destined in his parochial ministries (the name of the benefice). Information about the title was carefully entered in the register and any candidate who appeared for ordination without a title was banned from the sacrament unless the bishop himself agreed to sponsor him to a placement.[34]

The analysis of ordination titles for patterns of recruitment and placement is important for two reasons: since titles were taken seriously at ordination, any material or personal statement of support had to influence the make-up of the candidate pool. Second, there was again the chance that support for reception of orders was linked with subsequent support for placement.

One way to test the strength of ordination patronage regarding placement is to note the title and locate any other reference to the placement of a cleric in the records of the time. We can do this most easily with beneficed clergy since they usually appear both in the ordination lists and in the record of their institution to a benefice. But even among the less noteworthy stipendiaries, there are scattered references which help at least to trace some of these men from ordination to parish. In the end the sample of clergy whose titles can be compared with their placement is relatively small, not because we have fewer confident references to where they ended up, but because we need to limit our analysis of titles to those ordinands who obtained support from sources which could actually play a role in their placement, usually the owners of church advowsons.

Regarding beneficed clergy, the actual correspondence between patronage at ordination and patronage at institution is slim, given the large numbers of men noted in either record. But patrons might change, with every other circumstance in a cleric's life, from his ordination to the beginning of a career as a rector. There were only thirteen clerics, or a little over 5 percent of the total number of incumbents, who were supported from ordination to placement. But the illustrations of patronage in these cases were varied and suggested something of the complexity which characterized the system of medieval patronage. Most of the cases observed resulted from the activities of stable patrons, such as the cathedral chapter and the larger religious houses. For instance, Walter Bounde was ordained with a title given him by Abbey Dore in 1385, and three years later was presented by the same abbot and convent to Bacton chapel, a church appropriated to Dore.[35] The cathedral chapter sponsored John Ewyas' ordination to the priesthood in 1386, and presented him to the bishop as the new vicar of Lydney in 1402.[36] William de la More was ordained with a title from

Wigmore Abbey in 1352, and presented by the same house to Aymestrey parish church the following year.[37]

This sort of patronage could be individual as well as corporate: in 1343 Richard de Ketford, one of the vicars choral at Hereford Cathedral, was ordained with a title appropriately given him by the Dean and Chapter. In 1349 Richard was presented by one of the canons, William de Fownhope, for the vicarage at Westbury.[38]

There is a similar rate of correspondence in the ordination titles and placement sites of the wage-earning or non-beneficed clergy. But our records in this case are less dependable and certainly less uniform throughout the diocese. Clerical subsidy rolls survive from the later fourteenth century listing all clergy, beneficed and non-beneficed alike, for the diocese or portions thereof between 1379 and 1406.[39] These can be supplemented to some extent with chance references in the bishops' registers. But among the non-beneficed clergy recorded in the subsidy roll of 1406, 13 percent (64 of the 495 clerics listed) showed a correspondence with the names of ordinands. As with the similarly low degree of correspondence in the case of beneficed clerics, this does not mean that there was no connection between patronage and placement for the remaining 87 percent of clerics in the subsidy roll. Once again, stable patrons — usually institutions more than individuals — are the links between the two kinds of patronage. Five stipendiaries had won the patronage of the cathedral Dean and Chapter, one held a title from Monmouth Priory and was later recorded as being a chaplain in Monmouth parish, and another secular priest, John Montgomery, was ordained with a title from Wigmore Abbey and placed in the parish of Lydbury North under the patronage of the same house. John Davys, a Benedictine monk who was ordained under the title of his own house, St. Guthlac's, became the chaplain at St. Peter's parish in Hereford, one of the priory's appropriated churches. Another religious, an Austin friar named John Coston, became a chaplain at St. Lawrence in Ludlow where the friars had a large community. Perhaps most interesting was another patron from Ludlow, the Palmers' Guild, which gave clerics Thomas Sidler and Geoffrey Stynygton titles at ordination as well as chantry positions at their altars in St. Lawrence Church. In a similar case, the brothers of nearby St. John's Hospital supported John Hory through ordination to a chaplaincy in Ludlow.

These cases of correspondence between title at ordination and the placement of a cleric are too few to say that the two principles of promotion to orders and actual ministry were always linked. Too many discrepancies in

TABLE 4.1   Titles of Priest-Ordinands in Hereford, 1328–1404

Bishop	Priests	Patrimony	Religious houses	Property	Benefice	Other
			Ordination title (percent)			
Thomas Charlton (1327–44)	684	523 (77	76 (11)	13 (2)	52 (7)	20 (3)
John Trillek (1344–60)	669	376 (56)	200 (30)	1 (0.1)	60 (8.9)	32 (5)
Lewis Charlton (1361–69)	121	29 (24)	70 (57)	0	19 (16)	3 (3)
W. Courtenay (1370–75)	159	19 (12)	87 (55)	6 (4)	11 (7)	36 (22
John Gilbert (1375–89)	214	23 (11)	122 (55)	32 (16)	17 (8)	20 (10
John Trefnant (1389–1404)	137	6 (5)	89 (64)	22 (16)	14 (10)	6 (5)

the records have to be resolved for a clearer picture of this relationship to emerge. But the connection is there in enough cases to indicate that patronage was an important factor in clerical recruitment in the fourteenth century. And even if placement could not be assured at ordination — a cleric's title could change through the various levels of order — patronage at ordination itself helped determine who would and would not be ordained. The medieval church depended on systems of patronage at every level. When it came to institutions to benefices, it was the patron who provided the first step for pastoral leadership in the presentation of a candidate to the bishop. Patronage was at work as well, though perhaps in a less visible way, among the non-beneficed clergy whose hopes of obtaining a livelihood through the exercise of the functions of their office hinged upon the employment given them by a patron, if not at ordination then at some subsequent point. This type of patronage often took place in entirely modest ways, facilitated by the network of social and institutional relationships that grew among individuals, families, and parishes.

There is one final aspect to this relationship between patronage at ordination and clerical placement that needs to be acknowledged. This was the shift in the nature of ordination titles that took place shortly after the Black Death. Throughout the fourteenth century in Hereford most ordination titles came in one of the five types represented in Table 4.1. Most ordinands, at least before the plague, had patrimonial titles (*ad titulum patrimonii*) which implied some financial backing from their families. Religious houses, including the Cathedral Dean and Chapter, were also responsible for the ordination patronage of a sizeable number of diocesan ordinands. Personal property or promise of the same by some benefactor whose name was noted in the title form a third type. Perhaps the most secure title was an ecclesiastical benefice which showed a direct correlation between support at ordination and actual placement in a parish. A fifth type has been accorded the indefinite term "other" and denotes a wide range of titles, small in number, which came from a variety of sources: papal and episcopal provision, and parochial guilds.

In order to focus this discussion more clearly on pastoral provision, only priest-ordinands from the Hereford diocese have been included in the statistical representation below. Their titles may have changed in the course of their progression through the ranks of major orders, but here they are displayed according to the statement of support at ordinations to the priesthood. Each category of title is accompanied by two sets of figures. The left-hand column shows the total for that particular title presented during a bishop's reign while the right-hand parenthetical figure shows the volume in percentage of those ordained to that particular title. Thus, for example, 523 priests, or 77 percent of all priest-ordinands promoted by Thomas Charlton between 1328 and 1344, were ordained with patrimonial titles. This large proportion of titles based on family income and sponsorship had been typical of most ordinands before Charlton's reign, in his own dio-cese — as the ordination lists in Thomas Cantilupe's register of the late thirteenth century demonstrate — as well as in other English sees.[40] After patrimony, religious houses provided the next largest number of ordination titles but only at 11 percent of the total ordained over a seventeen-year period.

The figures could be traced in a more exacting fashion, but the point demonstrated here is a simple one. Throughout the course of the century all categories of ordination titles changed to some degree, but the most strik-ing changes occurred between patrimonial and religious titles. Though the former held the majority through the early part of the period and into the first years of John Trillek's pontificate, titles of patrimony witnessed an unremitting decline through the rest of the century, so that by John Tref-nant's pontificate a mere 5 percent of priest-ordinands showed this sort of title at their ordination. The story of titles from religious houses was exactly the opposite. In his lengthy pontificate, Thomas Charlton had ordained only 76 men to the priesthood with religious titles. But the numbers grew steadily during the Trillek years when one-third of all priest-ordinands were presented by religious houses, and in Lewis Charlton's pontificate the

TABLE 4.2   Ordination Titles, 1345–1369

Year	Total priests	Patrimony	Religious houses	Other
1345	42	27	10	5
1346	130	74	43	13
1347	23	16	6	1
1348	47	27	17	3
1349	159	107	37	15
1350	86	48	22	16
1351	43	24	16	3
1352	40	18	16	6
1353	26	13	8	5
1354	16	2	7	7
1355	15	9	4	2
1356	2	1	—	1
1357	—	—	—	—
1358	8	3	4	1
1359	22	7	10	5
1360	11	6	1	4
1361	—	—	—	—
1362	22	7	10	5
1363	16	5	9	2
1364	20	5	9	6
1365	12	3	7	2
1366	10	2	7	1
1367	20	2	15	3
1368	13	3	8	2
1369	8	2	4	2

numbers rose to 57 percent of the total ordained. The trend continued through the 1370s and 1380s, reaching their highest point for the century in Trefnant's pontificate, with 64 percent.

The significance of these changes is not immediately discernible. Though some defense for actual patronage behind the ordination title has already been presented, the sample remains small and difficult to generalize for the entire period or for all ordinands. At the same time it is difficult to accept the position that all or most of these titles were legal fictions, as some have stated, formalities whose real origins had been obscured behind social, religious, and economic changes over the centuries.[41] It is also true that these same changes in title occurred in other dioceses in the fourteenth century, though their relationship to the plague is easily arguable. In Lincoln diocese, patrimonial titles at ordination had been on the decline since the late thirteenth century. Up in Carlisle the change from patrimonial to religious titles would not show in the ordination lists until the end of the fourteenth century.[42] But in Hereford we can see that the change, evident through the reigns of John Trillek and Lewis Charlton, did take place very close to the Black Death. In the early 1350s, with the shrinking numbers of recruits for all orders, the traditional volume of patrimonial titles was maintained against other sources of patronage (Table 4.2).

But by the middle of that decade, the change would occur and predominate with rare exception for the rest of the century. What role the Black Death had to play in this change is impossible to detect. Its effects, as we have seen, were manifold and uneven. It may also be true, as one historian has suggested, that the shift in titles all over England was too sudden to show the more gradual changes that took place in the social status of ordinands.[43] But the social status of ordinands may not have changed that gradually. The more traditional bonds which strengthened the possession and transmission of property within families during times of relative calm were severely strained and, in some cases, altered permanently after the Black Death. The devaluation of property which occurred after the plague may have further challenged the tendency among ordinands to rely upon the support of family wealth.[44] With the increased mobility among laborers, including candidates for the clergy, customary structures of personal and material support traditionally linked with a stable community were no longer widely available.

What was lacking in patrimonial titles was, to some extent, made up for in titles provided by religious houses, not so much in the form of actual money but in the form of permanence. Some of the great monastic houses in the diocese, such as Wigmore and Wormley abbeys, could have made good on statements of patronage at ordination; as we have seen, some of these wealthier houses supported clergy to livings where they excercised their ministry. But many titles to religious houses were from the poorer places in the diocese: hospitals, almshouses, and convents of nuns whose financial operations were barely adequate for their own support, much less for that of clerics whose associations with those houses were often less than formal. If patronage was not forthcoming and if the houses themselves stood little to gain from their support of candidates at ordination, as both seem likely, it is difficult to say what precise meaning these relationships held. For one thing, the ordinand obtained a title from an institution, a source of stability and viability in its place within the local church and society, no matter how wealthy or poor the house was. It is also possible, as one historian has said, that religious houses rationalized their place in this system of patronage by participating in the scrutiny required of every candidate for orders. Their statements on behalf of ordinands more often had the appearance of the traditional presentation to the bishop, the original notion of the "testimony of clergy and people," than the declaration of property or income that had dominated the earlier part of the century.[45] Also, there was little chance in the post-plague church that backers of titles would have to actually pay for the support of their clerics. The conditions for such payment were almost exclusively based on employment and though salaries for non-beneficed clergy were often low in the decades following the Black Death, the positions they represented were in steady supply.

What bearing such changes had upon the patterns of recruitment in Hereford during the fourteenth century is hard to say. Titles, to the extent that they demonstrated some form of patronage and were consistently required from ordinands, played an important though not an exclusive part in the formation of the diocese's clerical population. The titles candidates displayed during the changeful times after the Black Death managed to meet the traditional requirements for ordination. But the purpose behind the requirement may have changed during the course of the century. The securities against unemployment customarily addressed in the title were of less concern after the Black Death, when clerical jobs were available in larger number. At the same time, guarantees of personal worth were needed and looked for in the title. It is true that changes in patronage had begun before the diocese was rocked by the Black Death, but as with other things, the depopulation, social dislocation, and economic changes which had been the first effects of plague certainly contributed to the altered conditions of patronage and personal testimony.

Clerical recruitment in the Hereford diocese had been greatly influenced by these and other changes during the course of this troubled century. The large numbers of clerics entering the diocesan work-force in the 1330s and 1340s had been severely reduced in the years following the Black Death. Although in the episcopal or papal registers of the time there were no urgent pleas for exceptions to normative procedures regarding recruitment and ordination in Hereford, it would take nearly a century for the downward trends in recruitment after the Black Death to reverse themselves. There were a number of factors within and outside the church in

Hereford that influenced the course of clerical recruitment. Changes in population were joined by fluctuations in the economy and contributed to an altered view of clerical life in a changed world. Within the church, regulations and controls continued to help determine the size and quality of its clerical members. Although ordinations were held regularly by the bishops of Hereford, how they measured the field of potential candidates to the standards of the clerical office cannot be known with certainty. It is possible that lower numbers in the latter half of the century indicated either a general deficiency in candidates who were less able than their clerical predecessors to meet canonical requirements, or a more rigorous screening of potential ordinands by church authorities. The former and not the latter has tended to carry the day in historical assessments of clerical life during this time. It is the rightness or error of this judgment to which we now turn.

5. Hereford Parish Clergy at the Century's End

Writing toward the close of the fourteenth century Henry Knighton, an Augustinian canon and chronicler of St. Mary's Priory, Leicester, had ample time to reflect on the changes that had taken place in the church since the great pestilence. He wrote a brief and vivid account of what had happened in church and society as a result of the plague and grieved especially that so few priests — and able ones at that — had survived the epidemic.[1] Henry complained of the deaths of many fellow priests, but also echoed his contemporary, Langland, in his disdain for those survivors who left their cures for wealthier livings. There were vacancies everywhere but not for long. In fact, it was probably this incentive in new markets for clerical positions more than any other single factor that helped produce a generation of recruits less-suited for the office they were seeking. Knighton wrote: "in very short time there came crowding into orders a great multitude whose wives had died in the pestilence. As might be expected of laymen, many of these were illiterate and those who knew how to read could not understand what it was they read."[2] Knighton belabored the differences between himself, an educated man, and these widowers who in the priest-scarce years following the plague were all but assured of parochial employment. Though he does not say it outright, Knighton knew that bishops had to be responsible for much of what had happened, in that they had the power to determine who would and who would not be ordained.

The Leicester chronicler and his fellow canons were not alone in their dilemma over the effects of the plague on the quality of clergy. Bishops Bateman of Norwich, Islip of Canterbury, and Wykeham of Winchester had to resort to the expensive efforts of founding their own schools to offset the intellectual poverty that had troubled their dioceses after the deaths of many "illustres vires" during the mid-century plagues.[3] Religious leaders mourned similar losses in their own communities; Lucas Wadding, though puzzling over the changes much later, echoed the sentiments of Knighton in attributing the declining standards in the Franciscan order with the many widowers who gained access to the decimated convents.[4]

All of this was confirmed in the vernacular literature of the time as well. Illiterate and lazy clerics pass through the works of Langland, Chaucer, and Gower, eager for the hunt or intent more on gold than the pursuit of learning or the cure of souls. Chaucer's clerical and religious pilgrims with few exceptions wend their way to Canterbury with ambiguous motives. Langland, who probably knew Hereford curates from his days in Malvern, consistently pointed out clerical failings in "Piers Plowman" and made a pointed judgment by assigning the role of Sloth to a parish priest.[5] Few writers of the day held up priests as men of learning and pastoral zeal; indeed, the references in Knighton, Langland, and Gower are often whistful recollections of how things once were in "daies old" when clerics seemed more accomplished in the *ars artium*.[6] These sentiments and satires were more than anticlerical: there had been a gathering mood of disappointment over the state of the church and the condition of the clergy in the late fourteenth century and, with it, a longing for restored rigor and pastoral nobility. This desire — more than the facile castigation of a dimmer clergy — was partly at work in Chaucer's portrait of the Parson in the "Canterbury Tales."

There is an immediate temptation to compare Chaucer's stalwart Parson with his real-life contemporaries, but such comparisons are in many ways bound to be unfair. For one thing, the Parson achieves all those ideals associated with his role as a local pastor. But even more important, he is a poetic construction and the various facets of his identity as pilgrim, teller of tales, and a character in his own right are too subtle and complex to stand in simple and direct relationship to the historical world around him. On the other side of the comparison, we lack any similar depth of character in the historical pastors of the time. They appear, when they appear at all, in the colorless language of court records and episcopal memoranda.[7] All of these concerns notwithstanding, it is hard not to make the comparisons in question, especially in a discussion about pastoral leadership in the half-century following the Black Death. This is, after all, the world in which Chaucer's Parson tended his flock. If he is an idealized representation of a pastor, it must also be said that his pastoral attributes come out of a long tradition in the medieval church that Chaucer did not invent.[8] His virtues are much the same as we find in the synodal statutes and pastoral *summae* of his own age: spiritually wealthy though materially poor, wise and compassionate, completely committed to the guidance of his parishioners.[9] The Host remarks perhaps for the whole company: "A bettre preest I trowe that nowhere noon ys."[10]

John Trefnant, bishop of Hereford from 1389 to 1404, was a contemporary of Chaucer and his Parson. He may have read some of the poet's lines from time to time, though his library reveals a far more serious reader of canon law and theology.[11] In April, 1397, Trefnant made a pilgrimage of his own: he set out with his retinue of advisors, scribes, personal attendants, and men-at-arms to visit all the parishes of his diocese. By an accident of preservation, the record of this visitation survives to reveal, albeit in flat legalese, a portrait of Hereford pastors and their parishioners at the century's end. It is a remarkable document, filled with the depositions of parishioners who served as members of delegations from their parish communities to respond to the bishop's inquiries regarding the physical state of their parish churches and the moral condition of their neighbors and pastors.[12] It is also incomplete for the purposes of this discussion. A visitation record is a detailed image of a moment in the history of the diocese and, as such, needs to be supplemented where possible with other diocesan records of the late fourteenth century.

Accepting that there are important differences between the literary figure of the Parson and the half-hidden pastors of Hereford, the intention of this final chapter is to measure the quality of Hereford clergy in the decades following the Black Death according to some of the Parson's more significant pastoral attributes. If the Parson realized many of the pastoral qualities of his day, how close were his contemporaries in Hereford to pursuing similar ideals? From another perspective, how true were the complaints of Knighton, Langland, and others regarding the clergy of Hereford diocese? Was there in this diocese, as Wadding had complained for the Franciscan order, a *multitudo promiscua* eroding traditional standards of pastoral? One could cull a number of details from Chaucer's portrait of the pastor and find parallels or opposites among his real contemporaries, but three major aspects of pastoral leadership stand out and are used in the following discussion: pastoral learning, the pastor's residence, and work in the cure and conduct of life.

Parish Priests and Instruction for the Cure of Souls

> A good man was ther of religioun,
> And was a povre Persoun of a toun,
> But riche he was of hooly thoght and werk.
> He was also a lerned man, a clerk,
> That Christes gospel trewely wolde preche;
> His parisshens devoutly wolde he teche. (ll. 477–82)

If there was anything exceptional about the Parson's learning in pastoral matters, it was not that he stood outside the educational standards of his day but rather seems to have fulfilled them. He was, writes Chaucer, a "lerned man," but beyond this we know nothing about his formal education. As a church rector he might have enjoyed a study leave and time at a university but he was, by his own admission, not very "textueel" and modestly left the discourse on Penance, which was his tale, to the correction of his intellectual betters.[13] That he did so was a greater testimony to his humility than his intelligence.

In some sense, what formal education he had is beside the point since a pastor's learning was not solely a matter of book knowledge. What he knew was built upon the twin foundations of *scientia* and *virtus* and it was this that he put to the service of his cure. His theological acumen and knowledge of the Scriptures had direct bearing on his personal character, his life as a Christian, and, hence, on his preaching and the building up of his parish community.[14]

All of this, of course, was hoped for in the everyday life of Hereford pastors. But educational opportunities for clerics were not always in keeping with expectations. The more precise educational requirements were not determined by any universal policies in the late medieval English church, but according to the application of local standards that were far from exact. At ordinations, bishops and their assistants charged with examining candidates looked for basic intellectual qualities, but what was essential was a sufficient knowledge of Latin and liturgy to allow the candidate to carry out the ministry of his order effectively. Any other learning for the cure of souls would come in time with experience.

This flexibility in the measurement of the qualifications for ordination was pastorally expedient, allowing church authorities to interpret broadly according to local needs. It also matched the remarkable diversity in background and education of late medieval clerics. But the absence of set standards also presented obvious problems as occurred at Garway parish at the end of the century. Parishioners there pointed out that their curate was wholly inept and knew nothing about the cure of souls.[15] In the neighboring vicarage of Garway, Welsh parishioners were frustrated by the fact that their curate could not speak their tongue nor could they speak English, leaving the pastoral care of that parish in considerable doubt.[16] In Coddington parish on the eastern borders of the diocese the rector was called "tepidus et negligens."[17] The vicar of Woolaston may have been more embarrassed than ignorant when he processed through the streets of his village, pyx in hand, on his way to the bed of a sick parishioner. The pyx was obviously empty, but, in spite of his parishioners' protests, the vicar ordered them to bow in reverence to the Blessed Sacrament.[18]

These are the only obvious cases of clerical ignorance in the extensive criticisms that make up the Hereford visitation record. There are similarly few references to this failing in other official records of the time, such as the bishops' registers. Few dispensations are recorded that might suggest liberality on a bishop's part regarding other qualifications for ordination. There were no changes to examination procedures before ordination, when the mental acumen of future pastors might be most effectively measured, nor were there any new laws or statutes in diocesan and provincial legislation covering intellectual deficiencies. If anything, the bishops of Hereford in the post-plague years seem to have sustained traditional requirements for ordination and pastoral service as best they could. By all appearances in the official records, the diocese was maintaining an adequate standard of clerical and pastoral competence.

But, once again, adequacy of learning is a difficult thing to measure and intellectual standards are hard to discern in a late medieval diocese. A look at the schools of the diocese and educational opportunties for clerics give us much more to go on in this regard. The greatest number of schools in the diocese were those modest enterprises attached to parish churches. None is mentioned specifically in plague-related memoranda of the bishops' registers, but a number of parishes collapsed in the years following the Black Death and many more suffered from increased poverty. Either circumstance would have impinged greatly upon a local school. The best example of a school that had fallen on hard times in the decades following the Black Death was Hereford's most distinguished school. Once a great center of scientific learning, the cathedral school had, by the 1380s, declined markedly. It was brought to Bishop Gilbert's attention that the grammar mastership of the school was vacant and had not been filled in a number of years. So the duty, which was customarily performed by the cathedral chancellor, was taken over by the bishop on this occasion and Gilbert appointed a reputable master, Richard Cornwall, to the cathedral post.[19] But it was later discovered that the mastership had been vacant for so long because there had been no chancellor to fill it or to oversee the school for at least twelve years. The cathedral chapter had leased the income from the position and had decided to make do without a grammarian for the school.[20] Why the chapter had done so is not clear. The chancellorship was caught up in a lengthy dispute over appointment and there had been chronic com-

TABLE 5.1   Dispensations for Non-Residence, 1283–1404

Bishop	Clerics given leave	Study licenses	Institutions to benefices
R. Swinfield (1287–1316)	64	64	593
A. Orleton (1317–27)	27	27	117
T. Charlton (1327–44)	42	34	224
J. Trillek (1344–60)	56	23	481
L. Charlton (1361–69)	10	6	133
W. Courtenay (1369–75)	0	0	54
J. Gilbert (1375–89)	6	0	138
J. Trefnant (1389–1404)	3	1	357

plaints from the cathedral clergy about diminished revenues and increased expenses. But one effect from all this was a decline in learning at that once celebrated school.

There were similar changes in opportunities for a clerical education in the post-plague church. The old custom of setting aside a small portion of the parish's income as a stipend for a young cleric's educational expenses had all but disappeared by the century's end. The recipient worked for this support as the holy water cleric or the *aquabajulus* for the parish. The stipend lasted for only a short period of time and, once it had helped educate one cleric, was passed on to another. But the stipend, as with any of the parish's revenues, was linked to the local economy and would be prey to all the factors that influenced the latter. Furthermore, it ceased being a high priority among prelates who had to face more urgent financial complaints from impoverished rectors or stipendiaries who were loathe to put up with traditional wages. When he was archbishop of Canterbury, William Courteny tried to revive the moribund office in 1393, but to little apparent effect.[21]

What was happening at the local level of the parish was occurring at the universities as well. Since Boniface VIII's decree *Cum ex eo* in 1296, parish rectors had been taking advantage of a university education with the support of their own church revenues. Hereford bishops had been rather liberal about such study leaves, but in the years following the Black Death, when diocesan policies on clerical residence became stricter, these leaves of absence for university study declined.

In Table 5.1 two things are immediately observable.[22] The first is that the proportion of dispensations granted for purposes of study to those given for other suitable reasons remained strong through most of the pontificates in the fourteenth century. Trillek and Gilbert seem the only exceptions to this pattern. Fewer than half the clerics given leave from their cures between 1344 and 1360 were licensed for study. The figures for the Gilbert years must remain inconclusive, as no reasons were specified for the licences issued during his pontificate. Still, it is likely that some of these were given to clerical students.

The second observation is that the strength of study leaves against other possible reasons for non-residence declined markedly after the Black Death. The decline among study licences for Hereford clergy began at some point in the later years of Thomas Charlton's pontificate. Perhaps his absence from the diocese on the king's business from 1337 to 1339 had something to do with a more restrictive policy. Only five clerics sought or were given leave from their cures for legitimate reasons. Greater liberality marked the early years of John Trillek's reign, but after 1346, when six of nine licensees were dispensed for study, the numbers in all categories drop rapidly.

The reasons for this gradual decline in study-leaves over the century varied with each pontificate and according to the circumstances of individual petitioners. But it is clear that this trend was not unique to Hereford.[23] There were educational and clerical reasons why this decline occurred. Educationally, the conditions which had prompted Boniface VIII to issue his famous constitution had been substantially altered by the mid-fourteenth century. Beneath the higher stratum of university education, local grammar and theology schools had continued to develop during the period and to draw scholars whose educational interests were more modest or whose non-beneficed status excluded them from taking advantage of the terms set out in *Super specula* and *Cum ex eo*. Also, the pastoral literature that had begun to develop in the thirteenth century had expanded in volume and rich variety by the later fourteenth century. These books, treatises, and homilaries would never take the place of a university education, but there was no intention that they should. Still, clerics who had sufficient Latin acquired new choices and opportunities for improving their pastoral education in studying books like William of Pagula's *Oculus sacerdotis* (1323) and John de Burgh's *Pupilla Oculi* (1384).

Another factor in the decline of study leaves was that fewer clerics below the rank of priest were being instituted to parochial cures in the second half of the fourteenth century, making it difficult to follow the exact terms of Boniface's constitution. As Table 5.2 indicates, there was a signifi-

TABLE 5.2   Status of Hereford Beneficed Clerics, 1283–1404

	Beneficed clerics			
	Priests	Deacons	Subdeacons	Acolytes/clerici
R. Swinfield	377	40	76	73
A. Orleton	80	5	8	23
T. Charlton	189	5	0	26
J. Trillek	341	3	3	34
L. Charlton	107	0	1	15
W. Courtenay	54	0	0	0
J. Gilbert	111	0	1	19
J. Trefnant	354	0	0	0

cant shift in the institution of priests to non-priests in the post-plague church. A full 30 percent of the clerics instituted by bishops Swinfield and Orleton had not received priest's orders at the time of their presentation. This changed in the period between John Trillek's elevation and Lewis Charlton's death, when the numbers of beneficed clerics below the rank of priest fell by half. There was a concomitant rise in the number of priests among the beneficed clergy, from 70 percent during the Swinfield years to 85 percent by the mid-fourteenth century. During the pontificates of Courtenay and Trefnant all beneficed clerics had been ordained to the priesthood by the time of their institution. Though bishops like Swinfield and Orleton had interpreted *Cum ex eo* more broadly and had granted study leaves to priests as well as lesser clerics, the fact that there were far fewer candidates who could apply to the exact terms of Boniface's decree by the latter part of the century did little to encourage study leaves in the diocese.

In sum, it was the changing economy that posed the greatest threat to schools and educational opportunities in the half century following the Black Death. In a time when many parishes were experiencing greater poverty and when material and human resources were in precious supply, priests simply could not afford to support themselves for a period of study at a university on the revenues of their parish. Nor were they encouraged to leave their parishes when there were so few other priests who might serve in their stead and less income to provide a worthy stipend for a vicar.[24]

After the Black Death and by the end of the fourteenth century, fewer parish clergy were able to take advantage of the same educational opportunities available decades before. The proliferation of schools attached to

chantries was still far off, a development more of the fifteenth than fourteenth century.[25] For the clergy of Chaucer's world, schools and scholars
endeavored as they could through the vagaries of local economies and the
chancy provision of good teachers. No doubt, most parish priests continued to learn as children their smatterings of Latin from the local curate
and, later, the more practical of sacramental ministry as clerics in minor
orders. Clearly, some were abler than others, but it had always been so.

Clerical Residence and Management of the Cure

> Ful looth were hym to cursen for his tithes,
> But rather wolde he yeven, out of doute,
> Unto his povre parisshens aboute
> Of his offryng and eek of his substaunce.
> He koude in litel thyng have suffisaunce . . .
> He set nat his benefice to hyre
> And leet his sheep encombred in the myre
> And ran to Londoun unto Seinte Poules
> To seken him a chaunterie for soules,
> Or with a bretherhed to been witholde;
> But dwelt at hoom, and kepte wel his folde. (ll. 486–90, 507–12)

The Parson was a model of extraordinary charity, forbearance, and
uncompromised duty to his flock: "Benygne he was, and wonder diligent,
And in adversitee ful pacient." The basis for his enduring fellowship with his
people was a simple and ancient principle in church law—that there should
be one priest to serve one church, just as there is one head to rule the body.[26]
The allusion to scripture had a dual purpose: it was descriptive not only of
the unity of government properly associated with a parish but also of the
manner in which the pastor should regard his people. Personal residence in
the cure, quite apart from the more practical features of sound administration, was suggestive of another scriptural image, that of the Good Shepherd
committed solely to the care of his sheep. The Parson "dwelt at hoom, and
kepte wel his folde." For him such residence was not an irksome responsibility to which he was legally bound but, rather, a matter of duty to which
he should willingly devote himself for the sake of his parishioners: he
visited his parishioners both near and far, provided hospitality and alms to
the poor of his parish even "out of doute," and instructed his people with
timely preaching and the example of his virtuous life.

The Parson's reputation as a good pastor lay not only in the fact that he did what the law of the Church required, but that his attentiveness to the cure went beyond mere compliance. Thus, it is as telling to note what the Parson did as what he did not do. He did not, for instance, make more of tithes than charity would allow. Had he been more concerned with the collection of parishioners' dues he might have turned his benefice or its tithes over to a 'farmer' who would manage the church's revenues in his stead. Neither did he consider quitting his church for any reason, including the lure of a well-endowed chantry or the less burdensome life in a conventual church ("Or with a bretherhed to been witholde"). Furthermore, while he was resident in his church and in full possession of office and benefice there was no need to employ a chaplain who would carry out the Parson's duties in his absence.

But some of his clerical contemporaries might rightly complain that to insist on tithes was not an evil but something that pastors had to do against begrudging parishioners.[27] They might also defend, though perhaps with less self-righteousness, that leaving their cures was also necessary to do from time to time. Still, non-residence was a reality in the fourteenth-century church and though there were provisions for such under canon law, there was always the concern that the exception would be abused and that non-residence could become absenteeism in one form or another. As we saw at the time of the Black Death, some rectors and vicars fled their parishes outright. Though reports of flagrant absenteeism subsided with the general restoration of order in the benefices, there would be occasions in the second half of the fourteenth century when bishops of Hereford had to deal with absentee clerics.

The clearest abuse against clerical residence was the absenteeism implicit in holding more than one church benefice, but Hereford was not a place much troubled by pluralism in the fourteenth century.[28] There are only a few scattered references to it in the registers in the first half of the century. After the Black Death, when Lewis Charlton submitted the names of all pluralists in the diocese to Archbishop Langham under the terms of the papal bull *Consueta* (1366), only 28 names appeared on the list from Hereford and most of these (23) were cathedral canons and prebendaries.[29] So it is unlikely that parish churches in Hereford suffered much from this particular abuse. But the sort of neglect associated with the evils of pluralism could come in other forms, all usually gathered under the rector's excessive regard for his benefice as a source of income rather than a setting for preaching and prayer. In such cases, the rector or vicar might be physically present but pastorally absent. This attitude can be seen in four particular abuses which were very much the concern of church law in the later middle ages: putting a benefice out to farm, the unlicensed exchange of benefices, inadequate employment and provision of assistant clerics, and the physical repair of church properties.

A benefice was put out to farm when an individual other than the rector was employed to manage the entire benefice or some portion of it, such as the income from tithes. While some would defend the practice as an efficient means of using church revenues, the potential for abuse was great. Farming not only encouraged absenteeism but it further undermined the integral relationship between the service of the altar and the curate's sustenance. There was always the concern that church revenues might the more easily be diverted from their proper purpose. This often happened, for example, with income meant for poor relief or the maintenance of the fabric. If nothing else, the arrangement caused further alienation between the parishioners and their rector.

By the time of the Black Death there had already been a lengthy history of ecclesiastical concern regarding the improper farming of churches.[30] Earlier in the century, the bishops of Hereford had been generally successful in keeping the abuse under control. Richard Swinfield allowed only one church to be farmed during his lengthy pontificate and Adam Orleton made grants for two.[31] Thomas Charlton allowed no benefices to be farmed, but by the middle of the century there was considerable relaxation of the rules governing the farming of churches, especially where religious houses were concerned. Between 1344 and 1358 John Trillek permitted seven churches to be farmed, all of which were in the possession of religious houses.[32] After 1358 no episcopal grants were issued in this regard for more than two decades. When the practice was resumed in 1380, significant changes in the terms of church-farming had taken place. John Gilbert approved the request of Great Malvern to farm Peterchurch for three years, but to a layman rather than a priest.[33] In the final years of the century only one license for farming was given by John Trefnant, and this was yet another to the monks at Great Malvern to farm their churches to any fit person, ecclesiastic or lay.[34]

During the course of the fourteenth century there was an increase in the numbers of churches put to farm by their rectors, although it might be said that the arrangement was never seen as a desireable thing by church authorities. Still, there was a marked difference between the policies maintained by bishops Swinfield and Orleton and those conveyed in the far more liberal grants of Trillek and Gilbert. Where the former had conceded the grants to individual rectors to hire priests, the latter were making provisions for religious houses to farm their churches to any fit person. The requirement that the farmer be a cleric seems to have disappeared altogether. The reasons for this are not immediately evident. Doubtless, they have much to do with the economic considerations involved in the farming of benefices. They probably indicate as well that the farmed benefices of religious houses were unlikely to suffer any further compromise to the cure of souls. Vicars had long been established in these churches, and, in the employment of a farmer, the collection of tithes would simply move from one set of hands to another. There was also the difference in what constituted a farm. When bishops Swinfield and Orleton permitted Hereford rectors to farm their benefices, the terms of these approvals were very much similar to the appointments of coadjutors. The management of the cure was in those earlier days inseparable from the fulfilling of pastoral obligations. In the half-century following the Black Death the terms are far more economic: religious corporations which had had little pastoral contact with the parish were rather keener to employ an effective manager for their parish revenues. To this extent it was perhaps the hope of bishops like Trillek and Gilbert that any advance in the economic state of these appropriators might reflect as positively on the parishes in their keeping. One last reason for the change in the required clerical status of the farmer may have had to do with the fact that fewer priests were to be had in the latter half of the century for the auxiliary roles of coadjutor, in the case of parochial duties, and receivers of tithes in farm for administrative duties.

The abusive nature of illegal farming was obvious. Unless the revenues of a church were responsibly managed, the spiritual provision of the parishioners for which they were intended was short-shrifted in favor of the rector's personal gain. When he toured his diocese in 1397, John Trefnant discovered through the depositions of parishioners that unlicensed farming was taking place in nine churches. Each of these cases involved an individual rather than a corporate rector, as monastic communities generally had an easier time obtaining a licence. In five of the nine cases the parishioners offer little detail, merely stating that the rector has had his church farmed for so many years.[35] But others indicate that the fears of churchmen regarding the farming of benefices were well-founded. The rector of Little Cowarne was accused by his parishioners of illegally farming his benefice. This led to further abuses such as unapproved non-residence and the refusal to find a chaplain to fulfill his pastoral obligations in his absence.[36] The rector of Wentnor showed a general disregard for his parish. He had set his benefice out to farm, only to spend "day and night" in the local tavern.[37] The parishioners of Ledbury accused the warden of St. Katherine'sHospital of failing to meet time-honored responsibilities to the poor of the parish. Ancient custom had required him to purchase food for thirteen poor folk daily, but any money for that purpose had been completely withheld. Part of this may have been due to the fact that the warden had also farmed all the hospital's lands and tenements ("omnia beneficia") to a layman, without the bishop's permission.[38] The rector of Montgomery was accused by his people of doing the same thing to the great neglect of the parish.[39]

The second abuse regarding the mismanagement of churches by rectors who had financial gain more than spiritual vigilance in mind was the exchange of benefices. In this case, the benefice was really seen as little more than property to be handed from one rector to another. There were plenty of motives behind exchanges, even some which were probably administratively sound. But in the years following the Black Death the practice threatened to undermine the traditional bond between a rector and his church. By the end of the century professional exchange agents or brokers had set up a thriving practice in negotiating exchanges between two rectors and profiting from the successful match. These so-called "choppe-churches" threatened to institutionalize the reductionist tenedencies in exchanges, and provoked the ire of reformers and prelates. In 1391 Archbishop Courtenay condemned the practice. Choppe-churches, he maintained, encouraged a number of evils to the detriment of the cure of souls. Simony was at the heart of the abuse, as benefices were regarded and marketed for their material value. The equal worth of benefices necessary for proper exchanges was often misrepresented by the choppe-churches to the clerical parties involved. The archbishop condemned most vehemently the gathering of church revenues by a cleric who legally possessed only one benefice. In such a case, an incumbent resigned his benefice for another but was able to keep the better share of his previous revenues by means of an arrangement with his successor. The abuse of exchanges lay in the shrewd manipulation of parish revenues at the expense of the *cura animarum*, and the archbishop condemned those clerics who, scarcely able to fulfill the requirements of one church, gathered to themselves several. With the diversion of church revenues to such as these, "divine services are greatly diminished, the obligations of hospitality are undermined and the cure of souls neglected."[40]

It is hard to measure how much this abuse was prevalent in the diocese of Hereford after the Black Death. In the case of licensed exchanges, the figures drawn from the Hereford registers indicate an increase rather than a

TABLE 5.3   Exchanges of Benefices in Hereford Diocese,
1327–1404

Bishop	Exchanges
T. Charlton (1327–44)	29
J. Trillek (1344–60)	55
L. Charlton (1361–69)	24
W. Courtenay (1370–75)	25
J. Gilbert (1375–89)	62
J. Trefnant (1389–1404)	120

decline in these licenses by the century's end (Table 5.3). Though some of these benefices were sinecures whose exchange would not have adversely affected the cure of souls, others were parishes. Whatever the circumstances, the greatest increase in licensed exchanges occurs in the last twenty years of the century, precisely when Archbishop Courtenay was expressing his concern over the abuse. But the increase is probably reflected in the fact that part of Courtenay's strategy against abusive exchange was to urge his suffragans to be far more vigilant about the practice in their dioceses. Liberality in this regard did not manifest laxity but, rather, increasing episcopal control over benefices, their clerics, and the "choppe-churches."

The third abuse associated with mismanagement of the parish, and perhaps the most influential regarding pastoral care, was in the employment of adequate clergy to assist in the spiritual mission of the parish. Certainly, in the case of the rector's non-residence the employment of a vicar was an urgent necessity. But such provision was not always a duty properly carried out. Also, in the period following the Black Death, pastoral provision for assistant clerics became increasingly difficult due to the overall decline in numbers of priests, fluctuations in the economy, and keener competition for wages among the *stipendarii*. This latter condition was only slightly mitigated by the swift and repeated application of wage restrictions on clergy of this class. Nevertheless, churches which had long suffered from poverty found it difficult to maintain their clergy even according to a traditional pay scale.[41]

In the visitation record from 1397, Hereford parishioners revealed twenty-five separate cases where there were too few clergy, most of these due to the inadequate provision of the parish rector. In two of these cases it was discovered that the church lacked any resident cleric at all. The parishioners of Castle Goodrich claimed that their church was without a vicar and since neither he nor any other chaplain had been celebrating divine services there, they believed their souls to be in great peril.[42] The peril of their souls may have been less threatened by the fact that there were two chantry chaplains, John Byterlowe and John Smyth, who celebrated masses twice a day ("celebrant bis die") at Castle Goodrich and Honsham. But these priests may have limited their religious duties in the parish to the low masses celebrated at chantry altars. The sacramental ministry to which the incumbent was obliged seems to have been far more neglected. At Gana-rew, not far from Castle Goodrich, the parishioners reported that no rector had been there since the death of their last rector, Maurice. Services had gone unperformed for at least half a year and in the rector's absence one enterprising parishioner took advantage of the empty manse and set up a tavern there.[43]

In both cases it is uncertain whether the patron had actually failed to present anyone to the bishop or whether the incumbent was notoriously lax in his duties to reside in and tend the church committed to his care. We find more evidence of the latter than the former in the record of Trefnant's visitation. There were at least eight cases in 1397 of curates failing to reside in their churches. The vicar of Monmouth, his parishioners reported, had gone off to Rome, leaving his large church in the hands of a single chaplain. Recognizing the worth of their claim, the bishop ordered the fruits of the church sequestered until a second chaplain had been hired.[44] The parishio-ners at Aston seemed not to mind the fact that their rector did not reside nor did they even know his whereabouts, yet "otherwise everything was well there."[45] Munsley's rector was also absent to the neglect of the divine services.[46] The parishioners of Woolaston and Coddington were subject to similar neglect. At Woolaston the vicar was said to have been absent from his church for five or six months continuously and the rector of Coddington was gone from his cure long enough to require parishioners to take their children elsewhere for baptism.[47] The vicar of Weobley was only absent for short periods of time, a fortnight here and there, and the rector of Pixley had been absent from his church long enough to allow the rectorial manse to fall into ruins.[48] The rector of Little Cowarne, who had put his church out to farm without the bishop's permission, neither resided in his parish nor provided for a chaplain to work there in his stead.[49] There was no one at Mainstone to manage the cure, and the parishioners at Clunbury claimed that no services had gone on in their church since the chaplain's last leave, however long ago that was.[50] Two chantrists, John Pole, a chaplain at

Weston, and Reginald Penymawe of Mansel Gamage, were absent from their altars. Parishioners at Weston claimed that Pole was absent from his church for three weeks to a month continuously, neglecting entirely the duties of his benefice.[51]

The adequate provision of clergy included the employment of chaplains for limited services in parish churchs or chapels and, more frequently, clerics in lesser orders to assist at the altar and with the care of liturgical books and vessels. The rector of Birley had failed to hire a chaplain for full service in his church. Parishioners there claimed that the priest who celebrated mass for them on Sundays was not their own chaplain but, rather, a stipendiary hired by a Leominster parishioner.[52] The chapels of Ursay and Snowdell, attached to Peterchurch, were not adequately provided for and the rector was ordered to see to their provision.[53] The same kind of report was made by the parishioners of Lugwardine regarding the chapels of St. Weonard's, Treferanon, and Penrose and their vicar's obligation to find the necessary chaplains.[54]

Although the employment of assisting clerics was not as critical to the general pastoral provision of the parish, it was a frequently expressed concern on the part of parishioners. It was also something which tended to be the more easily overlooked by rectors who did not reside in their churches and, hence, could not see as clearly as their parishioners the necessity of employing assistant clerics. The rector of Leominster had allowed his obligation in this regard to lapse for at least three years; the parishioners there asserted the need for a clerk who would ring the bells and carry a lit candle before the vicar on his visitations to the sick of the parish.[55] Wigmore Abbey had failed to find a deacon and a subdeacon for their vicarage, the rector of Wistanstow did not have a deacon in his church, the rector of Pontesbury was similarly lax in his duties to find a deacon and a clerk for the reading of lessons and the ringing of bells, and Hopesay was in need of a cleric "ad deserviendum in ecclesiam."[56] Vicars were equally negligent in this regard. The churches of Much Dewchurch, Castle Goodrich, Much Cowarne, Bishop's Frome, and Eardisley were all deficient in the assignment of assisting clerics "in defectu vicarii."[57] The method employed by the vicar of Eardisley, in view of his church's lack of assistant clergy, is worth describing in further detail. The parishioners claimed before the bishop their right to have a clerk "who knows how to read and sing, ring the bells, process before the vicar on his visitations to the sick, and do other things."[58] Whether it was to avoid providing for such a cleric out of his own portion or whether he simply lacked the necessary income, the vicar had his two servant women, Agnes and Isabella, acting as bellringers and assistants at the altar "contra honestatem ecclesiasticam."[59]

The scandalous provision for assistants at Eardisley prompts the question of why clerics were not properly employed. The reasons, of course, were various and had everything to do with local circumstances. But three general reasons for the deficiency in the number of parish clergy seem to emerge from the evidence. The first had to do with the willingness of the rector or vicar to employ necessary assistants. There was also the factor of economy and the difficulties faced by poor curates in hiring other clerics. And, thirdly, there were simply fewer clerics in the diocese during the latter half of the fourteenth century from which suitable assistants could be drawn.

The vicar of Eardisley is an example of how one form of neglect — the refusal to employ clerical assistants — was symptomatic of other pastoral ailments in the parish. The vicar's makeshift provisions for assistants at the altar has already been described. But it was also true that what pastoral work was required of the vicar was often carried out in a haphazard way. His parishioners noted that several of their number had died without the consolation of the sacraments "in defect of the vicar." A child had been baptized without chrism, and John Boley, a parishioner, was denied the final consolations of a peaceful interment when the vicar publicly cursed him at his burial.[60] Unlike the Parson, this vicar did not hesitate to curse for his tithes: the sacraments were denied those parishioners who had failed to contribute their tenth. The vicar also celebrated clandestine marriages and was widely known to be a profiteer and a usurer. It seems no surprise, then, that this same vicar should neglect to hire an assistant from his own portion.

Another reason why adequate clergy may not have been provided for in Hereford parishes had to do with the troubles of local economies or the paltry income of the parish vicar. The parishioners of Stokesay claimed that their vicar was obliged to find a priest for Aldon Chapel. But when the visitors pressed him with the charge, the vicar pleaded that he was unable to provide for the chapel in this manner "because of the smallness of his portion."[61]

Lastly, there is the possibility that local clerics found it impossible to secure the necessary number of priests for the churches and chapels under their supervision not because of their meager resources but, rather, on account of the fewer qualified priests to be had. What may give strength to this notion of clerical scarcity — apart from the general decline in numbers noted in the previous chapter — were reports of a kind of pluralism which existed among parish curates whose churches were visited in 1397. There are ten specific references to Hereford vicars and chaplains doing double duty in their cures as well as other neighboring churches. In most cases the parishioners asserted that their rector, chaplain, or vicar celebrated mass and other divine services twice or more times a day.[62]

What were the motives behind these cases of extra duty? Charity and pastoral zeal cannot be discounted, but neither can financial gain. The vicar of Eardisley, notorious for other crimes, probably had money on his mind when he sung services at neighboring churches. In some cases parishioners were explicit in stating the motives: the parishioners at Garway claimed their chaplain celebrated mass in their church and then set out to Wormbridge five miles away to celebrate mass and collect his "double pay."[63] Some clerics actually bore two titles: the parish chaplain of Foy was also the vicar of Llangaren, the vicar of Felton was a chaplain in Ocle Pychard, and the vicar of Burrington the chaplain at Elton.[64] It can be assumed that they, like the chaplain at Garway, held two jobs and drew income from two different churches. This was bound to have some ill effect on the community. The vicar of Stokesay celebrated mass in the neighboring church at Halford first and then returned to his own parish, where his people found him less inspiring.[65] The vicar evidently found something defensible in his actions and begged the bishop's tolerance and understanding, which he seems to have received.

Not all incidents of this sort of 'pluralism' necessarily involved compromise of the cure to which the vicar or chaplain was properly attached. In some cases such an arrangement could have appeared very similar to what was required of a coadjutor.[66] Whether or not the clergy named in the visitation record were proper coadjutors is less the point than the fact that some deficiency in the local provision of clergy had required their services.

The fourth abuse often associated with non-residence was the rector's deficiency in keeping the church in good repair and adequately provided with the proper liturgical vestments, books, and vessels. Practically a full third of all churches visited by Trefnant in 1397 were in need of some repair to chancels, naves, belltowers, and cemetery walls. Certainly, some of this was attributed to the neglect of parishioners rather than their clergy. In twenty-five of ninety churches found in need of repair, the parishioners were told to fix or restore naves, uncovered or damaged roofs, windows, and cemetery enclosures.[67] Some of the laity also had duties that were less common to parishioners: the people of Vowchurch were responsible for providing a service book, a cross, and vestments for processions and the parishioners of Donnington were expected to repair the chancel as well as the nave in their church.[68] But nearly half of the churches needing repair required work in the chancels and the sanctuary, the areas traditionally assigned to the rector. The sanctuary at Dixton was "obscurus et tenebrosus" and divine services, even at midday, could not be performed without the use of candles.[69] Ruardine's chancel was in ruins, and Yarkhill's in such bad condition that mass could not be celebrated when it rained.[70]

The neglect by rectors of their chancels extended to the condition of the parish house. Fourteen rectorial manses were reported in ruin or demolished. The house owned by the rector of Donnington was barely standing. The parishioners of Pauntley complained that their church manse had "fallen to the ground" and that the curate had nowhere to live in the parish where he could be at the service of his people, especially in emergencies."[71] In a similar case, the parish house at Monmouth was ruined and dangerous, especially at night, causing the vicar undue anxieties about his safety and his ability to tend to his flock.[72]

Numerous other churches were lacking in vessels, books, and vestments. Much Dewchurch needed a psalter, as did Ullingswych whose parishioners claimed their previous rector had made off with their only copy. When confronted, he quibbled and said the book was not a psalter but an antiphonary. Trefnant ordered him to return it to the parishioners.[73] The rector of Wentnor owed his church vestments and a candle to be carried to the homes of the sick. Waterdene was in need of vessels, a bookstand, an antiphonary, a psalter, and vestments for the celebration of masses.[74] A more somber note was rung at Leominster where the parishioners reported an insufficiency of burial books, especially in view of the great number of funerals held in the church during the recent plague.

In sum, it is important when reviewing this list of lost books and damaged churches not to lose sight of who was responsible for the upkeep of the churches and why. Without the right books or a worthy sanctuary for the celebration of the mass, the pastoral care assured by the church was seriously compromised. Absenteeism was often the root of many of these evils. There were plenty of monastic rectors who succumbed to the temptation to regard their churches as sources of revenues rather than centers of worship and pastoral care for which they were, at the very least, indirectly responsible. But they were by no means the only villains in the faults uncovered on Trefnant's visitation. Of the ninety churches that had reported some material neglect of the church, only half were administered by monastic or collegiate rectors. The other half, which included ruined church houses and darkened chancels, were neglected by individuals, not institutions. And the parishioners had to bear some blame in these matters themselves. In twenty-eight churches the people had failed to carry out their duties of provision and repair. Some of this no doubt was due to neglect, some, too, from the bad example shown by the clergy to their parishioners; but poverty was also a frequent defense for pastor and people alike.

I have already stated that non-residence pure and simple was not always a preliminary to decline and neglect in parish churches. But as the association of church and income, so happily united in the literary Parson's management of his cure, was based on a simple principle of religious and economic integrity, so, too, did the possibilities for neglect emerge from the division of benefice and pastoral office. This separation existed to some degree as soon as the canonically instituted incumbent removed himself from his cure. His absence, whether it was licensed or not, encouraged a system whereby the revenues of the parish were farmed out to a third party employed for their strict collection and management. Not only might this practice alienate the tithes of parishioners but often their hearts as well. As we have seen, this abuse did not occur very often in Hereford during the course of the fourteenth century. What did occur with greater frequency, and what continued to be a central difficulty in the proper exercise of the pastoral cure, was the poor record of clerical provision to churches in the half century following the Black Death. This was the result of an array of factors, including, especially, the declining numbers of clerical recruits for the diocese and the depressed economies of local parishes. But there was at the same time a growing stability among individual rectors and vicars in relationship to their cures. With bishops granting fewer dispensations from the requirements of personal residence, local incumbents were given less opportunity for leaving their cures for any reason. Violations of this policy were bound to occur, but the abuse of absenteeism was higher among wage-earning clerics than those whose residence was required according to the terms of canonical institution. If, as it seems, Hereford clerics tended to abide in their churches and chapels, it remains to be seen what quality of life they lead as pastors according to morals, doctrine, and discipline.

Clerical Life and Conduct

This noble ensample to his sheep he yaf,
That first he wroghte, and afterward he taughte.
Out of the gospel he tho wordes caughte,
And this figure he added eek therto,

That if gold ruste, what shal iren do?
For if a preest be foul, on whom we truste,
No wonder is a lewed man to ruste;
And shame it is, if a prest take keep,
A shiten shepherde and a clene sheep.
Wel oghte a preest ensample for to yive,
By his clennesse, how that his sheep sholde lyve. (ll. 496–506)

The way in which any pastor conducted himself was the most eloquent and perhaps the most attended-to sermon on Christian living. The lessons parishioners took from their curate came as often from what he said and did as what he did not say or do. Chaucer's Parson was well aware that "if a preest be foul, on whom we truste, No wonder is a lewed man to ruste."

Fourteenth-century pastors had some guidance regarding the life and bearing of their clerical state. The same church law that governed their learning and the disposition of their cures described, albeit in terse and formulaic style, the type of life that should precede and sustain the cure of souls. John de Burgh, who best represents the canonical tradition in England in the late fourteenth century, wrote that clerics should have minds washed clean with many virtues, but especially with charity, humility, and chastity. But their service to others should be graced as well with seemly learning (*competens scientia*). Though the former Cambridge chancellor refrained from dilating much on what he meant by seemly learning, he did emphasize that the higher the office in the church the more important a cleric's education.[75]

There was much more in the tradition that addressed the external bearing of pastors and clerics. John de Burgh reiterated ancient admonitions to priests regarding modesty in bearing and attire; they should be temperate in food and drink, display their tonsure so as to be known publicly as clerics, and keep a good distance from the snares of markets, courts, taverns, and other unsavory places. They should not carry weapons or go on hunts, rather they should be busy with their own work, manage their churches with diligence, and avoid inappropriate familiarity with women.[76] In a section longer than the others, de Burgh emphasizes the strict rule of continence for all in Holy Orders and sets out the usual penalties for those who lapse in this discipline. Fornication is to be abhorred among clerics, but they should not lose their office as a result unless their sin is a matter of public scandal.

John de Burgh's description of how a cleric should live was as complete

and as concise as any. What is especially noteworthy is the order in which
the interior and exterior virtues are described: the manner and bearing of
the cleric, the expected single-mindedness of his ministry, and his avoidance
of sins, which were the special concerns of his life were all placed within the
context of his spiritual and mental character. These wider and less observable aspects of the clerical life should be kept well in mind when comment-
ing upon the incidental references to clerical transgressions recorded in
episcopal registers and visitation documents. In what follows, we will be
concerned with three major areas of clerical transgression in the post-plague
church: felonious crimes, sins against morality, and heresy.

Members of the clerical state were protected under civil and canon law
from the full procedures of secular courts. Nevertheless, they were subject
to arraignment before one of the king's judges on charges of felony, after
which they were turned over to the bishop until their case could be tried
before the appropriate church court. Meanwhile, they were detained in one
of the bishop's prisons, either at the palace in Hereford or in the jail at Ross.
Neither was a comfortable place.[77]

The evidence of the registers suggests that the transfer of clerical felons
from secular to ecclesiastical authorities was a fairly common occurrence.
The more precise nature of the crimes is far less clear. Thomas Charlton
issued at least two commissions to his assistants to receive criminous clerks
for subsequent court hearings in 1331 and 1332.[78] During Trillek's pontificate, when the troubled times of the Black Death provoked more frequent
crimes, Hereford clergy were handed over to the bishop on six occasions.[79]
But there were actually fewer times when this procedure was carried out in
the second half of the century: only once in Lewis Charlton's reign, twice
when Gilbert was bishop, and once during Trefnant's pontificate.[80]

Though these memoranda covered the transfer of prisoners and were
not meant to be briefs of the charges leveled against Hereford clerics, we
sometimes get a glimpse of what they were accused of. For instance, a canon
from Llanthony was convicted of theft and imprisoned during Thomas
Charlton's pontificate.[81] In 1349 Henry de Shipton, the archdeaon of
Shropshire, was brought up on charges of accessory to murder.[82] The vicar
of Dilwyn, perhaps provoked by the incessant demands of royal taxation
and the hardness of the times, was to answer charges in the bishop's court
for assaulting an offical of the Exchequer.[83] Two clerics were vindicated
from charges of theft, and Bartholomew Tyrel was pardoned in the murder
of John of Hinton.[84] In 1383 the rector of Easthope was deprived of his
benefice on account of his conviction for murdering the patron of the

church, John de Easthope.[85] Later that same year Bishop Gilbert appealed to the king for aid in the capture of certain stiff-necked clerics who were contumacious in crimes not defined in the bishop's memorandum.[86] The sole case during Bishop Trefnant's reign involved a young Welsh cleric who was accused of stealing some pepper from a storehouse in Leominster. Tried before the king's justices, he was found guilty and condemned to death. It was fortunate for the young Welshman that he was handed over to the church authorities in accordance with the law, as he was later successfully purged of any wrongdoing with the testimony of many good priests and upstanding clerics.[87]

Memoranda such as these are not the best measure of bad behavior among clerics. This is in part due to the fact that clerical conduct was generally under the supervision of local church authorities such as the archdeacon and rural dean. When rumors spread or accusations were made public, these local leaders of the clergy were to bring the matter to a just conclusion. It was only when a cleric was contumacious or when his crime was much graver — as in matters of felony — that the bishop involved himself in the case. Thus the relative dearth of episcopal memoranda covering clerical misdeeds represents the fewer and graver crimes committed by clerics.[88] However, there were many more charges of clerical transgressions short of major crimes, most of these lapses in chastity.

Hereford parishioners in 1397 indicated that a good number of their clergy had so fallen. Forty-three clerics of varying rank were accused of incontinence, a charge that was only second in number to the rectors and vicars who neglected the church fabric and liturgical needs of the people. The deeds behind the charges no doubt varied as well: ecclesiastical visitors were constantly sifting through such reports to winnow the gossip from the truth. For instance, the parishioners of Orcob stated that their rector kept a certain Susanna in his house, though they were not quite certain whether or not this involved any sin.[89] There was also the curious case at Kinnersley where the parishioners stated that their chaplain, Walter Ondys, had been living with a certain Agnes, his "concubina." Still, the parishioners maintained, they believed them both to be free from any sins of impurity.[90] A few marginal comments in the manuscript register of Trefnant's visitation note that some of these charges had been dropped in light of further inquiry or the subsequent purgation by the necessary number of witnesses.[91]

Other more precise statements were made about clerical incontinence. John ap Adam, parish chaplain at Llanwaren, was accused by his parishioners of keeping Celia Veyr in his house "as though they were husband and wife." The priest appeared at a later date, confessed his crime, and was sentenced by the commissary to read the psalter and fast every Friday, apparently for life, taking only bread and water.[92] Parishioners from Westbury, not far from the Cistercian abbey at Flaxley, told the bishop that eight of the monks, including the abbot himself, had carried on amorously with women in the area and that the abbot had been doing this for thirteen years.[93] In another case, Richard Stoke, a cleric at Dymmok, had been ordained shortly before Trefnant's visitation but in the course of the inquiry was discovered to have been married. The bishop accordingly suspended Stoke from the exercise of his office.[94]

Lapses in celibacy were the most common flaws recorded in this visitation of Hereford clergy and parishes. But there were other, lesser crimes recorded as well. Six priests were charged with frequenting taverns and being drunk in the presence of parishioners.[95] Not surprisingly, most of these clerics were accused of other faults as well. The chaplain of St. Weonard's was "inept and ill-suited for carrying out the cure of souls." Thomas Folyot, the priest at Garway whose ignorance of Welsh made him ineffectual to most of his parishioners, spent more of his time in taverns than anywhere else and was probably in his cups when he publicly divulged the confession of one of his parishioners. The priest then began to invest in his favorite pastime by setting up his own drinking establishment, much to the alarm of his parishioners. John Scone, the chaplain at Leominster, provoked similar worry among his parishioners who saw him lurking in taverns and other suspicious places at night.[96]

Of course, the parishioners who provided the visitors with disclosures about their priests also had things to say about their neighbors. There were, for instance, fifty-two charges of fornication and twenty-four of adultery recorded among the depositions in 1397. A further fifty-four parishioners refrained from attending the services of their churches, nine were busy at work on religious feastdays, and eleven withheld some requisite due, usually tithes or altarage, from their parish priests. Certainly people will sin regardless of injunctions to the contrary, but the example of their parish clergy was an undeniable factor in the moral lives of parishioners. When parish priests were guilty of crimes against the laws of church and kingdom, their parishioners were more likely themselves to fall in similar ways: "if gold ruste, what shal iren do? For if a preest be foul, on whom we truste, No wonder is a lewed man to ruste." There were those parishioners as well who managed to veer from grave sin in spite of the errant qualities of their pastor. The good people of Eardisley could hardly be faulted for witholding their tithes — one of the few offences recorded of the parishioners there — given the scandalous behavior of their vicar.[97]

It was essential that the moral instructor of the faithful be himself a man of uncompromised morality. This same model of instruction pertained to the preaching of sound doctrine and this was especially important in the diocese in the last decades of the fourteenth century. The subject of heresy in Hereford requires a more extended discussion than can be adequately framed in these few pages, but we can at least summarize the extent to which heterodox opinions took hold of diocesan clergy and parishioners in the early years of the Lollard movement.[98]

It was probably a combination of the personal welcome of parishioners and the remoteness of the see which drew some of the early followers of John Wycliffe into the Hereford diocese in the late fourteenth century. When the Oxford Lollard John Aston was preaching in the Worcester diocese in the early 1380s he probably visited Hereford parishes in the Gloucestershire deanery of the Forest.[99] Other names associated with the movement in the diocese at this time were Nicholas Hereford, William Swynderby, and the layman Walter Brut. But none of these, save Hereford in a limited way, had any official or lasting contact with the clergy and people of the diocese. Nicholas Hereford had been granted the chancellorship of the cathedral in 1377 but was never confirmed in the dignity.[100] Hereford's grant of the cathedral dignity seems to have initiated the long confusion during which the office was effectively vacant with no little detriment to the administration of the cathedral and its grammar school.[101] Thus, between 1377 and 1394 when Hereford returned to the diocese as the newly appointed chancellor, there is little evidence that he spent any significant length of time at the cathedral or elsewhere in Hereford.[102] During this seventeen-year period, Hereford had moved from being a staunch Wycliffite to repenting his heretical views before Bishop Trefnant, and finally winning back his former dignities and privileges in the diocese. His redemption was complete when in October 1391 he assisted the bishop as one of the judges in the heresy trial of Walter Brut. Of his effect in the diocese as a Lollard or, for that matter, as a cathedral chancellor little can be said.

Though we know more about Walter Brut through the lengthy testimony associated with his trial in Hereford, his effect on the people of that diocese as a Lollard preacher seem minimal. He described himself in modest terms as "peccator, laycus, agricola, cristianus," but he could hardly have been typical of any of these classes given his impressive education at Merton College, Oxford.[103] His Hereford wanderings were brief; two years after he was first charged with heresy, Brut recanted and submitted himself to

Bishop Trefnant's authority. He seems not to have been linked with any particular parishes in Hereford, nor did any parishioners from the diocese state publicly that they were his followers.

It was a different matter for William Swynderby, whose trial preceded Brut's, and whose influence in the diocese, though not lasting, seems to have been taken most seriously by John Trefnant and his orthodox contemporaries. Unlike Nicholas Hereford, Swynderby had no official place in the Hereford diocese but this usual restriction was not accepted by a preacher who taught where he liked "noghtwithstanding forbading of the bishop."[104] A priest of Lincoln diocese, he found frequent refuge beyond the Severn and further west in the more remote parts of the Welsh march. His first appearance in the Hereford records occurs in 1388 when on November 10 the sheriff of Herefordshire was ordered to arrest Swynderby and turn him over to Bishop John Gilbert on charges of heresy.[105] From a combination of his own strong support among the Hereford gentry and the translation of John Gilbert to the Bangor diocese in the following year, Swynderby's case was left for the Dominican's successor, John Trefnant, to manage.[106] It is probably true that Trefnant, who had made quite a reputation for himself as a canonist at the papal court, was provided to Hereford as an effective force against the heretical opinions connected with the diocese in the 1380s. Shortly after his appointment Trefnant received special powers by the king

> to arrest and imprison maintainers and preachers of conclusions contrary to sound doctrine and subversive of the catholic faith, and further to search for, seize, and produce before the [king's] Council, books, pamphlets, sheets, and quires compiled both in English and Latin by Master John Wyclif, deceased, Master Nicholas of Hereford, Master John Aston, and John Purvey, and to make proclamation prohibiting the purchase or sale thereof or the maintenance or preaching of such opinions by any persons under pain of imprisonment and forfeiture of all they can forfeit.[107]

Thus one of Trefnant's first official acts was to issue a letter from his London palace condemning heresy in the diocese and warning all who held suspect opinions that he would attack these with the greatest severity.[108] Trefnant issued further letters on heresy and the opinions being popularized in his diocese by William Swynderby. Numerous citations were issued to the Lollard commanding his appearance before the bishop at various places in the diocese. Finally, in October 1391, Swynderby was brought to trial in Hereford and there given opportunity to state and defend his views.[109]

But the trial itself or even Swynderby's views, accessible enough in the

Trefnant register, cannot occupy us much here. What is of special importance is the question of his effect on the Hereford parishes where he preached from 1388 to 1391. He very likely preached in Crofte chapel and in the parish churches of Leominster, Kington, Almeley, Eardisley, Whitney, and Monmouth. With the exception of Monmouth, the southernmost place in Swynderby's Hereford sojourns, and Leominster, which was in the central and northern part of Herefordshire, the parishes were mainly in the western parts of the diocese very near the Welsh border whose thick woodlands and hills offered easy refuge.[110] Still, there are no indications in the Trefnant visitation record that these parishes were particularly troubled by heretical leanings or led by Lollard sympathizers. In fact, most of them show the usual list of sins. At Crofte, where Swynderby seemed to have spent a great deal of his time when in Hereford, the parishioners told the bishop "that all was well there."[111] But previous to the visitation John Crofte, a squire, had been urged by both king and bishop to formally renounce his erroneous beliefs.[112] The vicarage at Almeley, where John Oldcastle grew up, was in fairly good shape except for the fact that the vicar's portion was too small and the work too great.[113] At Kington and Whitney the reports were much the same.

Though Bishop Trefnant seemed so intent on eradicating Lollardy from his diocese, it is surprising that so few references to the heresy, apart from the lengthy records of Walter Brut's and William Swynderby's trials, are found in his register. Early in 1392 probable disciples of Swynderby were cited to appear before the bishop. Margaret Laborn and Juliana "filia David Smyth de Salopia" were summoned by Trefnant in February but refused to respond to the citation. The bishop's mandate was reissued in April and then again in December when others were included in the summons.[114] John Ely, a chaplain of Howel, Jevan ap Byvyde, and Matilda Bond were ordered to appear before Trefnant with Margaret and Juliana, cited nearly a year before. But if there were any answers to the citations, they do not appear in the Trefnant register. There may have been some connection between John Ely and a cleric of the same name who appears in the 1397 visitation record as vicar of Winforton, about a mile east of where Swynderby preached. There he was accused of being incontinent.[115] The solicited renunciation of John Crofte in 1395 and 1396 has been cited.[116] Isabella Prustes is the last-mentioned Lollard in fourteenth-century Hereford. Her unorthodox views may have been discovered when Trefnant toured the diocese in 1397, as it was later in that year that she repudiated her heretical beliefs and submitted to the authority of the bishop.[117]

It is possible that the movement took a greater hold on Hereford clergy and parishioners than the records of Trefnant's episcopal register or visitation book suggest. But this does not fit well with the bishop's wide reputation as a hammer of Lollards, nor with the patient and diligent composition of his register. On the other hand, the seeds of the movement had been planted in parts of the diocese and would be nurtured to new growth in the early years of the fifteenth century. John Oldcastle, who as a boy had probably heard William Swynderby preach in the parish church at Almeley, became one of the movement's great martyrs.[118] John Mar, the prior of Wenlock, had shown himself a sympathizer to the Lollard cause and assisted Oldcastle and his fellows on a number of occasions.[119] It was likely that others in Hereford worked to promote Lollardy, but the strength of the movement had been checked for a time, at least until the vigilant Trefnant's reign had ended and the new century had begun.

The life and conduct of Hereford clergy in the half-century following the Black Death are the most difficult to evaluate among the general attributes of pastoral care discussed in this chapter. Indeed, it is often in this area that the differences are greatest between the achieved excellence of Chaucer's Parson and the lapses great and small of Hereford clergy. We cannot ignore the fact that the crimes of the latter did appear in judicial records and episcopal registers, but neither can we conclude that all parish clergy were as likely to forget their vows, or frequent taverns, or nurse heretical sympathies. It was the nature of official church records to document on a far more regular basis the sins and failings of clergy and parishioners than their achievements or contributions. Even when Trefnant's scribe summarized the comments of parishioners in the visitation register by saying that "all was well" in a particular parish, he did not expand on what the phrase meant. Perhaps the good was privately praised, but the sins were almost always a matter of official record. One will occasionally find in the bishops' registers notes to the contrary, usually letters testimonial written as positive references for a cleric in search of new employment or on leave from his parish and the diocese. In one of these Bishop Trillek was more than usually descriptive. In a letter written on behalf of Ralph de Brugge, vicar of Bridge Sollers (the circumstances which prompted it are not given), the bishop called the curate a man of honesty, goodness, and eminently good conduct. According to his own parishioners he cared for his people by his good example and his praiseworthy leadership in liturgy and prayer.[120] The vicar of Bridge Sollers may well have been the exception to the rule. Certainly, our general impression of parish clergy at the end of the fourteenth century is not usually this flattering. But, perhaps, the real exception lies in the nature of this record. We find few references to good and able pastors, not because there were none but because they merely did what was expected of them and in so doing failed to draw the attention usually accorded their more infamous brothers. In any case, were we to know something more about Ralph de Brugge, he might come closer to the pastoral ideals represented in Chaucer's illustrious Parson.

To contemporaries, what was most attractive about Chaucer's Parson was the quality of his life and the ways in which the Christian virtues of faith, hope, and charity were so evident in his pastoral care. His integrity in this manner was enough, it seemed, to set him apart from the lesser lot of other clergy. The apparent disparities in moral rigor suggested here have almost become an accepted conclusion among historians of the late medieval English Church, and every record of clerical deficiency is an affirmation of this portrait of decline. But in the good vicar of Bridge Sollers there are other images of pastoral strength hidden among records which typically portray clerics in a harsher light. By the same token, there is little reason to believe that learning for the cure of souls was badly threatened in late fourteenth-century Hereford. It had certainly changed and clerics were faced with new challenges in the fewer opportunities available for formal education in preparation for Holy Orders. But there were no apparent concessions on the part of bishops of Hereford regarding the conditions of literacy and learning among clerical candidates; neither was there a suspicious rise in dispensations from the traditional impediments to the sacrament and ministry. Last, there was no clear evidence in the records that the post-plague influx of poorly qualified men to holy orders, reported by the canon of Leicester, much affected the churches west of the Severn. Certainly, clerics came in less number, but they came with the basic qualifications required of their order and, it must be remembered, the foundations — even the promise — of an education were considered hopeful beginnings for pastoral training. Ordination was an approbation of the promise and desire that each candidate possessed; pastoral life was something to be lived.

The challenges of the cure of souls the Parson seemed to have met with such firm resolve were to be found in the daily routine of every parish priest. But to do the work well meant that the curate had to have some learning and reside as a permanent member of his parish community. There were lapses in this requirement in post-plague Hereford, but they diminished rather than increased in number as the century passed. Part of this was owing to the fewer numbers of Hereford clergy and the restricted policies of leave-taking in the years following the Black Death. Although the scarcity of clerics was never critical enough to warrant emergency measures by the bishops, there were cases of a sort of low-level pluralism among the wage-earning clergy in the latter part of the century. This may have been necessitated to some degree by the thinning ranks of the parish clergy, but it may also have been prompted by the poverty which was a constant complaint among salaried priests.

The apparent stability in clerical residence did not indicate the quality of that presence. The visitation record of 1397 is evidence that the parish clergy were not always living according to the ideals of their calling. Parishioners frequently pointed out the sexual sins of their pastors, but the former were often more concerned with public drunkenness or patent abuses that brought scandal to their church. The notoriety that sprang from a cleric's sin was often deemed graver than the sin itself. There was little evident change after the Black Death in the number or nature of crimes which brought Hereford clerics to a secular court and then to a bishop's jail. Penances continued to be exacted here as in any determined violation of the clerical code. It was always a concern of bishops that sinful clergy posed the greatest danger to the spiritual well-being of their flocks. Thus, when heretical opinions were preached from Hereford pulpits in the last decades of the century, bishops Gilbert and Trefnant moved to cut short the growth of Lollardy in their diocese. What inclined certain churches to welcome enthusiasts like Swynderby and Brut is unclear, but some sympathy for their message must have been present in the clergy and parishioners of those churches. Yet the interest in heterodox opinions did not mean wholesale reception of the same; few Hereford clerics were brought up on charges of Lollardy before Bishop Trefnant or any other bishop for that matter. The laity seemed more receptive to Wycliffe's followers, but the men and women cited by the bishop to answer questions on heresy were very few indeed. The tendency is to focus attention on the few who left the orthodox fold and stood by the new teaching. But we must consider as well the many who were not so inclined and the local diligence necessary in checking the wider spread of heresy. Hereford pastors continued to preach right doctrine to their parishioners and may themselves have joined their bishop in attacking heretical sentiments in their own parishes. Some of these clerics may have been numbered among the many parishes where testators in 1397 asserted that "all was well" in their churches.

In the end it is clear that when John Trefnant toured his diocese in the last years of the fourteenth century, he was not looking for Chaucer's

Parson. Had he found him he might have suspected something in the man's marvelous detachment from church revenues or in his principled egalitarianism. Trefnant was looking for orthodox men, priests who showed basic abilities and good instincts when it came to leading their people on the road to salvation. The bishop did not overlook pecadillos of clerical incontinence or ministerial sloth, but neither did he make more of them than was required. Clerics were properly chastized or given the opportunity to purge themselves with witnesses to their innocence. More was at stake when parishioners were swayed by clergy who were unsound in their own beliefs. Given the evidence of his episcopal register, Trefnant was primarily concerned about the inroads of heresy in his diocese. For the time being, the followers of Wycliffe had not won too many converts among Hereford parishioners and clergy. There were some problems in Almeley and perhaps at Minsterworth and a few other parishes, but most Wycliffites in Hereford in this earlier stage were university men. It would be different in a decade or two.

The diocese of Hereford had changed considerably since Trefnant was a boy; the place had always been poor but by the end of the century the burden of poverty was even greater. Parishes were harder to manage in economically depressed times after the Black Death and the moral neglect of Hereford parishes by their rectors only exacerbated problems in pastoral care. Manses were in ruins, chancel roofs were open to the elements, and fewer churches could afford to hire assisting clergy from the meager revenues generated. But it was also true that there were simply fewer clergy around: Trefnant had ordained far fewer men than any of his predecessors in the fourteenth century. What he had to do, then, was secure the parishes as best he could and this was much of what was behind the visitation of 1397. Had he allowed himself the leisure of wistful recollections, Trefnant might have joined Knighton and Gower in pining for the days of old. The life of medieval pastors was as varied as the society in which they lived or as diversified as that company which left the Tabard for Canterbury. Numbered among the pastors of the fourteenth century were those who, like Chaucer's "poure Persoun" and the good vicar of Bridge Sollers, labored quietly and effectively in their parishes. There were also those, better known to us, who were less able and less devoted to the cure of souls.

Conclusion

Epidemic plague in England did not end with the fourteenth century. In the early years of John Trefnant's successor, the Carmelite Robert Mascall, plague would once again trouble the kingdom and the diocese. In August 1407 Bishop Mascall received a letter from Archbishop Arundel commanding him to oversee masses, prayers, and processions in the cathedral and parish churches of Hereford on account of the many ills that menaced England in those days. Numbered among them was the schism that refused to end and the current civil strife that threatened Henry IV's crown and the peace of England. But of all the trials Arundel recounted, the one that seemed gravest in the letter was the pestilence then threatening the country. The correspondence was all too similar to one shared by Bishop Stratford of London and John Trillek of Hereford nearly sixty years before.[1] And just as that first plague moved implacably towards Hereford's borders, so too did this latest.

The mandates *ad orandum pro pestilentia* had acquired a numbing familiarity to Hereford clergy and parishioners over the last decades. The news was always fearsome, but the novelty of special processions and prayers and, perhaps, the hope as well that should have been their fruit, had diminished. Countless families and communities had been touched by death over the long season of mortality, for there had been eleven separate outbreaks of epidemic plague since the Great Pestilence of 1348.[2] So, when Bishop Mascall had the news broadcast through the diocese there were doubtless those who responded anew with fitting expressions of piety while others wondered at the depth of human misery and sin or the unrelenting judgment of God.

More than ritual expressions surrounding sickness and death had changed in the diocese in the last sixty years. Nearly half the diocesan clergy had been struck down in the first plague and subsequent outbreaks continued to erode clerical and lay communities alike. In spite of the activities of the bishops to shore up the diminished numbers of local pastors, it would take another century and a half before the general population and its clerical cohort were restored to something approaching pre-plague levels.[3] Parishioners suffered the deaths of neighbor and kin, and poor parishes struggled to maintain an economic base adequate to support the church and its ministries. And what happened in the parish communities occurred in other places as well. Religious houses diminished in size, some never to recover from the ravages of plague. The number of religious advanced to Holy Orders soared during the plague years, telling of new needs for pastoral care to religious houses. Often struggling to keep their own communities financially secure, some houses were less vigilant in overseeing the pastoral care of the parish churches whose revenues they had appropriated. It was far more difficult for the poorer houses, hospitals, and places of charity.

All these changes in the religious and pastoral dimensions of the church took place within structures and institutions that been greatly tested during and after the Black Death and proved impressively resilient. The fourteenth-century church had inherited a strong institutional framework from the ecclesiastical reforms and the process of centralization that had been among the great legacies of the previous century. Certainly it was not merely the structures that kept the church going, but the individuals and communities who developed them and for whom they made sense. Still, however durable these structures were, the recovery they helped foster in the wake of the plague was only gradually achieved. Social and economic repercussions from the Black Death would continue to be felt long after the event. Even if we credit the foundations and walls of the pastoral edifice with a certain resilience, we have to concede that some aspects of the fabric had changed in significant ways.

The basic features of the parish community remained unchanged after the Black Death: ritual expressions of the faith of the local community went on much as they had before. But provision for prayer and ministry had changed. There were fewer curates to do the pastoral work in Hereford's parishes and those that held cures were stretched between increased responsibilities, either from a certain sense of priestly duty or out of a desire to augment their meager wages. Parishes that had once supported small communities of clergy of varying ranks in orders had to get by with far fewer and sometimes none. The solitude of the parochial cure, especially those churches in the remote and sparsely populated countryside, must have worn on the pastors of the late fourteenth century and accounted, in some measure, for the lapses in clerical celibacy. Local curates found assistance where they could, and this was one incentive for the further development of an office that had begun to appear in parish communities before the Black Death. The *custos* or churchwarden was a parochial administrator, a parishioner who had a mind for business and could provide some aid to the management of the cure by keeping the parish's financial operations and records in order. A further change occurred in patronage with clerical candidates moving increasingly away from traditional, familial sources of support to sponsorship by local religious communities. Schools and educational opportunities underwent changes as well over the course of the fourteenth century. The cathedral school's reputation had been tarnished, traditional if modest stipends for junior clerics in the parish had all but disappeared, and fewer rectors allowed themselves the hope of spending time at a university away from their cures. But here again restriction forced innovation and change: more clergy were acquring a pastoral education from the growing volume of pastoral manuals, homilaries, and mass-books available in the late fourteenth and early fifteenth centuries.

These changes that took place within the apparently durable structures of church life point to a question with which this study began: was there a decline in the standards of the parish clergy in the decades following the Black Death? Any answer to this question needs to be qualified in two general ways: first, the plague's effects were far from following a single direction of impact and response. In fact, the further one moves from the event of plague itself, the greater the possibility that other forces, perhaps only distantly related to the changes associated with the plagues, entered to influence developments in institutions and their management. Certainly, by the end of the fourteenth century there had been an accumulation of dismal events that had added greater burdens to the church and its pastoral mission. Men of letters would recall the plague as the watershed event between better days and the difficulties of the present. But their perceptions and others' had been shaded by some of the larger social and economic changes that had gone on in England and the church during the second half of the century. The schism that dominated the higher echelons of ecclesiastical power revealed the weakness that plagued even the greatest authorities in the church. Some priests had earned notorious reputations for leading crowds of peasants in their campaigns against customary obligations and traditional wage scales. Other preachers were drawn to the new and dangerous opinions of John Wycliffe and his followers, and Hereford pulpits became yet another source of dismay and division in some communities. Thus, there can be no easy connection between most plague-events and the status of the clergy by the century's end; yet the idea that the Black

Death presented a myriad of problems, institutionally and personally, and required an equally diffused range of responses, cannot be ignored.

Second, the whole question of clerical standards in the late medieval church needs to be weighed carefully. We know from their appearance in the records that medieval clerics were far from uniform in background, their sense of profession, patronage, education, and ecclesiastical status. The large and nondescript categories of "higher" and "lower" clergy reveal very little of the diversity that existed among their ranks, differences among the sons of promise and prosperity, university scholars, wage-earners who were the yeomen of pastoral care, guild chaplains, chantrists, royal clerks, and poor parsons. The pastoral effectiveness of any of these was based upon a few simple principles: that he have the ability to function freely in the exercise of the church's sacraments, that he do so with regularity and dignity and that he build up rather than neglect or tear down his community. There were almost limitless ways in which these things could be done (or not) and every pastoral act was in some sense shaped by the setting in which it occurred. If any one in the fourteenth century knew this, it was the bishop. As the first pastor of the diocese, he was meant to be the guardian of the apostolic tradition and the preserver of unity among his people. But he knew as well, through his ministers and by his own sight, the disparate nature of his diocese. Even in a place as remote and as small as Hereford, the variety of pastoral concerns was great; each community existed with its own spiritual and human needs; each had its own customs, honored or broken; each its measure of support in seasonal dues and offerings; each its curate by institution or appointment. All of this does not suggest that diversity reigned where unity was needed, but that religious life in the fourteenth century was much influenced by concerns which were, in the end, quite local. Though this was beginning to change somewhat by the end of the century, we look in vain for clear standards set out to be met by parish clergy. What standards did exist were tersely described and sometimes generously interpretated by ecclesiastical authorities. The greatest concerns bishops had at ordination were not so much in the decorous qualities of candidates but in their defects. If a man was free from those few impediments which could threaten his effectiveness as a minister, and if he showed promise for prospering in his office, then there was little reason to dismiss him from the ranks of *ordinandi*. The best standard of a man's work in the pastorate was observed in place, a standard in some sense clarified when parishioners answered the inquiries of diocesan visitors by saying that all was well in their parish.

Still, the picture of pastoral care in Hereford at the century's end is often not a flattering one. In their depositions at Trefnant's visitation, Hereford parishioners provide us with some glaring cases of misfits at the altar, men who were patently inept at exercising the art of arts, some on account of ignorance, poor training and spare opportunity for learning, others out of an incompetence that was not adequately challenged by the usual pastoral authorities of rural dean, archdeacon or bishop. But it must also be said that there was little that was new to the clerical follies of the late fourteenth century saving, perhaps, the first signs of the new heresy and the gathering strength of its first adherents. Priests well before the Black Death had been brought to justice as criminous clerks; they had to be reminded of the need for study; they were put back from ordination or delayed in their institution to a living if their learning was shamefully insufficient. Bishops always had trouble overseeing the work of their subordinates, not only the parish clergy themselves, but the rural deans, archdeacons, and cathedral dignitaries that had so much influence on pastoral care.

Thus the question of a decline in the quality of pastoral leadership does not so much revolve around the degree of change in the diocese as much as its resistance to change. Ecclesiastical structures and operations had withstood a great test in the catastrophe of the Black Death, but it was also true that some of these same institutions and approaches to them had become too fixed and brittle. For example, the institutional demands of the diocese remained pretty much the same after the plague as before, but there were far fewer priests to administer them and far fewer innovations provided by visionary leaders of the post-plague church. It could hardly come as a surprise, then, that the evils of pluralism should fall upon the church in such circumstances. There were plenty of grasping clergy who attempted to collect church benefices as other wealthy men collected land, but in Hereford, as elsewhere, curates already taxed by the ministry of their own parishes felt obliged or pressured to labor in more than one vineyard. Church leadership showed a similar institutional conservatism in the matter of clerical salaries. The wages set for stipendiaries even after the scandalous behavior of clerical mercenaries in the hard times following the plague continued to ignore the poverty of most chaplains and the changing economy of the times. This discrepancy only added to the anxieties over class and opportunity that distinguished the fewer beneficed clerics from their more numerous non-beneficed brothers. It was almost inevitable that bishops like John Trefnant should encounter a low morale and slackened discipline among the poorly paid and just as poorly trained stipendiaries in his tour through the diocese.

There were further changes in society that were too great to ignore: the

Black Death had provoked new struggles or revived old ones regarding the social and economic identities of common laborers. When local and national markets began to rebound in the years following the plague, and people availed themselves of new opportunities in work and status, the clerical life seemed a less desirous choice to many. As traditional forms of alliance and solidarity had changed in many places, so a greater mobility characterized much of society, including the emerging middle class from which most candidates for the clergy came. Old local loyalties declined, and testimonies for titles were steadily connected with institutions of stability such as religious houses, that offered a reputable or at least a familiar name to men little known in the territory.

Reprimanding the bishops of Hereford for not adjusting to the larger changes from without is perhaps too easy an accusation to make. In many ways it is hard to imagine that they could have done much otherwise. They were bound to act within certain limits established by custom, law, and the authorities to which they themselves were subject. Their conservatism was understandable to the extent that innovation of any kind is always cautiously regarded in times of change. Their efforts by and large were devoted to stabilizing the traditional means of assuring salvation. They naturally relied on the structures which had formed them and served as the basis of authority and order in the diocese. At least for Hereford, things might have been far different had a man of less talent and determination than John Trillek been bishop during the plague years. His own response to the pastoral crisis that gathered quickly with the advance of the plague was to be a pastor and to carry out his duties as best he could. We have little reason, given the evidence available, to conclude otherwise. Though the diocese was rocked by yet another plague only months after Trillek's death in 1360, Lewis Charlton was a man equal to his predecessor's talents and abilities. In many ways the challenges he faced were greater than those confronted by Trillek. Charlton witnessed the continuing decline in clerical recruits while attempting to secure the pastoral life of the diocese in spiritually and economically difficult times. The good fortune the diocese had in the quality of its bishops diminished slightly in the brief pontificate of William Courtenay. It was surely not that the young bishop was inept but rather that he seemed preoccupied with other things. His contributions were small and there is little reason to believe that he left the diocese in greater difficulty than he found it. But had Courtenay delivered there the power of his intellect and force of rule that characterized the man later as archbishop, some of the difficulties the diocese continued to experience during John

Gilbert's rule might have been eased. Gilbert, another able man, was too busy with the affairs of state to tend as vigilantly as he might to the local concerns of Hereford parishes and clergy. Indeed, during his years the diocese witnessed the first inroads of heterodox teaching from the followers of John Wycliffe. John Trefnant's arrival came at an auspicious time. Intelligent and self-possessed, he was content to busy himself with the cure of souls and the administration of his beleaguered diocese. Perhaps overly zealous in bringing errant Christians to trial — he was a litigious prelate — Trefnant was more devoted to the concerns at home than his immediate predecessors had been.

In the diocese of Hereford, as elsewhere, changes in institutions and attitudes gradually took on the accepted forms of church life. Though the Black Death and subsequent epidemics did not alter forever the basic manner of pastoral leadership and care in the diocese, what changes had taken place were far-reaching. They were at first immediate and devastating in the loss of lives occasioned by the plague and the attendant disruptions in society, economy, and religion. Past the crisis of plague, these effects merged with other great forces from within and without that marked this time as an age of adversity: the continued ruin of war, the scandal of the papal schism, and the new ways of thinking and believing that touched the very foundations of the Christian faith. Still, the plague, though one of many factors of change in this period, was the most significant and enigmatic event in the history of the late middle ages. Its origins were enshrouded in mystery and its operations buried in physical realities far beyond the ken of medieval people. Unlike wars and schisms which are the fruit of human folly, the plague was God's judgment on the age and its effects, even when they had disappeared from the superficial structures of church and society, lingered far longer than any military conflict or ecclesiastical argument devised by princes and popes. For generations medieval people would meditate on the violent and random nature of death and impress their musings in poetry, painting, and architecture.[4] Some had turned away in despair from a church that had revealed its human corruptablity and inconstancy in the face of trial. But most medieval Christians continued to search for meaning and identity in this calamity as in any other, through the comforts of the community at prayer and the pastoral care of the church.

Appendix: Statistics and Their Sources

The statistical analyses that appear in this book, mainly with regard to the filling of vacant benefices and clerical recruitment, are based on examinations of the records of those events in the Hereford registers from Thomas Charlton (1327–1344) to John Trefnant (1389–1404). As numbers can be used fast and freely, it is important to acknowledge here how the figures that reveal impressive changes in the pastoral provision of the diocese have been obtained.

There are two main sources of information about ecclesiastical benefices and how they were filled after reported vacancies. The largest and most complete record for the diocese are the memoranda of institutions to benefices, entered in the bishops' registers. The record of institution, even in its original and unabbreviated form, was the summation of an extended procedure. After a candidate was presented to the bishop, the latter issued a commission to the archdeacon or some other commissary to hold an inquiry in a full local chapter of the deanery in which the benefice lay or with several neighboring rectors, vicars, and chaplains, all under oath. The inquest was to conclude on the time and cause of the vacancy, who last presented to the benefice, its annual value, whether any pensions were attached, whether it was under litigation and, finally, some evaluation on the qualifications of the presentee were expected. The results, summarized from the sworn testimony of those individuals consulted, were sent back to the bishop. Only then was he free to institute to the benefice. If his own examination proved successful, the cleric was formally instituted and a record of the event entered into the bishop's register. Induction usually took place shortly thereafter.

The formulaic nature of these memoranda was carried over into the printed bishops' registers in the form of appendices or lists of institutions to benefices accompanying other usual and frequent episcopal acts, such as approval of exchanges, dispensations, and letters dimissory. By and large, the editors of the printed registers were careful to include all the basic information such as the date the institution took place, the name of the candidate, his patron (the one or ones who owned the church advowson), the name of the church, chapel or altar supported by the benefice if it were a cure, occasionally, the name of the person last presented, and the reason for the vacancy. Unfortunately, in the process of distilling all of this into readable information, editors regularly left out information thought inessential, such as where the institution took place, and who actually officiated at it, the bishop himself or a commissary delegated to the task. To supply information otherwise lost, I have compared all institutions noted in the printed registers as having taken place from 1348 to 1350 with their apperance in the form of memoranda in the original manuscript registers.

Not every act of presentation was realized in the form of an institution: some clerics lacked the necessary qualities, others found themselves competing for the benefice which could only be assigned to one, and still others' hopes were frustrated by the arguments of the courts over advowsons, rights of presentation, etc. Still, volume of presentation, whether it includes actual institution or not, can be a measure of change in parish churches, the promotion of certain candidates to the cures, and the exercise of patronage. The royal acts of presentation recorded in the patent rolls illustrate these latter qualities and have been used here as corroborating evidence for the rate of flux in Hereford benefices, especially during seasons of great change. They are also helpful as a complement to the more complete references in the episcopal registers since they sometimes note church vacancies and the deaths of previous incumbents in benefices not directly under episcopal jurisdiction, as in the cases of the cathedral deanery and royal free chapels.

In order to arrive at reasonably accurate statistics — complete figures are impossible as some vacancies and institutions were not recorded — I have examined all records of institution and presentation for the diocese from 1327 to 1404. Each institution was entered into a database in order to more easily manipulate the various data separately entered. For instance, one is able to observe changes in personnel and patronage in a benefice over a length of time by calling up all institutions under a particular church. By the same token, gaps can be seen in the names of deceased incumbents who did not appear as clerics newly instituted to the church in question.

The most extensive sources for the study of medieval clerical recruitment are the ordination lists which survive in Hereford in an unbroken series from 1328 to 1404, the years which embrace the present study. Starting with the register of Thomas Charlton (1322–1344), these lists were written on separate quires and joined to other portions of the register. They were accompanied by records of letters dimissory for Hereford clerics who wished to be ordained by a bishop other than their own. The lists include details about the ordinations themselves — who celebrated the sacrament, when, and where — but their greatest value lies in the names of ordinands, usually from acolyte to priest, sometimes their place of origin in toponymics, or family background in patronymics, and the title or statement of patronage under which they were ordained.

In my calculations for recruitment in the diocese before and after the Black Death, I emphasized provision for parish churches and, accordingly, marked off secular ordinands ordained for Hereford separately from their non-Hereford and regular counterparts. In the seventy-six year span between Thomas Charlton's election and John Trefnant's death in 1404, there were 243 separate ordination ceremonies. Each was celebrated by a bishop of Hereford or a suffragan commissioned for this and other episcopal duties. Of these, 214 ordinations were used as the basis of my statistical studies: 29 were excluded on the grounds that they involved only first tonsure or that no Hereford clerics were ordained on those occasions. (See, for example, the ordination of Exeter clerics by William Courtenay in his register, *Reg. Courtenay*, pp. 15–21, 24–25, 25–27, 27–30, 30–31.)

On a few occasions an ordination date has been corrected from the one given in the printed registers. At times (as in a number of John Gilbert's ordinations) it is merely a matter of adjusting the year from the old to the new style, at others a matter of scribal error.

The table on the next two pages offers annual totals for all three major groups of ordinands as well as grand totals per annum. As such, it does not show the different orders conferred nor the number of ordination ceremonies held that year. It is meant to illustrate only in the broadest terms the annual rate of ordinations according to the secular or regular status of the candidates and recruitment (Hereford seculars) that more directly affected the pastoral care of Hereford parishes. Blanks in a column indicate either the absence of ordinations that particular year or the loss of ordination records.

TABLE APP. 1. Annual Ordination Figures, 1328–1404

Year	Hereford seculars	Non-Hereford seculars	Regulars	Total
1328	475	56	55	586
1329	133	9	15	157
1330	354	89	29	472
1331	274	94	69	437
1332	337	39	62	438
1333	336	132	64	532
1334	394	114	38	601
1335	351	93	53	497
1336	234	108	46	388
1337	152	127	41	320
1338	—	—	—	—
1339	—	—	—	—
1340	285	39	31	355
1341	232	52	14	298
1342	160	42	21	223
1343	324	54	67	445
1344	—	—	—	—
1345	498	137	81	716
1346	545	399	81	1025
1347	86	56	7	149
1348	283	75	35	393
1349	686	505	116	1303
1350	297	651	287	1235
1351	189	287	139	615
1352	153	319	119	591
1353	84	244	79	407
1354	57	46	48	151
1355	68	30	73	171
1356	27	13	13	53
1357	—	—	—	—
1358	30	4	3	37
1359	142	27	15	184
1360	46	19	11	76
1361	—	—	—	—
1362	122	93	65	280
1363	101	37	58	196
1364	61	32	53	146
1365	69	32	49	150
1366	69	20	50	139
1367	114	25	77	216
1368	67	35	49	183

Year	Hereford seculars	Non-Hereford seculars	Regulars	Total
1369	100	24	37	161
1370	70	2	2	74
1371	104	7	19	120
1372	65	19	29	113
1373	121	10	49	180
1374	222	1	53	276
1375	137	1	21	159
1376	—	—	—	—
1377	63	4	24	91
1378	99	7	15	121
1379	153	80	39	272
1380	44	23	39	106
1381	67	2	2	71
1382	92	60	19	171
1383	87	14	11	112
1384	102	42	36	180
1385	185	28	43	256
1386	102	21	55	178
1387	115	38	44	197
1388	54	20	23	97
1389	—	—	—	—
1390	43	0	13	56
1391	80	9	46	135
1392	71	9	60	140
1393	89	47	75	211
1394	46	5	10	61
1395	64	12	29	105
1396	87	30	28	145
1397	69	20	27	116
1398	18	2	6	26
1399	42	16	18	76
1400	71	44	29	144
1401	—	—	—	—
1402	12	3	4	19
1403	1	0	0	1
1404	25	2	4	31

Notes

Introduction

1. Élizabeth Carpentier, "Autour de la Peste noir: Famines et épidémies dans l'histoire du XIVe siècle," *Annales E.S.C.* 17 (1962): 1062–92; and *Une ville devant la peste: Orvieto et la peste noire de 1348*, Démographie et société 7 (Paris: S.E.V.P.E.N., 1962); David Herlihy, "Population, Plague, and Social Change in Rural Pistoia, 1201–1430," *Economic History Review* 2d ser. 18 (1965): 225–44; Josiah Cox Russell, *British Medieval Populations* (Albuquerque: University of New Mexico Press, 1949); John Hatcher, *Plague, Population, and the English Economy, 1348–1530* (London: Macmillan, 1977); Barbara F. Harvey, "The Population Trend in England Between 1300 and 1348," *TRHS* 5th ser. 16 (1966): 23–42; J. Ambrose Raftis, "Changes in an English Village After the Black Death," *Mediaeval Studies* 29 (1967): 158–77.

2. J. F. D. Shrewsbury, *A History of the Bubonic Plague in the British Isles* (Cambridge: Cambridge University Press, 1970); see Christopher Morris's critique of Shrewsbury, "Plague in Britain," *The Plague Reconsidered* (Stafford: Local Population Studies, 1977), pp. 37–48; Graham Twigg, *The Black Death: A Biological Reappraisal* (London: Batsford, 1984); Mary Kilbourne Matossian, *Poisons of the Past: Molds, Epidemics, and History* (New Haven, CT: Yale University Press, 1989).

3. For example, Christopher Dyer, *Lords and Peasants in a Changing Society: The Estates of the Bishopric of Worcester* (Cambridge: Cambridge University Press, 1980); M. Mate, "Agrarian Economy After the Black Death: The Manors of Canterbury Cathedral Priory, 1348–91," *Economic History Review* 2d ser. 37 (1984): 341–54; E. Fryde, "The Tenants of the Bishops of Coventry and Lichfield and of Worcester After the Plague of 1348–49," in *Medieval Legal Records*, ed. R. Hunnisett and J. B. Post (London: H. M. Stationery Office, 1978), pp. 224–66.

4. Augustus Jessop, "The Black Death in East Anglia," in his *The Coming of the Friars and Other Historic Essays* (London: T. Fisher Unwin, 1895; reprint 1908), pp. 166–261; Francis A. Gasquet, *The Great Pestilence (A.D. 1348–49)* (London: George Bell and Sons, 1893); idem, *The Black Death of 1348 and 1349* (London: George Bell and Sons, 1893, 1908; rpt. New York: AMS Press, 1977); G. G. Coulton, *The Black Death* (London, 1929); *Medieval Panorama: The English Scene from Conquest to Reformation* (Cambridge: Cambridge University Press, 1938), pp. 493–506.

5. A. H. Thompson, "The Registers of John Gynewell, Bishop of Lincoln, for the Years 1347–1350," *Archaeological Journal* 68 (1911): 300–360; "The Pestilence of the Fourteenth Century in the Diocese of York," *Archaeological Journal* 71 (1914): 97–154.

6. J. Lunn, "The Black Death in the Bishops' Registers" (Ph.D. diss., Cambridge, 1937).

7. Coulton, *Medieval Panorama*, pp. 495–500, 747–50; Shrewsbury, *History of the Bubonic Plague*, pp. 54–125.

8. One exception is R. A. Davies, "The Effect of the Black Death on the Parish Priests of the Medieval Diocese of Coventry and Lichfield," *Historical Research* 62 (1989): 85–90.

9. Philip Ziegler, *The Black Death* (London: Collins, 1969); Robert Gottfried, *The Black Death: Natural and Human Disaster in Medieval Europe* (New York: Free Press, 1983); and Twigg, *The Black Death*. For a summary of much of the work done on the plague and English bishops' registers, see B. I. Zaddach, *Die Folgen Des Schwarzen Todes (1347–51) für den Klerus Mitteleuropas* (Stuttgart: G. Fischer, 1971).

10. Lateran IV, c. 22, Alberigo et al., *Decreta*, p. 245. See also Richard Palmer, "The Church, Leprosy and Plague in Medieval and Early Modern Europe," in *The Church and Healing*, ed. W. J. Shiels, Studies in Church History 19 (Oxford: B. Blackwell, 1982), pp. 79–99.

11. J. Raine, ed., *Historical Papers from the Northern Registers*, Rolls Series (London: Longman, 1873), pp. 395–97.

12. A. H. Thompson, "The Registers of John Gynewell," 309–10; Ziegler, *The Black Death*, pp. 123–24.

13. Coulton, *Medieval Panorama*, p. 494; Gasquet, *The Black Death*, p. 127.

14. *The Register of John de Grandisson, Bishop of Exeter (A.D. 1327–1369)*, ed. F. C. Hingeston-Randolph, part II, 1331–1360 (London and Exeter: George Bell and Sons, 1897), p. 1069; *Reg. Trillek*, p. 139.

15. Coulton, *The Black Death*, p. 69; William W. Capes, *The English Church in the Fourteenth and Fifteenth Centuries* (London: Macmillan, 1900), p. 257; Gottfried, *The Black Death*, p. 94.

16. David Smith, *Guide to Bishops' Registers of England and Wales* (London: Royal Historical Society, 1981), pp. 95–104. See also A. Daniel Frankforter, "The Reformation and the Register: Episcopal Administration of Parishes in Late Medieval England," *Catholic Historical Review* 63 (1977): 204–24.

17. The register of Edmund Audley (1492–1502) is the only pre-sixteenth-century register lost from the Hereford archives. D. Smith, *Guide*, p 95.

18. L. M. Midgley, *A Survey of Ecclesiastical Archives*, The Pilgrim Trust (Hereford, 1946–51), pp. 7–10; B. G. Charles and H. D. Emanuel, eds., *A Calendar of the Earlier Hereford Cathedral Muniments*, 3 vols. (1955) and, by the same editors, *A List of Hereford Account Rolls, Court Rolls, Rentals and Surveys* (1955); F. C. Morgan and Penelope E. Morgan, *Hereford Cathedral Libraries and Muniments* (Hereford: Hereford Cathedral Library, 1975), esp. pp. 31–9.

19. R. L. Storey, *Diocesan Administration in the Fifteenth Century*, St. Anthony's Hall Publications 16 (London: St. Anthony's Press, 1959), p. 6; R. M. Haines, *The Administration of the Diocese of Worcester in the First Half of the Fourteenth Century* (London: SPCK, 1965), pp. 3–9; A. Daniel Frankforter, "The Origin of Episcopal Registration Procedures in Medieval England," *Manuscripta* 26 (1982): 67–89.

20. William W. Capes, *Charters and Records of Hereford Cathedral* (Hereford, 1908); Morgan and Morgan, *Hereford Cathedral Libraries and Muniments*.

21. See pp. 82–86.

22. *Calendar of Patent Rolls*, Public Record Office, vols. 1301–1307 to 1404–1405 (London 1891–1916).

23. PRO E. 179 30/7 and 30/21.

24. W. H. Bliss, ed., *Calendar of Entries in the Papal Registers relating to Great Britain and Ireland, Petitions to the Pope A.D. 1342–1419*, vol. 1 (London: H. M. Stationery Office, 1896–); W. H. Bliss and J. A. Twemlow, eds., *The Calendar of Entries in the Papal Registers relating to Great Britain and Ireland, Papal Letters, 1198–*, 14 vols. (London: Eyre and Spottiswoode, 1893–).

25. Shrewsbury, *History of the Bubonic Plague*, p. 22; Twigg, *The Black Death*; Matossian, *Poisons of the Past*.

26. Carpentier, "Autour de la Peste Noire".

Chapter One

1. Joseph Hillaby, "The Origins of the Diocese of Hereford," *TWNFC* 42 (1976): 16–52; M. Deanesly, *Sidelights on the Anglo-Saxon Church* (London: A. & C. Black, 1962), pp. 4–5.

2. John Duncumb, *Collections Towards the History and Antiquities of the County of Hereford* 3 vols. (Hereford: E. G. Wright, 1804–82); Robert W. Eyton, *Antiquities of Shropshire*, 12 vols. (London: J. R. Smith, 1853–60); H. W. Phillott, *Diocesan Histories: Hereford* (London: SPCK, 1888); *VCH* Shropshire, ii, pp. 1–3; *VCH* Gloucestershire, ii, pp. 13–14.

3. *Reg. Mascall*, p. 87.

4. Russell, *British Medieval Populations*, pp. 118–46; "The Clerical Population of Medieval England," *Traditio* 2 (1944): 177–212.

5. *VCH* Shropshire, ii, p. 3. On deaneries and county hundreds, see A. H. Thompson, *English Clergy*, p. 64.

6. W. A. Pantin, *The English Church in the Fourteenth Century* (Cambridge: Cambridge University Press, 1955), pp. 9–26; J. R. L. Highfield, "The English Hierarchy in the Reign of Edward II," *TRHS* 5th ser. 6 (1956): 115–138; Kathleen Edwards, "Bishops and Learning in the Reign of Edward II," *Church Quarterly Review* 138 (1944): 57–86; "The Political Importance of the English Bishops during the Reign of Edward II," *EHR* 59 (1944): 311–47.

7. *Reg. Gilbert*, pp. ii, 19.

8. G. Le Bras, *Institutions ecclésiastiques de la Chrétienté medievale*, Histoire de L'Église, ed. A. Fliche et V. Martin (Paris: Bloud & Gay, 1964) vol. 12, part ii, pp. 355–76; J. Gaudemet, *Le gouvernement de l'Église a l'époque classique*, Histoire du Droit et des Institutions de l'Église en Occident, tôme 8, vol 2, Le Gouvernement Locale (Paris: Éditions Cujas, 1979), pp. 115–38. For England, see A. H. Thompson, *English Clergy*, pp. 1–39.

9. *Reg. Swinfield*, p. iv.

10. *Dist.* 25, c. 1; 93, c. 24.

11. For the importance of examination and recruitment, see Chapter Four, pp. 107–9.

12. Lateran III, c. 8.

13. *Statutes*, ii, p. 62.

14. On the important role of the bishop at visitation, see Christopher R. Cheney, *Episcopal Visitation of Monasteries in the Thirteenth Century* (Manchester: Manchester University Press, 1931); Nöel Coulet, *Les visites pastorales*, Typologie des Sources du Moyen Âge Occidental fasc. 23 (Turnhout: Brepols, 1977); A. H. Thompson, *Visitations in the Diocese of Lincoln, 1517–1531*, 3 vols., Lincoln Record Society nos. 33, 35, 37 (Lincoln, 1936, 1938 and 1940).

15. Duncumb, *Collections*, 1:506; Kathleen Edwards, *The English Secular Cathedrals in the Middle Ages*, 2d ed. (Manchester: Manchester University Press, 1967), pp. 155–58.

16. *Statutes*, p. 60; HCA 2710.

17. *Extra* I.23, c. 1; A. Amanieux, "Archdiacre," *DDC*; A. H. Thompson, "Diocesan Organization in the Middle Ages: Archdeacons and Rural Deans," *Proceedings, British Academy* 29 (1943): 153–67.

18. P. Andrieu-Guitrancourt, *Essai sur l'evolution du decanat rural en angleterre* (Paris: Librairie de Recueil Sirey, 1935); Thompson, "Diocesan Organization," 164–94; Jean Scammell, "The Rural Chapter in England from the Eleventh to the Fourteenth Century," *EHR* 86 (1971): 1–21.

19. *Reg. Trillek*, pp. 32, 34, 75; *Reg. Cantilupe*, pp. 46, 97, 131; *Reg. Orleton*, pp. 264, 313.

20. Irene Churchill, *Canterbury Administration* (London: SPCK, 1933), i, p. 81; Charles Trice Martin, ed., *Registrum Epistolarum Johannis Peckham Archiepiscopi Cantuariensis (1279–92)*, Rolls Series (London: Longman, 1882–85) i, p. 74.

21. A. H. Thompson, "Diocesan Organization," p. 185; Peter Heath, *The English Clergy on the Eve of the Reformation* (London: Routledge and Kegan Paul, 1969), p. 113.

22. *Reg. L. Charlton*, pp. 53–57; Churchill, *Canterbury Administration* i, pp. 161–240, 551–70.

23. *Reg. Trillek*, pp. 118–19; *Reg. Gilbert*, pp. 89–90. See also R. Storey, *Diocesan Administration*, pp. 9–16.

24. Cheney, *English Bishops' Chanceries, 1100–1250* (Manchester: Manchester University Press, 1950), pp. 1–21.

25. Cheney, *Chanceries*, p. 103; Frankforter, "Origins of Episcopal Registration Procedures," pp. 67–89.

26. *Reg. T. Charlton*, pp. 16–17; 67–68.

27. Statutes of Exeter II (1287), c. 28, *Councils and Synods* II, ii, 1025–26.

28. Statutes of Lincoln (1239?), *Councils and Synods* II, i, 273. See in general, P. H. Ditchfield, *The Parish Clerk* (New York: Dutton, 1907).

29. *Reg. T. Charlton*, pp. 67–68; see also R. A. R. Hartridge, *A History of Vicarages in the Middle Ages* (Cambridge: Cambridge University Press, 1930), pp. 130–37.

30. W. Lyndwood, *Provinciale*, Lib. III, tit. 23, c. 9.

31. See p. 24.

32. *Reg. Trillek*, pp. 395, 87.

33. *Reg. A. Orleton*, pp. 183–84.

34. Cheney, *Chanceries*, pp. 157–58; *VCH* Shropshire, ii, p. 147. See also *Reg.*

Trillek, pp. 500, 508, and 519 for references to ordination titles "scolarum de Ludlow."

35. A. H. Thompson, "Certificates of the Shropshire Chantries," *TSAS* 4th ser. (1911): 115–89; A. F. Leach counted schools for every chantry in the diocese: *The Schools in Medieval England* (London: Methuen, 1915) pp. 300–301. See also *Reg. Thomas Spofford* (Hereford), ed. A. T. Bannister (Canterbury and York Society, 23, 1919), pp. 281–88.

36. *Reg. Trillek*, p. 56; *Reg. T. Charlton*, p. 189. See also Nicholas Orme, *English Schools in the Middle Ages* (London: Methuen, 1973), pp. 59–65 and *VCH* Gloucester, ii, pp. 314–47.

37. Lateran III, c. 18; Lateran IV, c. 11.

38. *Councils and Synods* II, ii, 1026–27. For other references to the office of holy water clerk and its bearing on educational expenses, see ibid. II, i, 211 (Statutes of Coventry, cc. 5, 19); 309 (Worcester); 514 (Salisbury); 606 (Wells) and 713 (Winchester). On university licenses and their relationship to pastoral instruction, see L. E. Boyle, The Constitution 'Cum ex eo' of Boniface VIII," *Mediaeval Studies* 24 (1962): 274 and, by the same author, "Aspects of Clerical Education," *The Fourteenth Century*, pp. 22–26. For another opinion on the effectiveness of *Cum ex eo*, see R. M. Haines, "The Education of the English Clergy During the Later Middle Ages: Some Observations on the Operation of Pope Boniface VIII's Constitution *Cum ex eo*," *Canadian Journal of History* 4 (1968): 1–22. For a study of *Cum ex eo* licenses in a single diocese, see John R. Shinners, "University Study Licenses and Clerical Education in the Diocese of Norwich, 1325–35," *History of Education Quarterly* 28 (1988): 387–410.

39. Emma Mason, "The Role of the English Parishioner, 1100–1500," *JEH* 27 (1976): 17–29.

40. In general, see J. R. H. Moorman, *Church Life in England in the Thirteenth Century* (Cambridge: Cambridge University Press, 1945), pp. 115–25; R. A. R. Hartridge, *Vicarages*, pp. 1–22; Giles Constable, "Resistance to Tithes in the Middle Ages," *JEH* 13 (1962): 172–85. On the difficulties involved in determining tithe payment and parish membership, see Dorothy Owen, *Church and Society in Medieval Lincolnshire* (Lincoln: History of Lincolnshire Committee, v, 1971), p. 15.

41. Lyndwood, *Provinciale* Lib. I, tit. 3, c 1; see also Hartridge, *Vicarages*, pp. 37, 227–29.

42. Charles Drew, *Early Parochial Organization in England: the Origins of the Office of Churchwarden*, St. Anthony's Hall Publications 7 (London: St. Anthony's Press, 1954) and F. A. Gasquet, *Parish Life in Mediaeval England* (London: Methuen, 1906), pp. 102–12.

43. "Visitation" (1929): 449.

44. A. H. Thompson, "Ecclesiastical Benefices and their Incumbents," *Transactions, Leicestershire Archaeological Society* 22 (1944–45): 1–32.

45. Lateran I, c. 5; Lateran II, c. 10; Lateran III, c. 14; Lyndwood, *Provinciale*, Lib. III, tit. 9, cc. 1–3.

46. Pantin, *English Church*, p. 65.

47. *Reg. Orleton*, p. 388; *Reg. Trillek*, p. 375.

48. See *Registrum Caroli Bothe*, pp. 364–71; the possessions of the Hereford

dean and chapter are listed on pp. 364–65. See also Capes, *Charters and Records*, pp. ii–xii and Kathleen Wood-Legh, "The Appropriation of Parish Churches During the Reign of Edward III," *Cambridge Historical Journal* 3 (1929): 15–22.

49. *Registrum Edmundi Lacy*, pp. 67–81.

50. D. Knowles, *The Religious Orders in England* 3 vols. (Cambridge: Cambridge University Press, 1948–1959), ii, p. 159.

51. J. T. Driver, "The Papacy and the Diocese of Hereford, 1307–77," *Church Quarterly Review* 165 (1947): 31–47.

52. *CPL* ii, p. 195; *Reg. Swinfield*, p. 536; *CPL* ii, p. 405; *CPL* iii, pp. 201, 314; *CPP* i, pp. 103, 418; *Reg. Trillek*, p. 374.

53. *Reg. Cantilupe*, pp. 37, 48.

54. *Reg. Trillek*, pp. 20–21; *Reg. L. Charlton*, pp. 60–62.

55. Capes, *Charters and Records*, p. 70.

56. *Statutes*, ii, p. 78.

57. Edwards, *Secular Cathedrals*, p. 52.

58. *Statutes*, pp. 59–60; Capes, *Charters and Records*, pp. xxvii–xxviii.

59. *Statutes*, p. 71; Edwards, *Secular Cathedrals*, pp. 176–216.

60. Capes, *Charters and Records*, p. 228.

61. HCA 750, 1867; *CPL* iv, p. 390.

Chapter Two

1. *Reg. Trillek*, pp. 137–39.

2. Thompson, "The Registers of John Gynewell," pp. 309–10; and "The Pestilence of the Fourteenth Century," pp. 102–3; Ziegler, *The Black Death*, pp. 123–24.

3. *Reg. Trillek*, p. 139.

4. *Reg. Trillek*, pp. 267–68, 269–70, 277–78, 292–95, 312–16.

5. *Reg. Trillek*, pp. 15–16. When pressed on the matter, Trillek ended up going to the council: pp. 271–72.

6. *Reg. Trillek*, pp. 298–300, 308–9. Later in 1348 the king granted Trillek a bond for repayment of 48 pounds borrowed for the war effort (pp. 135–36).

7. *Reg. Trillek*, pp. 31–33, 62, 76, 90.

8. *Reg. Trillek*, pp. 34, 81–82, 102.

9. *Reg. Trillek*, pp. 60–61, 85–86, 110, 106–7.

10. *Reg. Trillek*, pp. 79, 80, 80–81, 84–85, 91–92, 109–10, 128.

11. *Reg. Trillek*, pp. 84–85, 99–100.

12. *Reg. Trillek*, pp. 141–42. Though the bishop's reprimand is addressed only to the church of "L," Leominster seems the likeliest place given its recent troubles in ecclesiastical discipline.

13. *Reg. Trillek*, p. vii.

14. *Reg. Trillek*, pp. vii, 207–10.

15. *Reg. Trillek*, pp. 174–76.

16. Trevor Rowley, *The Landscape of the Welsh Marches* (London: M. Joseph, 1986), p. 173.

17. Rowley, *Landscape*, p. 174.

18. Arthur T. Bannister, *The Cathedral Church of Herford* (London: SPCK,

1924), p. 116. For the impact of the plague on pilgrimages to the shrine of St. Thomas, see Penelope E. Morgan, "The Effect of the Pilgrim Cult of St. Thomas Cantilupe on Hereford Cathedral," *St. Thomas Cantilupe Bishop of Hereford: Essays in His Honour*, ed. M. Jancey (Leominster: Orphans Press, Ltd., 1982), p. 151.

19. Mary D. Lobel, ed., *Historic Towns: Maps and Plans of Towns and Cities in the British Isles*, I, "Hereford" (Baltimore: Johns Hopkins University Press, 1969), p. 8; *Reg. Trillek*, p. vii.

20. HCA 3210 and, Chapter Three.

21. See, pp. 82–83.

22. *Reg. Trillek*, pp. 171–74; *VCH* Gloucestershire, ii, p. 90.

23. *Reg. Trillek*, p. 89; David Knowles and R. Neville Hadcock, *Medieval Religious Houses, England and Wales* (London: Longmans, 1953), p. 137.

24. *CPR*, February 8, 1352, p. 219.

25. *CPR*, July 7, 1355, p. 259; February 10, 1355, p. 168.

26. See Appendix.

27. These are the rectors and vicars of Bucknell, Great Collington, Culmington, Little Withington, Llanwarne, Newland, Pontesbury, Preston, Stanton Lacy, Stokesay, Talsey, and Tedstone Delamere.

28. *Reg. Trillek*, p. 345; *CPR*, 1338–40, p. 429.

29. See Chapter Three, pp. 73–75.

30. See Moorman, *Church Life in England*, pp. 198–201.

31. See Appendix.

32. W. Maskell, *Monumenta Ritualia Ecclesiae Anglicanae* (1846–47), iii, p. 158.

33. *Reg. Trillek*, pp. 376, 380. For the mass pence rolls, see HCA 431, 423; confirmations of the deaths of Thomas de Staunton and John de Orleton's death can be found in *CPP* i, 169 and *Reg. Trillek*, p. 387 respectively.

34. *Reg. Orleton*, p. 389; *Reg. Trillek*, pp. 375, 377, 380.

35. *Reg. T. Charlton*, p. 81; *Reg. Trillek*, pp. 374, 375, 380.

36. *Reg. Trillek*, pp. 377, 382, 384.

37. *Reg. T. Charlton*, p. 82; *Reg. Trillek*, pp. 375, 376, 378, 379.

38. *Reg. T. Charlton*, p. 82; *Reg. Trillek*, p. 374.

39. *Reg. Trillek*, pp. 527–32, 545–51, 164–65.

40. For examples of smaller ordinations held by Trillek, see *Reg. Trillek*, pp. 419, 458, 464, 475, 497.

41. *Reg. Trillek*, p. 146.

42. "Mundi Thomas furores temperat, sanem pellit, a peste liberat, firmat pacem, salutem reparat, fugat mortem, et vitam comparat." *Hereford Breviary*, ed. W. H. Frere and L. E. G. Brown, 3 vols. (London: Harrison and Son, 1904), ii, p. 360.

43. *Reg. Trillek*, p. 148; *CPP* i, p. 163.

Chapter Three

1. *Reg. Trillek*, pp. 149–50; the royal mandate is also printed in Wilkins, *Concilia* II, p. 752.

2. J. E. Wells, *A Manual of Writings in Middle English 1050–1400* (New Haven, CT: Yale University Press, 1926), p. 389. See also M. Malvern, "An Earnest 'Monys-cyon' and 'Thinge Delectabyll' Realized Verbally and Visually in 'A Disputacion Betwyx the Body and Wormes,' A Middle English Poem Inspired by Tomb Art and Northern Spirituality," *Viator* 13 (1982): 415–43; K. Brunner, "Mittelenglische Todesgedichte," *Archiv für Neure Sprachen* 167, 168 (1935): 20–35.

3. *Reg. Trillek*, pp. 511–19, 519–27.

4. *Reg. Trillek*, pp. 154–55, 532–38, 538–45.

5. Trillek commissioned Ewe along with Bishop Ralph Stratford of London and the Abbot of Walden. *Reg. Trillek*, p. 153.

6. *Reg. Trillek*, p. 168. Trillek would ask to be excused from Parliament again the following summer and ask the king to accept his proctors, including his brother, Thomas Trillek, on his behalf (August 10, 1352), p. 181.

7. *Reg. Trillek*, p. 179.

8. *Reg. Trillek*, pp. 196–97.

9. *Reg. Trillek*, pp. 178–79.

10. *Reg. Trillek*, pp. 176–77; "As a cell this house appears to have maintained a prior and two monks at most." Knowles and Hadcock, *Medieval Religious Houses*, p. 71.

11. The case was finally resolved in the bishop's favor. *Reg. Trillek*, pp. 182, 236–38, 238–40.

12. *Reg. Trillek*, p. 194.

13. *Reg. Trillek*, pp. 227–30, 246–47.

14. *Reg. Trillek*, pp. 171–74.

15. *Reg. Trillek*, p. 176.

16. *Reg. Trillek*, pp. 246–47, 253.

17. *Reg. Trillek*, pp. 174–76.

18. *Reg. Trillek*, pp. 235–36.

19. *Reg. Trillek*, pp. 252–53.

20. Peter Heath, *Church and Realm 1272–1461* (London: Fontana, 1988), pp. 135–38.

21. *Reg. Trillek*, pp. 185–89, 338.

22. *Reg. Trillek*, p. 193.

23. *Reg. Trillek*, pp. 354–55, 357.

24. *Reg. Trillek*, pp. 357, 360.

25. *Reg. Trillek*, pp. 361–62, 368.

26. *Reg. Trillek*, pp. 371–72.

27. On clerical recruitment, see pp. 103–9.

28. *Extra* I.11, cc. 13, 15.

29. *Reg. Trillek*, pp. 485, 491, 495, 502.

30. *Reg. Trillek*, p. 379.

31. See, for example, petitions by Zouche of York (*CPP* i, p. 178; *CPL* iii, p. 332); Islip of Canterbury (*CPP* i, p. 189; *CPL* iii, p. 335) and the Abbot of Reading (*CPP* i, p. 282).

32. *CPP* i, p. 180; *CPL* III, p. 334.

33. *CPL* i, p. 189.

34. *Sext.* 1.6, 14.

35. *Extra* I.14, c. 5.

36. See Chapter Five, pp. 123–24.

37. *Reg. Trillek*, pp. 395–97.

38. The date of this exchange is given incorrectly in the printed register as 1355. See the institution for Neen Savage in *Reg. Trillek*, p. 382.

39. Bertha H. Putnam, *The Enforcement of the Statute of Labourers During the First Decade After the Black Death, 1349–1359*, Columbia University Studies in History, Economics, and Public Law 32 (New York: Columbia University Press, 1908) and Ada E. Levett, "A Note on the Statute of Labourers," *Economic History Review* iv (1932): 77–80.

40. *Reg. Trillek*, pp. 321–22.

41. *Reg. Trillek*, pp. 157–59 and Wilkins, *Concilia* III, pp. 1–2.

42. *Reg. Trillek*, pp. 323–24. Though the result of this case is unknown, the archdeacon must have been vindicated, as he continued in his post through Trillek's rule, was later Precentor of the cathedral, and appointed by Lewis Charlton to be his *officialis* in 1368: *Reg. L. Charlton*, p. 47.

43. *Reg. Trillek*, p. 231.

44. *Reg. Trillek*, p. 92.

45. *Reg. Trillek*, pp. 19–21.

46. *Reg. Trillek*, p. 232.

47. The licenses for preachers and confessors after 1355 are for the most part contained in the register of Lewis Charlton, where a fly-leaf from Trillek's register containing the names and presentors of these confessors was attached at some later date. See *Reg. L. Charlton*, pp. 61–62.

48. *Reg. Trillek*, pp. 364–68.

49. *Reg. Trillek*, pp. 369, 370–71, 629, 630–31.

50. *Reg. Trillek*, pp. x–xi.

51. *Reg. Trillek*, p. xi.

52. *CPR*, 1358–1361, p. 507.

53. *Reg. L. Charlton*, p. 1; *CPR*, 1361–1364, p. 106.

54. Phillott, *Diocesan Histories: Hereford*, p. 108.

55. *Anonimalle Chronicle*, ed. V. H. Galbraith (Manchester: Manchester University Press, 1927), p. 50. See also *VCH* Lincoln II, p. 315 for reports of death among children and, in general, Shrewsbury, *History of the Bubonic Plague*, p. 128.

56. See Chapter Two, pp. 51–52.

57. Thomas Rymer, *Foedera* (London: J. Tonson, 1726–35) v, p. 655.

58. PRO E, 179 6/28. The precise date of Trewlove's adjournment is not given.

59. *Reg. L. Charlton*, pp. 1–3.

60. *Reg. L. Charlton*, pp. 76–80.

61. *Reg. L. Charlton*, pp. 7–8.

62. *Reg. L. Charlton*, pp. 8–10.

63. The settlement was arranged on June 14, 1367. *Reg. L. Charlton*, pp. 42–43.

64. *Reg. L. Charlton*, p. 48.

65. *CPL* 4.32 (October 16, 1363).

66. *Reg. L. Charlton*, pp. 76–80, 80–82, 82–84.

67. *Reg. L. Charlton*, pp. 86–122 passim.
68. *Reg. L. Charlton*, pp. 32–33. In a letter written on September 15 the bishop of Llandaff reported to Charlton that his request had been carried out: p. 34.
69. *Reg. L. Charlton*, pp. 41–42.
70. *Reg. L. Charlton*, pp. 38, 45–46.
71. *Reg. L. Charlton*, pp. 47, 50.
72. *Reg. L. Charlton*, pp. 50–51.
73. Many of the documents that emerged in the course of this *"lis immortalis,"* as contemporaries called it, were destroyed, but a lengthy court roll of some thirty-one of these documents is preserved in the archives of the Hereford Dean and Chapter: HCA 3024–3212. In the mid-1950s Prebendary S. H. Martin wrote an article surveying the major points of the case; his research into these fascinating documents serves as the basis for much of what follows here. See S. H. Martin, "The Case of Roger Syde Versus the Dean and Chapter of Hereford," *TWNFC* 35 (1955–7): 156–62.
74. *Reg. Swinfield*, pp. 15–16, 213; *Reg. Orleton*, pp. 66–67; *Reg. Trillek*, pp. 105–6, 121, 122, 124–25. See also Julia Barrow, ed. *English Episcopal Acta VII: Hereford 1079–1234* (Oxford: Oxford University Press, 1993), p. 104.
75. Celia Wenlock led the group of witnesses with her testimony on September 22, 1363: HCA 3210.
76. The owners of the advowson to St. Peter's, the Benedictine priory of St. Guthlac's in Hereford, disagreed with this assertion. See Martin, "Syde Versus the Dean," p. 159 and HCA 3206.

Chapter Four

1. According to one chronicler, this plague was said to affect both humans and larger animals. *Adam of Murimuth's Chronicle*, p. 178; Shrewsbury, *History of the Bubonic Plague*, p. 134.
2. Courtenay was consecrated in March, 1370 and enthroned in the cathedral later that year on September 15. *Reg. Courtenay*, pp. 1–5.
3. *Reg. Courtenay*, pp. 6–7.
4. *Reg. Courtenay*, pp. 15–21.
5. R. L. Storey, "Recruitment of English Clergy in the Period of the Conciliar Movement," *Annuarium Historiae Conciliorum* 7 (1975): 290–313; R. K. Rose, "Priests and Patrons in the Fourteenth Century Diocese of Carlisle," in *The Church in Town and Countryside*, Studies in Church History 16 (Oxford: B. Blackwell, 1979): 207–18; JoAnn Hoeppner Moran, "Clerical Recruitment in the Diocese of York, 1340–1530: Data and Commentary," *JEH* 34 (1983): 19–54; Heath, *The English Parish Clergy*, p. 16.
6. See Chapter Three, pp. 67–70.
7. F. Clayes Bouaert, "Dimissoriales (Lettres)," *DDC* 4, cols. 1244–50; see also David Robinson, "Ordination of Secular Clergy in the Diocese of Coventry and Lichfield, 1332–1358," *Archives* 73 (1985): 3–21. For a contrary opinion on letters dimissory, see Storey, "Recruitment of English Clergy," p. 293.

8. For a more complete view of the data on clerical recruitment, see Appendix.

9. It should be noted that any discrepancies in the lists — repetitions among ordinands or the disqualifying instructions which occasionally appear alongside an ordinand's name — have been calculated into the figures here. Given the small number of such modifications, the changes with regard to the larger trends in clerical recruitment are negligible.

10. *Reg. Trillek*, pp. 468–70.

11. *Reg. Trillek*, pp. 515–51; see also R. M. Haines, ed., *A Calendar of the Register of Wolstan de Bransford, Bishop of Worcester, 1339–49* (London: H. M. Stationery Office, 1966), pp. li–lii.

12. Thomas Charlton received his Crown appointment in July, 1337 when he was ordered to assume the responsibilities formerly held by his brother John. He left the diocese shortly after receiving the king's mandate and did not return until April 1340. He resumed his ordination activity in Hereford the following June. *Reg. T. Charlton*, p. v, 177–81 and *CPR*, 1327–1330, p. 381.

13. *Reg. Trefnant*, p. 230.

14. *Reg. Mascall*, pp. 125–27.

15. Compare, for example, the studies of J. C. Russell, *British Medieval Population* and "The Pre-plague Population of England," *Journal of British Studies* 5 (May, 1966): 23–42 with M. M. Postan, "Some Economic Evidence of the Declining Population in the Later Middle Ages," *Economic History Review* 2d. ser. 2 (1950): 221–46. See also G. Ohlin, "No Safety in Numbers: Some Pitfalls of Historical Statistics," in *Industrialization in Two Systems: Essays in Honor of Alexander Gerschenkron*, ed. K. Rosovsky (New York: Wiley, 1966), pp. 68–90.

16. T. H. Hollingsworth, *Historical Demography* (Ithaca, NY: Cornell University Press, 1969). See also Barbara Harvey, "The Population Trend in England Between 1300 and 1348," *TRHS* 5th ser. 16 (1966): 23–42 and J. Z. Titow, *English Rural Society 1200–1350*, Historical Problems: Studies and Documents 4, ed. G. R. Elton (London: Allen and Unwin, 1969), pp. 66–73.

17. John of Reading described the plague of 1361 as taking with it most of the male population. See *Anonimalle Chronicle*, p. 169. On plague and demography, see M. F. and T. H. Hollingsworth, "Plague Mortality Rates by Age and Sex in the Parish of St. Botolph's Without Bishopsgate, London, 1603," *Population Studies* 25 (1971): 131–46 and *The Plague Reconsidered* (Stafford: Local Population Studies, 1977), p. 8; E. A. Wrigley and R. S. Schofield, *The Population History of England, 1541–1871* (London: Edward Arnold, 1981), pp. 228–48, 363–68.

18. T. H. Hollingsworth, *Historical Demography*, pp. 378–79.

19. R. A. Butlin, "The Late Middle Ages, c. 1350–1500," in *An Historical Geography of England and Wales*, ed. R. A. Dodgshon and R. A. Butlin (London: Academic Press, 1978), pp. 119–50.

20. R. Storey, "Recruitment," p. 304; Ziegler, *The Black Death*, pp. 248–59.

21. B. Putnam, *The Enforcement of the Statute of Labourers* and, by the same author, "Maximum Wage-Laws for Priests after the Black Death," *American Historical Review* 21 (1915–16): 12–32.

22. Wilkins, *Concilia* III, pp. 1–2.

23. H. G. Richardson, "The Parish Clergy in the Fourteenth and Fifteenth Centuries," *TRHS* 3rd ser. VI (1912): 89.

24. Wilkins, *Concilia* III, 50–51 (November 16, 1362) and pp. 135–36 (November 26, 1378).

25. Ada E. Levett, *Studies in Manorial History* (Oxford: Clarendon Press, 1938), p. 255; Fryde, "The Tenants of the Bishops of Coventry and Lichfield and of Worcester," p. 226.

26. Wilkins, *Concilia* III, p. 135. See also Storey, "Recruitment," pp. 290–91. See Hartridge, *Vicarages*, in which the author points out that the complaints in the 1360s about excessive wages demanded by stipendiary clergy show that the latter were profiting by the "vacancies in the profession created by the Black Death" (p. 111).

27. "Piers Plowman," A. Prol., ll. 80ff.

28. Gottfried, *The Black Death*, pp. 131–33. These are recorded outbreaks of epidemic disease on a national scale. Local bouts of plague would have only added to the short and long-term problems faced by any community. See John Hatcher, *Plague, Population, and the English Economy, 1348–1530* (London: Macmillan, 1977), p. 17.

29. See Chapter Five, pp. 139–42.

30. *Reg. T. Charlton*, pp. 104–5; *Reg. Trillek*, p. 471; *Reg. Courtenay* (Hereford), pp. 15–31.

31. See, for example, *Reg. Trillek*, pp. 631–32, *Reg. Courtenay*, pp. 31–5, *Reg. Gilbert*, pp. 101–2; 174–75; 175–76; 176–77; 178–79; 179–81; 181–82.

32. Dohar, "Medieval Ordination Lists," pp. 21–25.

33. John de Burgh provides a summary of the examination in the section *de aetate et qualitate ordinandorum* in his *Pupilla Oculi* (London, 1516), lib. 7, cap. iv.

34. R. Naz, "Titre d'ordination," *DDC* vii, col. 1279; on sanctions against fraudulent titles, see *Extra* I.14, c. 13; III.3, c.4; III.5, c. 16; IV.3, c. 45. See also John de Burgh, *Pupilla Oculi* VII, cap. ii and *Reg. A. Orleton*, pp. 303–4 and *Reg. Trillek*, pp. 26–28, 46, 47.

35. *Reg. Gilbert*, pp. 168, 121.

36. *Reg. Gilbert*, p. 173; *Reg. Trefnant*, p. 186.

37. *Reg. Trillek*, pp. 577, 387.

38. *Reg. T. Charlton*, p. 102; *Reg. Trefnant*, p. 375.

39. The three rolls are listed in the PRO as E 179 30/7; 30/10b; and 30/21 respectively.

40. *Reg. T. Cantilupe*, pp. 299–312 passim.

41. Robert Rodes, *Ecclesiastical Administration in Medieval England* (Notre Dame, IN: University of Notre Dame Press, 1977), pp. 115–16.

42. R. N. Swanson, "Titles to Orders in Medieval English Episcopal Registers," in *Studies in Medieval History: Presented to R. H. C. Davies*, ed. Henry Mayr-Harting and R. I. Moore (London: Hambledon Press, 1985) pp. 234, 242. For Carlisle, see R. K. Rose, "Priests and Patrons," pp. 211–12.

43. Robinson, "Ordination of Secular Clergy," p. 14.

44. Henry S. Bennett, "Medieval Ordination Lists in the English Episcopal

Registers," in *Studies Presented to Hilary Jenkinson*, ed. J. Conway Davies (London: Oxford University Press, 1957), pp. 26–27.

45. Swanson, "Titles to Orders," p. 24.

Chapter Five

1. *Chronicon Henrici Knighton, vel Cnitthon, monachi Leycestrensis*, ed. J. R. Lumby, Rolls Series (London: Eyre and Spottiswoode, 1889–95), i, pp. 61–64.

2. *Chronicon*, p. 63.

3. W. A. Pantin, *Canterbury College, Oxford* (Oxford Historical Society, ns VIII, 1950), 3, p. 159; Ziegler, *The Black Death*, pp. 262–63.

4. Lucas Wadding, *Annales minorum seu trium ordinum a S. Francisco Institutorum* (Florence: Quaracchi, 1931-), vol. viii, p. 25.

5. William Langland, *The Vision of William Concerning Piers the Plowman*, ed. W. W. Skeat (Oxford: Oxford University Press, 1886) I, A ii: 148–166; iii: 216–20; B v: 392–441.

6. John Gower, *Confessio Amantis*, ed. H. Morley (London: Routledge and Sons, 1889), p. 34; G. R. Owst, *Preaching in Medieval England* (Cambridge: Cambridge University Press, 1926), p. 26.

7. References to Chaucer's Canterbury Tales are from *The Riverside Chaucer*, ed. F. N. Robinson (Oxford: Oxford University Press, 1988). On the complexity of the Parson's character as well as the other pilgrims, see Lee Patterson, "The 'Parson's Tale' and the Quitting of the 'Canterbury Tales,'" *Traditio* 34 (1987): 331–80 and *Chaucer and the Subject of History* (Madison: University of Wisconsin Press, 1991), especially pp. 3–46; Jill Mann, *Chaucer and Medieval Estates Satire* (Cambridge: Cambridge University Press, 1973); E. Talbot Donaldson, "The Ordering of the 'Canterbury Tales,'" *Medieval Literature and Folklore Studies: Essays in Honor of Francis Lee Utley*, ed. Jerome Mandel and Bruce A. Rosenberg (New Brunswick, NJ: Rutgers University Press, 1970), pp. 193–204.

8. Mann, *Medieval Estates Satire*, pp. 55–67. See also Germaine Dempster, "The Parson's Tale," in *Sources and Analogues of Chaucer's Canterbury Tales*, ed. W. F. Bryan and Germain Dempster (New York: Humanities Press, 1958), pp. 723–60 and Alfred L. Kellogg, "St. Augustine and the Parson's Tale," *Chaucer, Langland, Arthur: Essays in Middle English Literature* (New Brunswick, NJ: Rutgers University Press, 1972), pp. 343–52.

9. The "General Prologue," ll. 477–528.

10. Allegations of Lollard sympathies cannot be fully entertained here, but the very fact that the Parson is on pilgrimage to England's holiest shrine underscores his orthodox qualities. Patterson, *Chaucer and the Subject of History*, p. 44; Margaret Aston, *Lollards and Reformers: Images and Literacy in Late Medieval Religion* (London: Hambledon, 1984), p. 16, n. 61; Anne Hudson, *The Premature Reformation: Wycliffite Texts and Lollard History* (Oxford: Clarendon Press, 1988), pp. 390–92.

11. At his death, Trefnant bequeathed a large number of volumes to the cathedral library, some 66 books in canon and civil law, theology, and liturgy,

including Hugh of St. Victor's *de Sacramentis*, John of Freiburg's *Summa confessorum*, and the *Racionale divinorum officiorum* of William Durandus. *BRUO* iii, p. 1901.

12. HCA 1779. A. T. Bannister transcribed the document, though not completely, in "Visitation Returns in the Diocese of Hereford in 1397," *EHR* 44 (1929): 279–89; 444–53; 45 (1930): 92–101; 444–63. There is no record of the questions Trefnant asked the parish delegations, but judging from their answers he was probably relying on a customary *inquisitio* meant to cover every aspect of parish life from illicit marriages to Sunday markets. See, for example, the *inquisitiones* in *Annales Monasterii de Burton, 1004–1263*, ed. H. R. Luard, *Annales Monastici* i, Rolls Series (London: Longman, Green, Longman, Roberts and Green, 1864–69), pp. 307–10.

13. "But nathelees, this meditacioun I putte it ay under correccioun Of clerkes, for I am nat textueel; I take but the sentence, trusteth weel" (Prologue to the Parson's Tale, ll. 55–58.)

14. John de Burgh, *Pupilla Oculi*, lib. VII, c. 4.

15. "Visitation" (1929): 288.

16. "Visitation" (1929): 289.

17. "Visitation" (1930): 94.

18. "Visitation" (1930): 94.

19. *Reg. Gilbert*, p. 48.

20. *Reg. Gilbert*, pp. 107–8.

21. Wilkins, *Concilia* III, p. 220.

22. The figures in this table represent the number of clerics licensed for study rather than the actual number of licenses granted. All renewals of *Cum ex eo* and other licenses for non-residence are calculated in the figures.

23. Haines, "The Education of the English Clergy," pp. 11ff.

24. Haines, "The Education of the English Clergy," p. 17 and R. N. Swanson, "Universities, Graduates and Benefices in later Medieval England," *Past & Present* 106 (1985): 37.

25. *Reg. T. Spofford*, ed. A. T. Bannister (Canterbury and York Society, 1919), pp. 281–88.

26. 1 Cor. 12: 12–30. Legatine Constitutions of Otto (1237), c. 12; *Councils and Synods* II, i, p. 250; the Constitutions of Ottobono (1268), c. 11, *Councils and Synods* II, ii, p. 761.

27. John Myrk, *Instructions for Parish Priests*, ed. E. Peacock, EETS o.s. xxxi (London, 1868), ll. 947–50.

28. The subject is well described by A. H. Thompson in "Pluralism in the Medieval Church," *Associated Architectural Society Reports and Papers* 33 (1915): 37–73; 34 (1917): 1–26; 35 (1919): 87–108; 36 (1921): 1–21.

29. *Reg. Orleton*, pp. 79–81; *Reg. Trillek*, pp. 43, 83. The returns for the Province of Canterbury are found in *Registrum Simonis de Langham, Cantuariensis Archiepiscopi*, ed. A. C. Wood (Canterbury and York Society 53, 1956), pp. 1–109. The returns for Hereford clergy are located on pp. 39–47. See also Thompson, "Pluralism," pp. 36–38.

30. Council of Oxford (1222), c. 43, *Councils and Synods*, II, i, pp. 119–20.

The Statutes of York, 1241 x 1255, c. 28 prohibited farming parish churches to regulars, especially the patrons of the benefice and absolutely forbade this arrangement with laymen: II, i, p. 491. See also the Constitutions of Ottobono (1268), c. 20, II, ii, p. 769 and c. 15 of the Council of Lambeth (1281), II, ii, p. 910.

31. *Reg. Swinfield*, p. 85; *Reg. Orleton*, pp. 97–98, 239–240.

32. The benefices of St. Guthlac's in Hereford were put out to farm (*Reg. Trillek*, p. 49); Clifford Priory farmed Dorstone for a five-year period (p. 116); Brecon Priory, the church of Bodenham for two years (p. 120); Abbey Dore leased Avenbury for five years (p. 122); Gloucester Abbey, the church of Much Cowarne for five years (p. 246); Aconbury, the church of Wolferlow for five years (p. 247); and Ewyas Priory was licensed to farm Foy church for three years (p. 253).

33. *Reg. Gilbert*, pp. 19, 90, 94.

34. *Reg. Trefnant*, pp. 28–29.

35. See the statements of parishioners in "Visitation" for Vowchurch (1929): 284; Llanrothal: 299; Ruardine (1930): 446; Brilley: 449; Montgomery: 459–60.

36. "Visitation" (1930): 18.

37. "Visitation" (1930): 457.

38. "Visitation" (1930): 93.

39. "Visitation" (1930): 459–60.

40. "Litera . . . contra choppe-churches," Wilkins, *Concilia* iii, p. 216.

41. Putnam, *The Enforcement of the Statute of Labourers*. See also "Statutes of Westminster III," 1262 x 1265, c. 27 which states that all churches taxed at a minimum of 50 marks should have a deacon and a subdeacon "continue ministrantes." *Councils and Synods* II, i, p. 709.

42. "Visitation" (1929): 444.

43. "Visitation" (1929): 445.

44. "Visitation" (1929): 445.

45. "Visitation" (1929): 447.

46. "Visitation" (1929): 93.

47. "Visitation" (1930): 450, 93; the vicar of Weobley was absent for shorter periods of time (1929): 296.

48. "Visitation" (1929): 296, 93.

49. "Visitation" (1930): 98.

50. "Visitation" (1930): 457, 458.

51. "Visitation" (1929): 282.

52. "Visitation" (1930): 98.

53. "Visitation" (1929): 283.

54. "Visitation" (1929): 288. Further examples of this included provision for the chapel of Docklaw by the vicar of Leominster (1930): 100; the chapel of Bollinghull by the vicar of Eardisley: 447; and Diddlebury's obligation to the chapel at Mydelhope: 455.

55. "Visitation" (1930): 99.

56. "Visitation" (1930): 452 for Wigmore and Wistanstow; Pontesbury: 462; Hopesay: 458.

57. "Visitation": Much Dewchurch (1929): 287; Castle Goodrich: 444; Much Cowarne (1930): 95; Bishop's Frome: 97; Eardisley: 447.

58. "Visitation" (1930): 447.

59. "Visitation" (1930): 447.

60. "Visitation" (1930): 447.

61. "Visitation" (1930): 455.

62. "Visitation," Peterchurch (1929): 283; Churcham: 452; Pixley (1930): 53; Eardisley: 447; and Habberley: 462.

63. "Visitation" (1930): 289.

64. "Visitation," Llangaren (1929): 447; Felton (1930): 95; Burrington: 451.

65. "Visitation" (1930): 455. Bannister's "Aldon" is a mistranscription of Halford.

66. See, for example, John Trillek's commissions of coadjutors for Ledbury and Lydham. In both cases the clergy, themselves vicars (Coddington and Bishop's Castle), were to carry out the pastoral duties of their incapacitated confreres. *Reg. Trillek*, pp. 233, 236.

67. "Visitation," Bredwardine (1929): 284; Sellack: 446; and Stow (1930): 453. The vicar of Foy was required to repair the walls of his churchyard (1930): 447.

68. "Visitation" (1929): 283; (1930): 454.

69. "Visitation" (1929): 445.

70. "Visitation" (1929): 446, 96.

71. "Visitation" (1930): 95, 452–3. Trefnant had Pauntley's revenues sequestrated until the house was repaired at the expense of the rector, Newent Priory. The *custos* of St. Katherine's Hospital was also the rector of Kempley church; the rectorial manse there was found to be in a similarly bad state and the bishop ordered its immediate repair (453).

72. "Visitation" (1929): 445.

73. "Visitation" (1929): 287; (1930): 95–96. Dilwyn and Bishop's Castle had similar need of liturgical books (1930): 445, 456.

74. "Visitation" (1930): 457, 459.

75. John de Burgh, *Pupilla Oculi*, lib. VII, cap. x.

76. John de Burgh, *Pupilla Oculi*, lib. X, "de vita et honestate clericorum."

77. J. H. Parry, the editor of John Trillek's episcopal register, comments on the jail at Ross: "The punishment of offenders sentenced by ecclesiastical courts was severe enough; nothing could be imagined more dreadful than the bishop's prison discovered in the last century at Ross; an undergound chamber without air, light, or drainage, of which the stone bench and rusty chains shewed plainly the use, could scarcely have been better than the king's gaol." *Reg. Trillek*, pp. viii–ix.

78. *Reg. T. Charlton*, pp. 7, 15.

79. *Reg. Trillek*, pp. 75, 82, 102, 113–14, 231.

80. *Reg. L. Charlton*, pp. 41–42; *Reg. Gilbert*, pp. 45, 113–14; *Reg. Trefnant*, pp. 158–59.

81. *Reg. T. Charlton*, p. 5.

82. *Reg. Trillek*, pp. 323–24; *Reg. L. Charlton*, p. 47.

83. *Reg. Trillek*, pp. 371–72.

84. *Reg. Trillek*, pp. 256–57; 260.

85. *Reg. Gilbert*, pp. 24–25.

86. *Reg. Gilbert*, p. 34.

87. *Reg. Trefnant*, pp. 158–59.

88. *Reg. Trillek*, pp. 35, 108; *Reg. Gilbert*, pp. 77–78, 84.

89. "Visitation" (1929): 287. See also John de Burgh's gloss on Gratian's text on clerical incontinence in the *Decretum*, *Dist.* 32, 81; *Pupilla Oculi*, lib. VII, cap. 10.

90. "Visitation" (1930): 448.

91. Canon Bannister neglected to transcribe the majority of references written in a later hand, attesting to the solutions of some of these cases. He does, however, include several which underline the fact that not every reported transgression was judged a punishable offense. See, for instance, the purgations of the chaplain at Newland (1930): 449 and the priest at Ledbury accused by their parishioners of being incontinent (93).

92. "Visitation" (1929): 297; but the bishop's sentence is not transcribed in Bannister. See HCA 1779, f. 4.

93. "Visitation" (1930): 451–52.

94. "Visitation" (1929): 453.

95. These were the chaplain of St Weonard's (1929): 288, the parish priest at Garway (288), the chaplain at Goodrich (1930): 444, the priest at Howelsfield (450), the chaplain at Leominster (99), and the rector of Wentnor (457).

96. "Visitation" (1929): 288; (1930): 99.

97. "Visitation" (1930): 447.

98. A more thorough discussion of early Lollardy is Charles Kightly's "The Early Lollards, A Survey of Popular Lollard Activity in England, 1382–1428," unpub. Ph.D. thesis, University of York, 1975, pp. 153–216. See also Kenneth B. McFarlane, *Wycliffe and English Nonconformity* (London: English Universities Press, 1972), pp. 107–23; Phillott, *Diocesan Histories*, pp. 129–34; and Owst, *Preaching*, pp. 121–43.

99. Kightly, "The Early Lollards," p. 153.

100. The royal grant for the chancellorship was issued on February 22, 1377: CCR 1374–77, p. 429; Capes, *Charters and Records*, p. 238.

101. *Reg. Gilbert*, pp. 105–7; Emden, *BRUO* ii, p. 914; LeNeve, *Fasti* (Hereford), p. 12.

102. The grant was made on February 16, 1394; CPR 1391–96, p. 372.

103. *Reg. Trefnant*, p. 285; *BRUO* i, p 270.

104. *Reg. Trefnant*, p. 241.

105. CCR 1385–89, p. 543.

106. *Reg. Trefnant*, p. 237.

107. CPR 1388–92 (December 16, 1389), p. 172.

108. The letter was written on December 31, 1389: *Reg. Trefnant*, pp. 234–35.

109. For the full account of Swynderby's trial see *Reg. Trefnant*, pp. 231–85.

110. McFarlane, *Nonconformity*, p. 115.

111. "Visitation" (1930): 100.

112. *Reg. Trefnant*, pp. 147–50. The business of John Crofte's renunciation began in September, 1395 and extended to the record of his oath in the following March.

113. "Visitation" (1930): 448. See also Philott, *Diocesan Histories*, p. 122.

114. *Reg. Trefnant*, p. 108.

115. "Visitation" (1930), p. 444; Kightly, "The Early Lollards," p. 179; see also *Reg. Gilbert*, p. 126 and *Reg. Trefnant*, p. 188.

116. *Reg. Trefnant*, pp. 147–50.

117. *Reg. Trefnant*, pp. 144–45.

118. McFarlane, *Nonconformity*, pp. 143–66.

119. McFarlane, *Nonconformity*, p. 164.

120. *Reg. Trillek*, p. 35.

Conclusion

1. *Reg. R. Mascall*, pp. 50–2.

2. Hatcher, *Plague, Population*, pp. 11–20.

3. Heath, *Parish Clergy*, pp. 72–37; Moran, "Clerical Recruitment," pp. 19–54.

4. T. S. R. Boase, *Death in the Middle Ages* (New York: McGraw-Hill, 1972); Philippa Tristram, *Figures of Life and Death in Medieval English Literature* (New York: New York University Press, 1976), pp. 152–83; Joan Evans, *English Art, 1307–1461* (Oxford: Oxford University Press, 1949), pp. 81–112; *Dies Illa: Death in the Middle Ages*, ed. Jane H. M. Taylor (Liverpool: F. Cairns, 1984).

Bibliography

PRIMARY SOURCES

MANUSCRIPT

Hampshire Record Office
  HRO A1/8,9 *Registrum* William Edendon (1346–1366)
Hereford Cathedral Archives
  HCA 1779 (Depositions from the visitation of Bishop John Trefnant, 1397)
  HCA 1975 (A memorandum concerning mortuary rights at Hopton Church, 1311)
  HCA 1155 (A citation concerning Archbishop Arundel's visitation, 1399/1400)
  HCA 2386 (Bishop John Trillek's ordinance on the office of cathedral peniten-tiary, 1355)
  HCA 1340, 1341, 3021, 3023, 3033, 3210, 3211, 3212 (Dispute between Here-ford Dean and Chapter and Roger Syde, vicar of St. Peter's: Documents and Depositions, c. 1362–1385/6)
Hereford Diocesan Registry
  HDR *Registrum* Thomas Cantilupe (1275–1282)
  HDR *Registrum* Richard Swinfield (1283–1317)
  HDR *Registrum* Adam Orelton (1317–1327)
  HDR *Registrum* John Trillek (1344–1360)
  HDR *Registrum* Lewis Charlton (1361–1369), John Gilbert (1375–1389), Robert Mascall (1404–1416)
  HDR *Registrum* John Trefnant (1389–1404)
Lambeth Palace Library
  LPL *Registrum* Simon Islip (1349–1366)
  LPL *Registrum* Thomas Arundel (1369–1397; 1399–1414)
Public Record Office, London
  PRO E 179 6/28 (Court records, Hereford vacancy, 1361)
  PRO E 179 30/7 (Clerical Subsidy, Hereford, 1379)
  PRO E 179 30/10 b (Clerical Subsidy, Hereford, 1406)
  PRO E 179 30/21 (Clerical Subsidy, Hereford, temp. Rich. II)

PRINTED

Alberigo, J. et al., eds. *Conciliorum Oecumenicorum Decreta*. Editio Tertia. Bologna: Istituto per le Scienze Religiose, 1973.

Bannister, A. T., ed. *Registrum Caroli Bothe, episcopie Herefordensis, A.D. MCXVIV–MDXXV*. Canterbury and York Society 28, 1921.

——. *Registrum Edmundi Lacy, episcopi Herefordensis, A.D. MCCCCXVII–MCCCCXX*. Canterbury and York Society 22, 1918.

——. *Registrum Ade de Orleton, episcopi Herefordensis, A.D. MCCCXVII–MCCCXXVII*. Canterbury and York Society 5, 1908.

Barrow, Julia, ed. *English Episcopal Acta VII: Hereford 1079–1234*. Oxford: Oxford University Press, 1993.

Bliss, William Henry, ed. *Calendar of Entries in the Papal Registers relating to Great Britain and Ireland, Petitions to the Pope A.D. 1342–1419*, vol. 1, London: H. M. Stationery Office, 1896.

Bliss, William Henry and J. A. Twemlow, eds. *The Calendar of Entries in the Papal Registers relating to Great Britain and Ireland, Papal Letters, 1198–*. 14 vols. London: Eyre and Spottiswoode, 1893–.

Bradshaw, Henry and Christopher Wordsworth, eds. *Hereford Consuetudines: Statutes of Lincoln Cathedral*. 2 parts in 3 vols. Cambridge: Cambridge University Press, 1892–97.

Browne, Edward, ed. *Fasciculus rerum expetendarum*. 2 vols. London: R. Chiswell, 1690.

Burgh, John de. *Pupilla Oculi*. London, 1516.

A Calendar of Close Rolls Preserved in the Public Record Office. vols. 1302–1307 to 1399–1402. London: H. M. Stationery Office, 1892–1954.

A Calendar of Patent Rolls Preserved in the Public Record Office. vols. 1301–1307 to 1404–1405. London: H. M. Stationery Office, 1891–1916.

Capes, William Wolfe, ed. *Charters and Records of Hereford Cathedral*. Hereford: Cantilupe Society, 1908.

——. *Registrum Thome de Charlton, episcopi Herefordensis, A.D. MCCCXXVII–MCCCXLIV*. Canterbury and York Society 9, 1913.

——. *Registrum Willelmi de Courtenay, episcopi Herefordensis, A.D. MCCCLXX–MCCCLXXV*. Canterbury and York Society 15, 1915.

——. *Registrum Ricardi de Swinfield, episcopi Herefordensis, A.D. MCCLXXXIII–MCCCXVII*. Canterbury and York Society 6, 1909.

——. *Registrum Johannis de Trefnant, episcopi Herefordensis, A.D. MCCCLXXIIX–MCCCCIV*. Canterbury and York Society 20, 1916.

Charles, Bertie G. and Hywel D. Emanuel. *A Calendar of the Earlier Hereford Cathedral Muniments*. 3 vols. 1955.

Frere, Walter Howard and L. E. G. Brown, eds. *Hereford Breviary*. 3 vols. London: Harrison and Son, 1904.

Haines, Roy Martin, ed. *A Calendar of the Register of Wolstan de Bransford, Bishop of Worcester 1339–49*. London: H. M. Stationery Office, 1966.

Hingeston-Randolph, F. C., ed. *The Register of John de Grandisson, Bishop of Exeter (A.D. 1327–1369)*. London and Exeter: George Bell and Sons, 1897.

Jacob, E. F., ed. *The Register of Henry Chichele, Archbishop of Canterbury, 1414–1443*, vol. I. Canterbury and York Society 45, 1943; vol. II, ed. E. F. Jacob and H. C. Johnson, Canterbury and York Society 42, 1938; vol. III, ed. E. F. Jacob, Canterbury and York Society 46, 1945; vol. IV, ed. E. F. Jacob, Canterbury and York Society 47, 1947.

Johnson, Charles, ed. *Registrum Hamonis Hethe, diocesis Roffensis, A.D. 1319–1352.* Canterbury and York Society 49, 1948.

Le Neve, John. *Fasti Ecclesiae Anglicanae 1300–1541.* II. Hereford Diocese, comp. Joyce M. Horn. London: Athlone Press, 1962.

Luard, H. R., ed. *Annales Monastici.* Rolls Series, London: Longman, Green, Longman, Roberts and Green, 1864–69.

Lumby, J. R., ed. *Chronicon Henrici Knighton, vel Cnitthon, monachi Leycestrensis.* Rolls Series. London: Eyre and Spottiswoode, 1889–95.

William Langland, *The Vision of William Concerning Piers the Plowman,* ed. W. W. Skeat. Oxford: Oxford University Press, 1886.

Lyndwood, William. *Provinciale seu constitutiones Angliae.* Oxford: R. Davis, 1679.

Martin, Charles Trice, ed. *Registrum Epistolarum Johannis Peckham Archiepiscopi Cantuariensis (1279–92).* 2 vols. Rolls Series. London: Longman, 1882–85.

Maskell, W. ed. *Monumenta Ritualia Ecclesie Anglicanae.* 2d ed. 4 vols. Oxford: Oxford University Press, 1882.

Murimuth, Adam (d. 1347). *Continuatio chronicarum.* Ed. E. M. Thompson, Rolls Series, London: Eyre & Spottiswoode, 1889.

Myrc, John. *Instructions for Parish Priests.* Ed. E. Peacock. EETS o.s., xxxi, 1868.

Parry, J. H., ed. *Registrum Ludowici de Charltone, episcopi Herefordensis, A.D. MCCCLXI–MCCCLXX.* Canterbury and York Society 14, 1914.

——. *Registrum Johannis Gilbert, episcopi Herefordensis, A.D. MCCCLXXV–MCCCLXXXIX.* Canterbury and York Society 18, 1915.

——. *Registrum Roberti Mascall, episcopi Herefordensis, A.D. MCCCCIV–MCCCCXVI.* Canterbury and York Society 21, 1917.

——. *Registrum Thome de Charlton, episcopi Herefordensis, A.D. MCCCXLIV–MCCCXLIV.* Canterbury and York Society 8, 1912.

Powicke, F. M. and C. R. Cheney, eds. *Councils and Synods with Other Documents Relating to the English Church.* vol. II, parts 1 & 2 (1205–1313). Oxford: Clarendon Press, 1964.

Raine, J., ed. *Historical Papers from the Northern Registers.* Rolls Series. London: Longman, 1873.

Record Commission. *Taxatio ecclesiastica Angliae et Walliae auctoritate Nicolai IV, c. 1291.* London: G. Eyre and A. Strahan, 1802.

——. *Valor ecclesiasticus temp. Henr. VIII.* 6 vols. London, 1810–34.

Rymer, Thomas, ed. *Foedera, conventiones, litterae et cujuscunque generis acta publica inter reges Angliae et alios imperatores.* 10 vols. 3rd edition. London: 1745

Smith, Waldo E. L., ed. *The Register of Richard Clifford Bishop of Worcester, 1401–1407. A Calendar.* Subsidia Mediaevalia 6. Toronto: Pontifical Institute of Mediaeval Studies, 1976.

Taylor, John, ed. "A Wigmore Chronicle, 1355–77." *Proceedings, Leeds Philosophical and Literary Society* 11 (March 1964–April 1966): 81–94.

Wadding, Lucas. *Annales minorum seu trium ordinum a S. Francisco Institutorum.* Florence: Quaracchi, 1931–.

Wilkins, David, ed. *Concilia Magnae Britanniae et Hiberniae,* 4 vols. London: R. Gosling, 1737.

Wood, A. C., ed. *Registrum Simonis de Langham, Cantuariensis Archiepiscopi.* Canterbury and York Society 53, 1956.

Woodruff, C. E. ed. *Calendar of Institutions by the Chapter of Canterbury* sede vacante. Kent Records 8. Canterbury: Gibbs and Son, 1924.

SECONDARY SOURCES

Adams, Reginald H. *The Parish Clerks of London: A History of the Worshipful Company of Parish Clerks of London*. London: Phillimore, 1971.

Addleshaw, G. W. O. *The Development of the Parochial System from Charlemagne (768–814) to Urban II (1088–1099)*. St. Anthony's Hall Publications 6. London: St. Anthony's Press, 1954.

Anderson, Mary Désirée. *History and Imagery in British Churches*. London: J. Murray, 1971.

Aston, Margaret. *Lollards and Reformers: Images and Literacy in Late Medieval Religion*. London: Hambledon, 1984.

Auden, Thomas. *Shropshire*. Oxford County Histories. Oxford: Oxford University Press, 1912.

Ault, Warren O. "The Village Church and Community in Medieval England." *Speculum* 45 (1970): 197–215.

Baker, Denise N. "From Plowing to Penitence: *Piers Plowman* and Fourteenth Century Theology." *Speculum* 55 (1980): 715–25.

Bannister, Arthur T. *The Cathedral Church of Hereford*. London: SPCK, 1924.

———. *A Descriptive Catalogue of the Manuscripts in the Hereford Cathedral Library*. Hereford: Wilson & Phillips, 1927.

———. "Parish Life in the Fourteenth Century." *The Nineteenth Century* 102 (1927): 399–404.

———. "Visitation Returns in the Diocese of Hereford in 1397." *EHR* 44 (1929): 279–89; 444–53; 45 (1930): 92–101; 444–63.

Barraclough, Geoffrey. *Papal Provisions: Aspects of Church History, Constitutional, Legal, and Administrative, in the Later Middle Ages*. Oxford: B. Blackwell, 1935.

Bean, J. M. W. "The Black Death: the Crisis and its Social and Economic Consequences." *The Black Death: The Impact of the Fourteenth-Century Plague*, ed. Daniel Williman. Binghamton, NY: Center for Medieval and Early Renaissance Studies, 1982, pp. 23–38.

Beck, Egerton. "Regulars and Medieval Churches in Medieval England." *Catholic Historical Review* n.s. III (1923): 205–16.

Bennett, Henry S. "Medieval Ordination Lists in the English Episcopal Registers." *Studies Presented to Hilary Jenkinson*, ed. J. Conway Davies. London: Oxford University Press, 1957, pp. 20–34.

Bennett, M. J. "The Lancashire and Cheshire Clergy, 1379." *Transactions, Historical Society of Lancashire and Cheshire* 124 (1974): 1–30.

Berlière, Ursmer. "L'exercice du ministère paroissial par les moines dans le haut moyen âge." *Revue Bénédictine* 39 (1927), pp. 227–50, 340–64.

Bettey, J. H. *Church and Community*. Wiltshire: Moonraker Press, 1979.

Bill, Peter Antony. *The Warwickshire Parish Clergy in the Later Middle Ages*. Dugdale Society Occasional Papers 17. Stratford-upon-Avon: Dugdale Society, 1967.

Biraben, Jean-Noël. "Current Medical and Epedemiological Views on Plague." *The Plague Reconsidered: A New Look at Its Origins and Effects in 16th and 17th Century England*. Stafford: Local Population Studies, 1977.

——. *Les hommes et la peste en France et dans les pays européens et méditerranéans*. 2 vols. Civilisations et Sociétés. vols. 35, 36. Paris: Mouton, 1976.

Boase, T. S. R. *Death in the Middle Ages*. New York: McGraw-Hill, 1972.

Boyle, Leonard E. "Aspects of Clerical Education in Fourteenth-Century England." *The Fourteenth Century. Acta IV*. Binghamton, NY: Center for Medieval and Early Renaissance Studies, 1977, pp. 19–32.

——. "The Constitution *Cum ex eo* of Boniface VIII." *Mediaeval Studies* 24 (1962): 263–302.

——. "The Oculus Sacerdotis and Some Other Works of William of Pagula." *TRHS* 5th ser. 5 (1955): 81–110.

Bridbury, A. R. "Before the Black Death." *Economic History Review* 2nd ser. 30 (1977): 393–410.

Brooke, C. N. L. "Rural Ecclesiastical Institutions in England: The Search for Their Origins." *Settimane de studio centro italiano di studi sull'alto medievo* 28 (1982): 685–712.

Brooke, Zachary and C. N. L. Brooke. "Hereford Cathedral Dignitaries." *Cambridge Historical Journal* 8 (1944): 1–21.

Brunner, K. "Mittelenglische Todesgedichte." *Archiv für Neure Sprachen* 167, 168 (1935): 20–35.

Burgess, Clive. "For the Increase of Divine Service: Chantries in the Parish in Late Medieval Bristol." *JEH* 36 (1985): 46–65.

Butlin, R. A. "The Late Middle Ages, c. 1350–1500," in *An Historical Geography of England and Wales*, ed. R. A. Dodgshon and R. A. Butlin (London: Academic Press, 1978), pp. 119–50.

Campbell, Anna. *The Black Death and Men of Learning*. 1931. Reprint New York: AMS Press, 1966.

Capes, William W. *The English Church in the Fourteenth and Fifteenth Centuries*. London: Macmillan, 1900.

Carpentier, Élizabeth. "Autour de la Peste Noire: Famines et épidémies dans l'histoire du XIVe siècle." *Annales E.S.C.* 17 (1962): 1062–92.

——. *Une ville devant la peste: Orvieto et la peste noire de 1348*, Démographie et société 7. Paris: S.E.V.P.E.N., 1962.

Cheney, Christopher R. *English Bishops' Chanceries, 1100–1250*. Manchester: Manchester University Press, 1950.

——. *Episcopal Visitation of Monasteries in the Thirteenth Century*. Manchester: Manchester University Press, 1931.

Chibnall, Marjorie. "Monks and Pastoral Work: A Problem in Anglo-Norman History." *JEH* 18 (1967): 165–72.

Churchill, Irene. *Canterbury Administration*. 2 vols. London: SPCK, 1933.

Clebsch, William and Charles Jaeckle. *Pastoral Care in Historical Perspective*. Englewood Cliffs, NJ: Prentice hall, 1964.

Cook, G. H. *The English Medieval Parish Church*. 3rd ed. London: Phoenix House, 1961.

Coulet, Noël. *Les visites pastorales*. Typologie des sources du Moyen Âge Occidental. Fasc. 23. Turnhout: Brepols, 1977.

Coulton, George, G. *The Black Death*. London: Benn's Sixpenny Library, 1929.

———. *Medieval Panorama: The English Scene from Conquest to Reformation*. Cambridge: Cambridge University Press, 1938.

Courtenay, William. "The Black Death and English Higher Education." *Speculum* 45 (1980): 695–714.

Cox, John Charles. *Churchwardens' Accounts from the Fourteenth Century to the Close of the Seventeenth Century*. London: Methuen, 1913.

Creighton, C. *A History of Epidemics in Britain*. 2 vols. Cambridge: Cambridge University Press, 1891, 1894.

Cutts, Edward Lewes. *Parish Priests and Their People in the Middle Ages in England*. London: SPCK, 1895. Reprint New York: AMS Press, 1970.

Davies, R. A. "The Effect of the Black Death on the Parish Priests of the Medieval Diocese of Coventry and Lichfield." *Historical Research* 62 (1989): 85–90.

Deanesly, Margaret. *Sidelights on the Anglo-Saxon Church*. London: A. & C. Black, 1962.

Dempster, Germaine. "The Parson's Tale," in *Sources and Analogues of Chaucer's Canterbury Tales*, ed. W. F. Bryan and Germain Dempster, New York: Humanities Press, 1958, pp. 723–60.

Ditchfield, P. H. *The Parish Clerk*. New York: Dutton, 1907.

Denton, J. H. "The *Communitas Cleri* in the Early Fourteenth Century." *BIHR* 51 (1978): 72–78.

Dohar, William J. "Medieval Ordination Lists: the Origins of a Record." *Archives* 20 (1992): 17–35.

Donaldson, E. Talbot. "The Ordering of the 'Canterbury Tales.'" *Medieval Literature and Folklore Studies: Essays in Honor of Francis Lee Utley*, ed. Jerome Mandel and Bruce A. Rosenberg. New Brunswick, NJ: Rutgers University Press, 1970, pp. 193–204.

Drew, Charles. *Early Parochial Organization in England: the Origins of the Office of Churchwarden*. St. Anthony's Hall Publications 7. London: St. Anthony's Press, 1954.

Driver, J. T. "The Papacy and the Diocese of Hereford, 1307–77." *Church Quarterly Review* 165 (1947): 31–47.

Dugdale, William. *Monasticon Anglicanum*. 6 vols. Repr. London: Longman et al., 1846.

Duncumb, John. *Collections Towards the History and Antiquities of the County of Hereford*. 3 vols. Hereford: E. G. Wright, 1804–82.

Dunstan, G. R. "Parish Clergy in the Diocese of Exeter in the Century after the Black Death." M.A. Thesis, Leeds University, 1939.

Dyer, Christopher. *Lords and Peasants in a Changing Society: The Estates of the Bishopric of Worcester, 600–1540*. Cambridge: Cambridge University Press, 1980.

Edwards, Kathleen. *The English Secular Cathedrals in the Middle Ages*. 2nd ed. Manchester: Manchester University Press, 1967.

———. "Bishops and Learning in the Reign of Edward II." *Church Quarterly Review* 138 (1944): 57–86.

——. "The Political Importance of the English Bishops during the Reign of Edward II." *EHR* 59 (1944): 311–47.

Emden, A. B. *Biographical Register of the University of Oxford to A. D. 1500.* 3 vols. Oxford: Clarendon Press, 1957–59.

Evans, Joan. *English Art, 1307–1461.* Oxford: Oxford University Press, 1949.

Finucane, Ronald. *Miracles and Pilgrims: Popular Beliefs in Medieval England.* London: J. M. Dent and Sons; Totowa, NJ: Rowman and Littlefield, 1977.

Fournier, Paul. *Les officialités au moyen âge.* Paris: Plon et cie, 1880.

Frankforter, A. Daniel. "The Origin of Episcopal Registration Procedures in Medieval England." *Manuscripta* 26 (1982): 67–89.

——. "The Reformation and the Register: Episcopal Administration of Parishes in Late Medieval England." *Catholic Historical Review* 63 (1977): 204–24.

Fryde, E. "The Tenants of the Bishops of Coventry and Lichfield and of Worcester After the Plague of 1348–49." *Medieval Legal Records*, ed. R. Hunnisett and J. B. Post. London: H. M. Stationery Office, 1978, pp. 224–66.

Garlick, V. "The Provision of Vicars in the Early Fourteenth Century." *History* 3 (1949): 15–27.

Gasquet, Francis A. *The Black Death of 1348 and 1349.* London: George Bell and Sons, 1897, 1908. Reprint New York: AMS Press, 1977.

——. *Parish Life in Mediaeval England.* London: Methuen, 1906.

Gaudemet, J. *Le gouvernement de l'église à l'époque classique.* Histoire du Droit et des Institutions de l'Église en Occident, ed. Gabriel Le Bras et Jean Gaudemet. Tôme 8, vol. 2, IIe partie, Le Gouvernement Locale. Paris: Éditions Cujas, 1979.

Gilchrist, John Thomas. *The Church and Economic Activity in the Middle Ages.* London: Macmillan; New York: St. Martin's Press, 1969.

Godfrey, C. J. "Non-residence of Parochial Clergy in the Fourteenth Century." *Church Quarterly Review* 162 (1961): 433–46.

Goering, Joseph. "The Changing Face of the Village Parish: the Thirteenth Century." *Pathways to Medieval Peasants*, ed. J. Ambrose Raftis. Toronto: Pontifical Institute of Mediaeval Studies, 1981.

Gottfried, Robert. *The Black Death: Natural and Human Disaster in Medieval Europe.* New York: Free Press, 1983.

Grandsen, A. "A Fourteenth Century Chronicle from the Grey Friars at Lynn (1349, 1360–77)." *EHR* 72 (1957): 270–78.

Haines, Roy Martin. *The Administration of the Diocese of Worcester in the First Half of the Fourteenth Century.* London: SPCK, 1965.

——. "The Education of the English Clergy in the Later Middle Ages: Some Observations on the Operation of Pope Boniface VIII's Constitution *Cum ex eo* (1298)." *Canadian Journal of History* 4 (1969): 1–22.

Hair, P. E. H. "Mobility of Parochial Clergy in Hereford Diocese c. 1400." *TWNFC* 43 (1980): 164–80.

Hartridge, R. A. R. *A History of Vicarages in the Middle Ages.* Cambridge: Cambridge University Press, 1930.

Harvey, Barbara F. "The Population Trend in England Between 1300 and 1348." *TRHS* 5th ser. 16 (1966): 23–42.

Hatcher, John. *Plague, Population, and the English Economy, 1348–1530*. London: Macmillan, 1977.

Havergal, Francis T. *Fasti Herefordensis and Other Antiquarian Memorials of Hereford*. Edinburgh: R. Clark, 1869.

Heath, Peter. *Church and Realm 1272–1461*. London: Fontana, 1988.

——. *The English Parish Clergy on the Eve of the Reformation*. London: Routledge and Kegan Paul, 1969.

Herlihy, David. "Population, Plague, and Social Change in Rural Pistoia, 1201–1430." *Economic History Review* 2d ser. 18 (1965): 225–44

Highfield, J. R. L. "The English Hierarchy in the Reign of Edward II." *TRHS* 5th ser. 6 (1956): 115–138.

——. "The Origins of the Diocese of Hereford." *TWNFC* 42 (1976): 16–52.

Hilton, R. H. "Small Town Society in England before the Black Death." *Past & Present* 105 (1984): 53–78.

Hollingsworth, T. H. *Historical Demography*. Ithaca, NY: Cornell University Press, 1969.

Hollingsworth, T. H. and M. F. "Plague Mortality Rates by Age and Sex in the Parish of St. Botolph's Without Bishopsgate, London, 1603." *Population Studies* XXV (1971): 131–46.

Hudson, Anne. *The Premature Reformation: Wycliffite Texts and Lollard History*. Oxford: Clarendon Press, 1988.

Hunnisett, R. and J. B. Post, eds. *Medieval Legal Records*. London: H. M. Stationery Office, 1978.

Jacob, E. F. "Petitions for Benefices from English Universities During the Great Schism." *TRHS* 4th ser. 27 (1945): 41–59.

Jessop, A. A. *The Coming of the Friars and other Historic Essays*. London: T. Fisher Unwin, 1895. Reprint 1908.

Kellogg, Alfred L. "St Augustine and the Parson's Tale," *Chaucer, Langland, Arthur: Essays in Middle English Literature*. New Brunswick, NJ: Rutgers University Press, 1972, pp. 343–52.

Kemp, Brian. "The Monastic Dean of Leominster." *EHR* 83 (1968): 505–15.

Kershaw, Ian. "The Great Famine and Agrarian Crisis in England 1315–1322." *Past & Present* 59 (1973): 3–50.

Kightly, Charles. "The Early Lollards. A Survey of Popular Lollard Activity in England, 1382–1428." Ph.D. dissertation, University of York, 1975.

Knowles, David. *The Religious Orders in England*. 3 vols. Cambridge: Cambridge University Press, 1948–1959.

Knowles, David and R. Neville Hadcock. *Medieval Religious Houses, England and Wales*. London: Longmans, 1953. Reprint New York: St. Martin's Press, 1972.

Langford, A. W. "The Plague in Herefordshire." *TWNFC* 35 (1955–57): 146–53.

Le Bras, Gabriel. *Institutions ecclésiastiques de la Chrétienté medievale*, Histoire de L'Église, ed. A. Fliche and V. Martin. vol. 12, part ii. Paris: Bloud & Gay, 1964.

Leach, A. F. *The Schools of Medieval England*. 2nd ed. London: Methuen, 1916.

Lerner, Robert E. "The Black Death and Western European Eschatalogical Mentalities." *The Black Death: The Impact of the Fourteenth-Century Plague*, ed. D. Williman. Binghampton, NY: Center for Medieval and Early Renaissance Studies, 1982, pp. 77–105.

Levett, Ada E. "A Note on the Statute of Labourers." *Economic History Review* 4 (1932): 77–80.

———. *Studies in Manorial History*. Oxford: Clarendon Press, 1938.

Levett, Ada E. and Adolphus Ballard. *The Black Death on the Estates of the See of Winchester*. Oxford Studies in Social and Legal History 5. Oxford: Clarendon Press, 1916.

Little, A. G. "The Black Death in Lancashire." *EHR* 5 (1890): 24–30.

Lobel, Mary D., ed. *Historic Towns: Maps and Plans of Cities in the British Isles*. Vol. 1. Baltimore: Johns Hopkins University Press, 1969.

Lunn, J. "The Black Death in the Bishops' Registers." Ph.D. dissertation, Cambridge University, 1937.

Matossian, Mary Kilbourne. *Poisons of the Past: Molds, Epidemics, and History*. New Haven, CT: Yale University Press, 1989.

McFarlane, Kenneth B. *Wycliffe and English Nonconformity*. London: English Universities Press, 1952.

Malvern, M. "An Earnest 'Monyscyon' and 'Thinge Delectabyll' Realized Verbally and Visually in 'A Disputacion Betwyx the Body and Wormes,' A Middle English Poem Inspired by Tomb Art and Northern Spirituality." *Viator* 13 (1982): 415–43.

Mann, Jill. *Chaucer and Medieval Estates Satire*. Cambridge: Cambridge University Press, 1973.

Martin, S. H. "The Case of Roger Syde Versus the Dean and Chapter of Hereford." *TWNFC* 35 (1955–7): 156–62.

Mason, Emma. "The Role of the English Parishioner, 1100–1500." *JEH* 27 (1976): 17–29.

Mate, Mavis. "Agrarian Economy After the Black Death: The Manors of Canterbury Cathedral Priory, 1348–91." *Economic History Review* 2d ser. 37 (1984): 341–54.

Mode, P. "The Influence of the Black Death on the English Monasteries." Ph.D. dissertation, University of Chicago, 1916.

Moorman, J. R. H. *Church Life in England in the Thirteenth Century*. Cambridge: Cambridge University Press, 1945.

Moran, JoAnn Hoeppner. "Clerical Recruitment in the Diocese of York, 1345–1530: Data and Commentary." *JEH* 34 (1983): 19–54.

Morgan, F. C. and Penelope E. Morgan. *Hereford Cathedral Libraries and Muniments*. Hereford: Hereford Cathedral Library, 1975.

Naz, R. "Titre d'ordination." *DDC* 7, cols. 1278–88.

Orme, Nicholas. *English Schools in the Middle Ages*. London: Methuen, 1973.

Owen, Dorothy M. *Church and Society in Medieval Lincolnshire*. Lincoln: History of Lincolnshire Committee, 1971.

Owst, G. R. *Preaching in Medieval England*. Cambridge: Cambridge University Press, 1926.

Palmer, Richard. "The Church, Leprosy, and Plague in Medieval and Early Modern Europe." *The Church and Healing*, ed. W. J. Shiels. Studies in Church History 19. Oxford: B. Blackwell, 1982, pp. 79–100.

Pantin, W. A. *The English Church in the Fourteenth Century*. Cambridge: Cambridge University Press, 1955.

———. *Canterbury College, Oxford*. Oxford Historical Society, n.s. VIII, 1950, 3.

Patterson, Lee. *Chaucer and the Subject of History*. Madison: University of Wisconsin Press, 1991.

———. "The 'Parson's Tale' and the Quitting of the Canterbury Tales." *Traditio* 34 (1987): 331–80.

Phillott, H. W. *Diocesan Histories: Hereford*. London: SPCK, 1888.

Postan, M. M. "Some Economic Evidence of the Declining Population in the Later Middle Ages." *Economic History Review* 2d ser. 2 (1950): 221–46.

Putnam, Bertha H. *Enforcement of the Statute of Labourers During the First Decade After the Black Death, 1349–1359*. Columbia University Studies in History, Economics and Public Law 32. New York: Columbia University Press, 1908.

———. "Maximum Wage-Laws for Priests After the Black Death." *American Historical Review* 21 (1915–16): 12–32.

Raftis, J. Ambrose. "Changes in an English Village After the Black Death." *Mediaeval Studies* 29 (1967): 158–77.

Rawlinson, Richard. *The History and Antiquities of the City and Cathedral-Church of Hereford*. London: R. Gosling, 1717.

Reynolds, Susan. *Kingdoms and Communities 800 to 1300*. Oxford: Clarendon Press, 1983.

Richardson, H. G. "The Parish Clergy of the Thirteenth and Fourteenth Centuries." *TRHS* 3rd ser. 6 (1912): 89–128.

Robinson, David. "Beneficed Clergy in Cleveland and the East Riding, 1306–1340." *Borthwick Papers* 37. York: St. Anthony's Press, 1970.

———. "Ordination of Secular Clergy in the Diocese of Coventry and Lichfield, 1322–1358." *Archives* 73 (1985): 3–21.

Robinson, F. N., ed. *The Riverside Chaucer*. Oxford: Oxford University Press, 1988.

Rodes, Robert. *Ecclesiastical Administration in Medieval England*. Notre Dame, IN: University of Notre Dame Press, 1977.

Rose, R. K. "Priests and Patrons in the Fourteenth Century Diocese of Carlisle." *The Church in Town and Countryside*, ed. Derek Baker. Studies in Church History 16. Oxford: B. Blackwell, 1979, pp. 207–18.

Rowley, Trevor. *The Landscape of the Welsh Marches*. London: M. Joseph, 1986.

Russell, Josiah Cox. *British Medieval Population*. Albuquerque: University of New Mexico Press, 1948.

———. "The Clerical Population of Medieval England." *Traditio* 2 (1944): 177–212.

———. "The Pre-Plague Population of England." *Journal of British Studies* 5, 2 (1966): 23–42.

Scammell, Jean. "The Rural Chapter in England from the Eleventh to the Fourteenth Century." *EHR* 86 (1971): 1–21.

Sheehan, Michael M. *The Will in Medieval England*. Studies and Texts 6. Toronto: Pontifical Institute of Mediaeval Studies, 1963.

Shinners, John. "University Study Licenses and Clerical Education in the Diocese of Norwich, 1325–35." *History of Education Quarterly* 28 (1988): 387–410.

Shrewsbury, J. F. D. *A History of the Bubonic Plague in the British Isles*. Cambridge: Cambridge University Press, 1970.

Smith, David. *Guide to Bishops' Registers of England and Wales*. London: Royal Historical Society, 1981.

Storey, R. L. *Diocesan Administration in the Fifteenth Century*. St. Anthony's Hall Publications 16, London: St. Anthony's Press, 1959.

——. "Recruitment of English Clergy in the Period of the Conciliar Movement." *Annuarium Historiae Conciliorum* 7 (1975): 290–313.

Swanson, R. N. "Titles to Orders in Medieval English Episcopal Registers." *Studies in Medieval History: Presented to R. H. C. Davies*, ed. Henry Mayr-Harting and R. I. Moore. London: Hambledon Press, 1985, 233–45.

Tanner, Norman. *The Church in Late Medieval Norwich 1370–1532*. Studies and Texts 66. Toronto: Pontifical Institute of Mediaeval Studies, 1984.

Taylor, Jane H. M., ed. *Dies Illa: Death in the Middle Ages*. Liverpool: F. Cairns, 1984.

Thompson, A. H. "Diocesan Organization in the Middle Ages: Archdeacons and Rural Deans." *Proceedings, British Academy* 29 (1943): 153–94.

——. "Ecclesiastical Benefices and Their Incumbents." *Transactions, The Leicestershire Archaeological Society* 22 (1944): 1–32.

——. *The English Clergy and Their Organization in the Later Middle Ages*. Oxford: Clarendon Press, 1947.

——. "The Pestilence of the Fourteenth Century in the Diocese of York." *Archaeological Journal* 71 (1914): 97–154.

——. "Pluralism in the Medieval Church." *Associated Architectural Society Reports and Papers* 33 (1915): 35–73; 34 (1917): 1–26; 35 (1919): 87–108; 36 (1921): 1–41.

——. "The Registers of John Gynewell, Bishop of Lincoln, for the Years 1347–1350." *Archaeological Journal* 68 (1911): 300–360.

——. "Certificates of the Shropshire Chantries." *TSAS* 4th ser. (1911): 115–89.

——. *Visitations in the Diocese of Lincoln, 1517–1531*. 3 vols, Lincoln Record Society nos. 33, 35, 37. Lincoln: Lincoln Record Society, 1936, 1938 and 1940.

Tierney, Brian. *Medieval Poor Law: A Sketch of Canonical Theory and Its Application in England*. Berkeley and Los Angeles: University of California Press, 1959.

Titow, J. Z. *English Rural Society 1200–1350*. Historical Problems: Studies and Documents. Edited by G. R. Elton. London: Allen & Unwin, 1969.

Tristram, Philippa. *Figures of Life and Death in Medieval English Literature*. New York: New York University Press, 1976.

Twigg, Graham. *The Black Death: A Biological Reappraisal*. London: Batsford, 1984.

Viard, J. "La messe pour la peste." *Bibliothèque de l'École des Chartes* 61 (1900): 334–38.

Wells, J. E. *A Manual of Writings in Middle English 1050–1400*. New Haven, CT: Yale University Press, 1926.

Williams, Glanmor. *The Welsh Church from Conquest to Reformation*. Cardiff: University of Wales Press, 1962.

Williams, J. F. "Ordination in the Norwich Diocese During the Fifteenth Century." *Norfolk Archaeology* 31 (1957): 347–58.

Williman, Daniel, ed. *The Black Death: The Impact of the Fourteenth Century Plague*. Medieval and Renaissance Texts and Studies. Binghamton, NY: Center for Medieval and Early Renaissance Studies, 1982.

Wood-Legh, Kathleen L. "The Appropriation of Parish Churches During the Reign of Edward III." *Cambridge Historical Journal* 3 (1929): 15–22.

———. *Studies in Church Life in England Under Edward III*. Cambridge: Cambridge University Press, 1934.

Wrigley E. A. and R. S. Schofield, *The Population History of England, 1541–1871*. London: Edward Arnold, 1981.

Yates, W. Nigel. "The Fabric Roll of Hereford Cathedral, 1290/1 and 1386/7." *Library of Wales Journal* 18 (1973): 79–86.

Zaddach, B. I. *Die Folgen des Schwarzen Todes (1347–51) für den Klerus Mitteleuropas*. Stuttgart: G. Fischer, 1971.

Ziegler, Philip. *The Black Death*. London: Collins, 1969.

Index

Abbey Dore, 30, 177n. 32; Abbot of, 67, 110
absenteeism, by clergy, 127–37
absolution, and Penance, 4–5
acolytes, 22, 51, 58, 68, 91, 97–103
Aconbury Convent, 66, 177n. 32
Alderbury Priory, 80
Aldon Chapel, 134
anti-clericalism, 89, 106, 119
aquabajulus (water-bearer or holy water
    cleric), 24, 123
archdeacons: registers of, 9; role and respon-
    sibilities of, 19
Arundel, Thomas, 149
Aston parish, 132
Augustinian order, 30, 39
Austin friars, 76, 111
Awre church, 39, 65
Aymestrey church, 111

Bacton Chapel, 110
Ball, John, 107
Bangor diocese, 143
Bannister, A. T., 176n. 12, 179n. 91
Barnet, John, 78
Bateman, William (bishop of Norwich), 118
Benedictine order, 29–30, 32, 39, 81
Birley parish, 133
bishops: assistants to, 18–20; description of,
    15–18; placement of clergy by, 17–18, 56–
    59; registers of, 2, 8–9, 20, 90–91, 111,
    122, 145, 157–61; role and responsibilities
    of, 6, 17–18, 107–8, 152
Bishop's Frome church, 133
Black Death (1347–50): and clerical recruit-
    ment, 94, 96, 99, 103–6, 115, 116; extent
    of, 1; impact on role of clergy in church
    life, 7, 37, 151–55; mortality in Hereford
    diocese, 37–55; recovery from, 61–63; re-
    percussions of, xi, 1–2; scholarly study of,
    1–3
Bold church, 65

Boniface VIII (pope), 123, 124, 125
Boomcraft township, 38
Bosbury parish, 54
Bransford, Wulstan de (bishop of Worces-
    ter), 57, 59, 94
Brantingham, Thomas (bishop of Exeter),
    88
Brecon Priory, 65–66, 177n. 32
Bromfield Priory, 65
Bromyard parish, 108
Brosley chapel, 77
Brut, Walter, 142–43, 144, 147
bubonic plague. *See* Black Death; plague
Burford deanery, 15
burial rights, 82

canon law: and clerical examinations, 90,
    107, 108–9, 117, 121; and ordination, 17
Canterbury Tales (Chaucer), 119, 120–21,
    126, 137–38, 145–48
Cantilupe, Thomas (saint), 8, 18, 59–60, 61,
    113; feast, 18
Carles, Walter, 42, 53
Carlisle diocese, 115
Castle Goodrich, 132, 133
Castle Holdgate, 30
Cathedral of St. Mary and St. Ethelbert
    (Hereford): building interrupted at, 38–
    39; clergy of, 18, 30–32; grammar school
    at, 122–23; ordinations at, 108; role in
    Hereford diocese, 30–32; tomb of St.
    Thomas Cantilupe at, 59–60. *See also*
    Dean and Chapter of Hereford Cathedral
chancellor, 31
chaplains: as clerical assistants, 133; mor-
    tality rate of, 49–50; placement of, 73–74;
    of private oratories, 23; scarcity of, 80
Charlton, John, 173n. 12
Charlton, Lewis: bishop's register of, 62,
    171n. 47; and clerical discipline, 81; cleri-
    cal recruitment by, 93, 99, 101; and con-

Charlton, Lewis (*cont.*)
  solidation of Puddleston and Whyle parishes, 79–80; and crimes by clergy, 139; death of, 86, 88, 125; diocesan administration under, 79, 154; and dispute over burial rights, 86; ordinations by, 79, 80, 89, 95–96, 101, 108, 113–14, 115; and pluralism of benefices, 127; political connections of, 15, 16; and recovery following the Black Death, 62; and Second Plague (1361–62), 63, 78–81; as successor to John Trillek, 8, 78
Charlton, Thomas: appointment as bishop, 173n. 12; bishop's register of, 41, 158; changes in benefices under, 43; and clerical assistants, 22; and clerical education, 124; clerical recruitment by, 93, 97; and crimes by clergy, 139; and farming of benefices, 128; management of diocese by, 35; ordinations by, 70, 91, 97–99, 103, 108, 113; political connections of, 15, 16; as predecessor to John Trillek, 78
Charlton, William de, 79
Chaucer, Geoffrey, 119, 120–21, 126, 137–38, 145–48
Cheney, Christopher, xi
"choppe-churches," 130–31
churches, repair of, 19, 25–26, 128, 135–37
churchwardens (*custos*), 26, 151
Cistercian order, 30, 141
clergy: abandonment of benefices by, 12, 45, 118, 127; absenteeism of, 127–37; assistants to, 128, 131–35; associated with castles, 13; bishop's placement of, 17–18, 56–59; canonical examination of, 90, 107, 108–9, 117, 121; as coadjutor, 135; conduct of, 137–48; criticism of, 106–7, 118–19; dispensations for, 70, 88, 89, 108, 123, 137, 146; education of, 21, 23–24, 71–72, 121–26, 138, 146, 150; exchange of benefices by, 41, 42, 43, 48, 49, 73, 128, 130–31; and farming of benefices, 128–30, 137; felonious crimes by, 139–40; heresy by, 139, 142–45, 147; impact of Black Death on role of, 7, 37, 151–55; leaves of absence for, 71–75, 123–25; and management of the cure, 126–37; moral supervision of, 19, 20, 138–39, 140; mortality rate of, 2–3, 5, 12, 39, 40–55, 103, 118, 149; ordination of, 17, 23–24, 50–52, 56, 57, 58, 63–64, 67–71, 77, 78, 79, 80, 88, 90, 107–8,

146, 159–61; ordination titles for, 109–17; papal authority over, 16, 28–29; of parish, 21–24; patronage of, 90, 109–17, 150; pluralism of benefices among, 127, 134–35, 147, 153; recruitment of, 8, 68–70, 80, 88–117, 159; resignation of, 41, 42, 43, 48, 49, 54, 73; responsibility for souls, 120–26; royal patronage of, 10, 16, 27, 28; salaries of, 22, 74–75, 104–6, 116, 131, 153; sins against morality by, 139, 140–42. *See also* bishops
Clifford Priory, 177n. 32
Close Rolls, 10
Clun deanery, 15
Cluniac order, 30
Clunstone parish, 132
Coddington parish, 121, 132
commissary general, 20
competens scientia (seemly learning), 138
confessors, 76–77, 81
Constitutions of Ottobono (1268), 176–77n. 30
Consueta (papal bull), 127
Cornwall, Richard, 122
Coulton, G. G., 2, 3
Council of Lambeth (1281), 176–77n. 30
Council of Oxford (1222): and clergy salaries, 22, 104; and farming of benefices, 176–77n. 30
Courtenay, William: appointment as bishop, 88, 154; and *aquabajulus,* 123; background of, 16; bishop's register of, 88; and clerical education, 125; clerical recruitment by, 93, 101; diocesan administration by, 154; and exchange of benefices, 130, 131; ordinations by, 88, 96, 101, 108; political connections of, 16
Court of Arches, 10, 83, 84
Crofte chapel, 144
Cum ex eo (papal decree), 24, 71, 73, 123, 124, 125

Dean and Chapter of Hereford Cathedral: clerical patronage by, 111; and dispute over funerary dues, 82–86; records of, 9–10, 40; role and responsibilities of, 18, 28. *See also* Cathedral of St. Mary and St. Ethelbert (Hereford)
Deanery of the Forest, 15, 45, 142
deans: of the cathedral, 31; role and responsibilities of, 18–19. *See also* rural deans

University of Pennsylvania Press
MIDDLE AGES SERIES
Edward Peters, General Editor

F. R. P. Akehurst, trans. *The* Coutumes de Beauvaisis *of Philippe de Beaumanoir.* 1992

Peter L. Allen. *The Art of Love: Amatory Fiction from Ovid to the* Romance of the Rose. 1992

David Anderson. *Before the Knight's Tale: Imitation of Classical Epic in Boccaccio's* Teseida. 1988

Benjamin Arnold. *Count and Bishop in Medieval Germany: A Study of Regional Power, 1100–1350.* 1991

Mark C. Bartusis. *The Late Byzantine Army: Arms and Society, 1204–1453.* 1992

Thomas N. Bisson, ed. *Cultures of Power: Lordship, Status, and Process in Twelfth-Century Europe.* 1995

Uta-Renate Blumenthal. *The Investiture Controversy: Church and Monarchy from the Ninth to the Twelfth Century.* 1988

Daniel Bornstein, trans. *Dino Compagni's* Chronicle *of Florence.* 1986

Maureen Boulton. *The Song in the Story: Lyric Insertions in French Narrative Fiction, 1200–1400.* 1993

Betsy Bowden. *Chaucer Aloud: The Varieties of Textual Interpretation.* 1987

Charles R. Bowlus. *Franks, Moravians, and Magyars: The Struggle for the Middle Danube, 788–907.* 1994

James William Brodman. *Ransoming Captives in Crusader Spain: The Order of Merced on the Christian-Islamic Frontier.* 1986

Kevin Brownlee and Sylvia Huot, eds. *Rethinking the* Romance of the Rose: *Text, Image, Reception.* 1992

Matilda Tomaryn Bruckner. *Shaping Romance: Interpretation, Truth, and Closure in Twelfth-Century French Fictions.* 1993

Otto Brunner (Howard Kaminsky and James Van Horn Melton, eds. and trans.). Land *and Lordship: Structures of Governance in Medieval Austria.* 1992

Robert I. Burns, S.J., ed. *Emperor of Culture: Alfonso X the Learned of Castile and His Thirteenth-Century Renaissance.* 1990

David Burr. *Olivi and Franciscan Poverty: The Origins of the* Usus Pauper *Controversy.* 1989

David Burr. *Olivi's Peaceable Kingdom: A Reading of the Apocalypse Commentary.* 1993

Thomas Cable. *The English Alliterative Tradition.* 1991

Anthony K. Cassell and Victoria Kirkham, eds. and trans. *Diana's Hunt/Caccia di Diana: Boccaccio's First Fiction.* 1991

John C. Cavadini. *The Last Christology of the West: Adoptionism in Spain and Gaul, 785–820.* 1993

Brigitte Cazelles. *The Lady as Saint: A Collection of French Hagiographic Romances of the Thirteenth Century*. 1991

Karen Cherewatuk and Ulrike Wiethaus, eds. *Dear Sister: Medieval Women and the Epistolary Genre*. 1993

Anne L. Clark. *Elisabeth of Schönau: A Twelfth-Century Visionary*. 1992

Willene B. Clark and Meradith T. McMunn, eds. *Beasts and Birds of the Middle Ages: The Bestiary and Its Legacy*. 1989

Richard C. Dales. *The Scientific Achievement of the Middle Ages*. 1973

Charles T. Davis. *Dante's Italy and Other Essays*. 1984

William J. Dohar. *The Black Death and Pastoral Leadership: The Diocese of Hereford in the Fourteenth Century*. 1994

Katherine Fischer Drew, trans. *The Burgundian Code*. 1972

Katherine Fischer Drew, trans. *The Laws of the Salian Franks*. 1991

Katherine Fischer Drew, trans. *The Lombard Laws*. 1973

Nancy Edwards. *The Archaeology of Early Medieval Ireland*. 1990

Margaret J. Ehrhart. *The Judgment of the Trojan Prince Paris in Medieval Literature*. 1987

Richard K. Emmerson and Ronald B. Herzman. *The Apocalyptic Imagination in Medieval Literature*. 1992

Theodore Evergates. *Feudal Society in Medieval France: Documents from the County of Champagne*. 1993

Felipe Fernández-Armesto. *Before Columbus: Exploration and Colonization from the Mediterranean to the Atlantic, 1229–1492*. 1987

Jerold C. Frakes. *Brides and Doom: Gender, Property, and Power in Medieval Women's Epic*. 1994

R. D. Fulk. *A History of Old English Meter*. 1992

Patrick J. Geary. *Aristocracy in Provence: The Rhône Basin at the Dawn of the Carolingian Age*. 1985

Peter Heath. *Allegory and Philosophy in Avicenna (Ibn Sînâ), with a Translation of the Book of the Prophet Muḥammad's Ascent to Heaven*. 1992

J. N. Hillgarth, ed. *Christianity and Paganism, 350–750: The Conversion of Western Europe*. 1986

Richard C. Hoffmann. *Land, Liberties, and Lordship in a Late Medieval Countryside: Agrarian Structures and Change in the Duchy of Wrocław*. 1990

Robert Hollander. *Boccaccio's Last Fiction: Il Corbaccio*. 1988

Edward B. Irving, Jr. *Rereading* Beowulf. 1989

Richard A. Jackson, ed. *Texts and Ordines for the Coronation of Frankish Kings and Queens in the Middle Ages, Vol. 1*. 1994

C. Stephen Jaeger. *The Envy of Angels: Cathedral Schools and Social Ideals in Medieval Europe, 950–1200*. 1994

C. Stephen Jaeger. *The Origins of Courtliness: Civilizing Trends and the Formation of Courtly Ideals, 939–1210*. 1985

Donald J. Kagay, trans. *The Usatges of Barcelona: The Fundamental Law of Catalonia*. 1994

Richard Kay. *Dante's Christian Astrology*. 1994

Ellen E. Kittell. *From* Ad Hoc *to Routine: A Case Study in Medieval Bureaucracy*. 1991

Alan C. Kors and Edward Peters, eds. *Witchcraft in Europe, 1100–1700: A Documentary History.* 1972

Barbara M. Kreutz. *Before the Normans: Southern Italy in the Ninth and Tenth Centuries.* 1992

Kuczynski, Michael. *Prophetic Song: The Psalms as Moral Discourse in Late Medieval England.* 1995

E. Ann Matter. *The Voice of My Beloved: The Song of Songs in Western Medieval Christianity.* 1990

A. J. Minnis. *Medieval Theory of Authorship.* 1988

Lawrence Nees. *A Tainted Mantle: Hercules and the Classical Tradition at the Carolingian Court.* 1991

Lynn H. Nelson, trans. *The Chronicle of San Juan de la Peña: A Fourteenth-Century Official History of the Crown of Aragon.* 1991

Barbara Newman. *From Virile Woman to WomanChrist: Studies in Medieval Religion and Literature.* 1995.

Joseph F. O'Callaghan. *The Learned King: The Reign of Alfonso X of Castile.* 1993

Odo of Tournai (Irven M. Resnick, trans.). *Two Theological Treatises:* On Original Sin *and* A Disputation with the Jew, Leo, Concerning the Advent of Christ, the Son of God. 1994

David M. Olster. *Roman Defeat, Christian Response, and the Literary Construction of the Jew.* 1994

William D. Paden, ed. *The Voice of the Trobairitz: Perspectives on the Women Troubadours.* 1989

Edward Peters. *The Magician, the Witch, and the Law.* 1982

Edward Peters, ed. *Christian Society and the Crusades, 1198–1229: Sources in Translation, including* The Capture of Damietta *by Oliver of Paderborn.* 1971

Edward Peters, ed. *The First Crusade: The* Chronicle of Fulcher of Chartres *and Other Source Materials.* 1971

Edward Peters, ed. *Heresy and Authority in Medieval Europe.* 1980

James M. Powell. *Albertanus of Brescia: The Pursuit of Happiness in the Early Thirteenth Century.* 1992

James M. Powell. *Anatomy of a Crusade, 1213–1221.* 1986

Susan A. Rabe. *Faith, Art, and Politics at Saint-Riquier: The Symbolic Vision of Angilbert.* 1995

Jean Renart (Patricia Terry and Nancy Vine Durling, trans.). *The Romance of the Rose or Guillaume de Dole.* 1993

Michael Resler, trans. Erec *by Hartmann von Aue.* 1987

Pierre Riché (Michael Idomir Allen, trans.). *The Carolingians: A Family Who Forged Europe.* 1993

Pierre Riché (Jo Ann McNamara, trans.). *Daily Life in the World of Charlemagne.* 1978

Jonathan Riley-Smith. *The First Crusade and the Idea of Crusading.* 1986

Joel T. Rosenthal. *Patriarchy and Families of Privilege in Fifteenth-Century England.* 1991

Teofilo F. Ruiz. *Crisis and Continuity: Land and Town in Late Medieval Castile.* 1994

Pamela Sheingorn, ed. and trans. *The Book of Sainte Foy.* 1995.

Robin Chapman Stacey. *The Road to Judgment: From Custom to Court in Medieval Ireland and Wales.* 1994

Sarah Stanbury. *Seeing the* Gawain-Poet: *Description and the Act of Perception.* 1992

Robert D. Stevick. *The Earliest Irish and English Bookarts: Visual and Poetic Forms Before A.D. 1000.* 1994

Thomas C. Stillinger. *The Song of Troilus: Lyric Authority in the Medieval Book.* 1992

Susan Mosher Stuard. *A State of Deference: Ragusa/Dubrovnik in the Medieval Centuries.* 1992

Susan Mosher Stuard, ed. *Women in Medieval History and Historiography.* 1987

Susan Mosher Stuard, ed. *Women in Medieval Society.* 1976

Jonathan Sumption. *The Hundred Years War: Trial by Battle.* 1992

Ronald E. Surtz. *The Guitar of God: Gender, Power, and Authority in the Visionary World of Mother Juana de la Cruz (1481–1534).* 1990

William H. TeBrake. *A Plague of Insurrection: Popular Politics and Peasant Revolt in Flanders, 1323–1328.* 1993

Patricia Terry, trans. *Poems of the Elder Edda.* 1990

Hugh M. Thomas. *Vassals, Heiresses, Crusaders, and Thugs: The Gentry of Angevin Yorkshire, 1154–1215.* 1993

Mary F. Wack. *Lovesickness in the Middle Ages: The* Viaticum *and Its Commentaries.* 1990

Benedicta Ward. *Miracles and the Medieval Mind: Theory, Record, and Event, 1000–1215.* 1982

Suzanne Fonay Wemple. *Women in Frankish Society: Marriage and the Cloister, 500–900.* 1981

Jan M. Ziolkowski. *Talking Animals: Medieval Latin Beast Poetry, 750–1150.* 1993

This book has been set in Linotron Galliard. Galliard was designed for Mergenthaler in 1978 by Matthew Carter. Galliard retains many of the features of a sixteenth-century typeface cut by Robert Granjon but has some modifications that give it a more contemporary look.

Printed on acid-free paper.